have power." —HOWARD SAPERS, Correctional Investigator of Canada (2004–2016)

"Solitary confinement is meant to break people. Rik McWhinney survived more than thirty-four years of isolation, and in that time discovered a gift for language. His words sing and startle, bringing the unimaginable into view. This book is a searing indictment of the violence of the prison system and an urgent reminder that harm finds no antidote in the cruel punishments of the penitentiary." —BRETT STORY, author of *Prison Land: Mapping Carceral Power across Neoliberal America*

"A creatively damning reflection on the politics, culture, and absurdity of imprisonment. An incredible example of the power of prisoner writing. Brought me to tears with its stories of human caging. Riled me up with its subtle and wily analysis of systemic injustice." —KEVIN WALBY, co-editor *Journal of Prisoners on Prisons*, Associate Professor and former Chancellor's Research Chair (2015–2018) in the Department of Criminal Justice at University of Winnipeg

I0086281

ADVANCE PRAISE FOR
The Life Sentences of Rik McWhinney

⸺ ✿ ⸻

"Thanks to the editing of Jason Demers, Rik McWhinney's written record of a long season in hell has emerged to shine light on a very dark place. My hat goes off to both of them." —DAVID CARPENTER

"*The Life Sentences of Rik McWhinney* takes you into the heart of prison darkness. The savagery and brutality found within, however, can only be understood in the context of an institution that cages human beings; those whose life circumstances have mostly been a trail of violent displacement, dispossession, and deprivation. And yet even in the darkest recesses of such confinement, a spirit of camaraderie, creativity, and community prevail. This book is an important commemoration of not only Rik, but of all the souls lost in modernity's violent advancements." —VICKI CHARTRAND, founder and director of Centre for Justice Exchange

"The most visceral and literate first-hand account I've seen of the brutal realities of prison life in Canada." —GARY GARRISON, author of *Human on the Inside: Unlocking the Truth about Canada's Prisons*

"This study is timely. An emerging academic demand in criminology and penology is the need to take into account the prisoner (criminalized) as an essential actor in the study of criminal justice and incarceration. This book addresses that demand." —ROBERT GAUCHER, editor of *Writing as Resistance*

"Rik McWhinney's harrowing *testimonio* calls for an abolitionist reckoning with the Canadian criminal justice system." —P.J. MURPHY, co-editor of *Sentences and Paroles: A Prison Reader*

"McWhinney's posthumously published book is a major contribution to prison writing in Canada because it reveals so much about recent prison history, including practices of solitary confinement under several other names, involuntary transfers, medical neglect, and the abuse of power in general. Through a uniquely articulate testimonial and literary voice, including a series of interviews with his editor, the author relives the realities of prison culture, from its codes of conduct and brutal memories to its numbing carceral logic. A penal subject for over three decades, McWhinney conveys his profound rage and frustration and the post-traumatic shock of doing time in Canadian prisons that are themselves imperfect and dehumanizing, if not corrupt. A gripping and heartbreaking read. A cry from the dark for meaningful prison reform, if not abolition." —ROXANNE RIMSTEAD, author of *Remnants of Nation: On Poverty Narratives by Women*

"Rik takes the reader through the life and daily routine of a prisoner. From meals and programs to solitary confinement and navigating the prison 'code.' As we read, we experience what Rik has experienced. His words

The Life Sentences of
Rik McWhinney

RIK McWHINNEY

Edited with an introduction by

JASON DEMERS

COVER AND TEXT DESIGN: Duncan Noel Campbell
COPY EDITOR: Ryan Perks
PROOFREADER: Alison Strobel
COVER PHOTO: "Closeup of a deep narrow prison window with bars on a white wall" by Wirestock / Adobe Stock

The CBC interviews on pages 101–103 and 116–121 have been reprinted with permission of CBC Licensing.

Library and Archives Canada Cataloguing in Publication

TITLE: The life sentences of Rik McWhinney / Rik McWhinney; edited with an introduction by Jason Demers.

NAMES: McWhinney, Rik, –2019, author. | Demers, Jason, 1979– editor.

SERIES: Regina collection.

DESCRIPTION: Series statement: The Regina collection ; 19 | Poetry, letters, essays, and   interviews. | Includes bibliographical references.

IDENTIFIERS: Canadiana (print) 20220259348 | Canadiana (ebook) 20220259402 | ISBN 9780889778979   (softcover) | ISBN 9780889778986 (PDF) | ISBN 9780889778993 (EPUB)

CLASSIFICATION: LCC PS8625.W58 L54 2022 | DDC C818/.6—dc23

10   9   8   7   6   5   4   3   2   1

University of Regina Press

University of Regina, Regina, Saskatchewan, Canada, S4S 0A2
TEL: (306) 585-4758 FAX: (306) 585-4699
WEB: www.uofrpress.ca

We acknowledge the support of the Canada Council for the Arts for our publishing program. We acknowledge the financial support of the Government of Canada. / Nous reconnaissons l'appui financier du gouvernement du Canada. This publication was made possible with support from Creative Saskatchewan's Book Publishing Production Grant Program.

Canada Council Conseil des arts   Canadä   creative
for the Arts   du Canada   SASKATCHEWAN

Contents

VII) POSTTRAUMATIC STRESS DISORDER

Acknowledgements

WORK ON THIS BOOK BEGAN WHEN RIK WAS IN solitary confinement in BC Pen almost half a century ago. Rik continued to write in large part because he was encouraged to do so by Peter J. Murphy and Wayne Knights, two university professors he encountered during the early years of his incarceration on the West Coast. Although writing is usually a solitary exercise, it is through relationships that portfolios grow, voices are developed, and insight into unknown regions and experiences is gleaned. I was fortunate to meet Rik when I moved to Regina in 2012. By that time, he had already amassed his portfolio and he was eager to share it. Thanks are owed to Sister RéAnne Letourneau for introducing me to Rik, for being a remarkable ally to Rik while he was living, and for continuing to exchange stories with me after he passed. Rik's death left a gap in both of our lives; our continued friendship helps to bridge that gap, and our exchange of stories keeps Rik animated in our memories. Helmed by Ruth Robillard,

Friends on the Outside provides a venue for coffee and friendship between incarcerated and non-incarcerated people. Indeed, it was over weekly coffee that Rik and I got to know each other, and we were able to build a friendship that was important to us both. I am extremely grateful to Rik's sister Dale Marcano for her permission to publish Rik's work posthumously, and for trusting me to finish the work Rik and I had started.

David Carpenter, Michael Jackson, Peter J. Murphy, and colleagues in the Department of English at the University of Regina provided support and encouragement when the project was in its formative stages. With the help of a Faculty of Arts Creative Research Award, combined with funds from the Faculty of Graduate Studies and Research at the University of Regina, I was able to have recorded conversations transcribed, and I was able to hire a remarkable research assistant, Jesse Desjarlais, who helped me to compile the book.

It was a pleasure to work with the team at University of Regina Press. Karen May Clark ferried the book through the review process and into production. As the book made its way through the production process, it was in the capable hands of a brilliant editing, design, and distribution team. Special thanks to Kelly Laycock, Duncan Noel Campbell, David McLennan, Melissa Shirley, and Curran Faris for their work on this book. The book benefited greatly from Ryan Perks's expert copy-editing work and Alison Strobel's careful proofreading.

Thanks to PASAN for their permission to publish "In Remembrance," which originally appeared in *Cell Count* no. 30.

Thanks to CBC Licensing for permission to publish "Televised Debate on the Death Penalty, CBC's Crossfire at Edmonton Max," a transcript of an episode of the television show Crossfire that originally aired on CBC Alberta in 1987, and "CBC Radio Interview: Prison Justice Day," the transcript of a segment that originally aired on CBC Radio Edmonton on August 10, 1995.

Introduction
by Jason Demers

"RIK? . . . RIK?!"

"Yeah. What do you want?"

"I did it."

"That's good, buddy."

"I finally did it."

"Did what?"

Rik hears footsteps coming down the walkway that runs in front of his cell. He's in solitary confinement, where sound is generally a prisoner's only stimulus and mode of interaction. There's conversation and camaraderie, to be sure, but screaming, groaning, and the pounding of heads, hands, and feet against steel punctuate the hours; in a concrete and steel dungeon that's lit 24/7, there's no such thing as circadian rhythm. Rik hears more footsteps—hurried footsteps—and some commotion. He walks over to the thick steel door at the front of his cell and lines his eyes up with a small judas window so that he can try to see what's happening, but because the window has been built so that he can be observed, and not the other way around, he doesn't have the luxury of peripheral vision. After a few minutes, he can hear several men coming back in his direction. Eventually, Rik sees that his friend has been removed from his cell; he's flanked by guards holding him up by his elbows and armpits, his head hunched over a blood-drenched towel. He's letting out a series of guttural moans, the most chilling sound that Rik has ever heard.

Later on that day, Rik finds out that his friend has slashed out both of his eyes with the piece of rusted blade that the men on the range circulated, via a hiding spot in the shower, for the purpose of self-mutilation. Such behaviour was the only release the men could find, and one of their only routes to human touch as wounds required stitching and dressing at the nurse's station. Rik would never see his friend again, but those all-too-human groans are forever imprinted in his memory. Though the images and sounds of that day plague him recurrently, their violent intrusion always catches him off guard and sends him reeling. Post-release, Rik is always tense. But as guarded as he is about every element of his environment and his place within it, one is never prepared to be interrupted by such violent memories.

I invite Rik into my prison writing class and he shares an excerpt from his poem "Slash Solitary." It's a poem that he's rearranged many times. Themes and variations. It's a poem, it would seem, that has proven impossible for him to escape, work through, or get in order. It makes reference to this episode with his friend, so he shares the story with the class. Although Rik insists that he be able to share his story every chance he gets, especially with students, I know he will be woken by nightmares and plagued by invasive thoughts for the next week.[1] Rik has been diagnosed with posttraumatic stress disorder, or PTSD. It's a condition he wasn't aware of and didn't fully understand when he was first told he had it, so he sought out a second opinion, confirmed the diagnosis, and ultimately endured the symptoms without much hope that he'd receive assistance: If military veterans and first responders were struggling to access available remedies, what chance did a lifer—someone who'd spent thirty-four and a half years in Canada's federal penitentiary system, about sixteen of them in solitary confinement—have to get the help that he needed to make his post-incarceration life bearable?

Rik always had complete command of the room as he divulged to the class, on the basis of his first-hand experience of life behind barbed wire fences and concrete walls, some of Canada's hidden history. On what ended up being his final visit, I introduced him to my students by telling them about his PTSD; I had just set him off on the way to class. Rik had been awake most of the night with a Crohn's flare-up and he was feeling quite rough, so when it seemed we'd have it to ourselves, I suggested we take the elevator rather than walk up the four flights of stairs to the classroom. Each time the elevator doors started to shut, however, two or three more students would charge in. In addition to Rik's low tolerance for small, enclosed spaces, I quickly learned that introducing a crowd into such a space was a definite faux pas. His body tensed and his eyes darted around. No one in the elevator was in danger from Rik, but they all represented potential threats to him. Rik had endured a great number of stabbings while incarcerated. Over the course of three and a half decades, Rik had been trained not to allow himself any vulnerabilities. After his release, he always stayed with his back to a wall, and close to an unobstructed exit.

That Rik suffered from PTSD meant that it had become difficult for him to function in society *because* of his incarceration. From seeing a friend slash his eyes out, to hearing and smelling a young, freshly admitted prisoner burn himself to death with leather glue, to witnessing and enduring all manner of beatings and stabbings, to living year upon year surrounded by never-ending lamplight and barely human screams, Rik had spent decades in institutions that were built to rehabilitate but that in fact did the opposite, making post-incarceration life overwhelming and almost impossible to endure. Because of the prevalence of traumatic experiences in prison, the nightmares and invasive thoughts associated with PTSD tend to begin quite early in one's sentence: posttraumatic stress is endemic in an environment where trauma is ongoing. So while it's easy to recognize that a post-incarceration stress response to crowds is irrational—it's rooted in the prison context, a place where crowds are unpredictable and dangerous—it's equally important to recognize that one's response to crowds and volatile situations within prison isn't rational either. As Rik notes in our conversation about his experiences in a Special Handling Unit, where men were always on edge, and where the nightmares that he now understands to be a symptom of his P T S D had already begun (see "In Conversation 1," in section 2), prison is always already an environment brimming with posttraumatic stress. In a sort of self-fulfilling prophesy, this, in turn, makes crowds within prison unpredictable and dangerous.

Due to his lengthy incarceration, Rik had developed many tics that made social outings a challenge, but because he was prone to depression and self-seclusion in the cement-floored Salvation Army bachelor's pad he wryly called his "cell," such outings were a must. Rik was unforgiving of anyone who took a long time at a cash register, especially if paying with cards that Rik himself had never used and didn't understand. Rik's experience had taught him that one entered the commissary line with a defined list of items and didn't ask questions; any delay could mean that those at the back of the line wouldn't make it to the front in time to be served. Rik wasn't always quiet about his contempt, not only for inefficient customers, but also and especially for gatekeepers like security guards and store managers who didn't like Rik's tattoos, or his gait, and singled him out for extra scrutiny. Rik had done his time and simply wanted to be free to walk through the world. He posed no harm, but he didn't exactly look or act like the typical twenty-first-century consumer. Going out with Rik in his neighbourhood was especially difficult because he had been banned from a number of establishments. That his neighbourhood was "in transition" meant that being banned was a common experience for those locals deemed "unsightly." Rik never bought much, but he never stole or vandalized, and he only let his tongue loose when cornered and provoked. His preference was to leave any premises where he was uncomfortable.

Rik "shopped" because the world was a curious place. After spending more than thirty-four years in the federal penitentiary system, Rik was granted conditional release in 2007. This meant that a parole board decided that he could serve the remainder of his sentence in the community while under the supervision of a parole officer. When he was brought to a grocery store upon release, he was confused by the presence of winter jackets, rubber boots, pots and pans, electronics, and stationery, so he asked if he had been brought to the wrong store—he just wanted to pick up some bread and milk. Rik could easily spend an hour in a tiny store, and many hours in much larger ones, picking up and examining any and every object that grabbed his attention. The completely logical outcome of decades of deprivation it turns out, was prototypical suspicious behaviour, and assuring security guards that there was nothing to worry about, that he was just curious about the world because he had spent most of his life in prison, was never the best option for defusing a situation.

I remember the first time I met Rik. He was wearing jeans, a denim shirt and leather jacket, cowboy boots, a fedora, and blue-tinted glasses. He was quiet and reserved. His hands—with "LOVE" and "HATE" tattooed across the fingers—were clasped together in front of him. Rik watched and listened to me intently. I could tell that I was being sized up. As our conversation veered toward Allen Ginsberg, William S. Burroughs, George Jackson, James Baldwin, and Edmund White's biography of Jean Genet, it was pretty clear from his animation and smile that I had not only passed his test, but we had quite a lot in common. But then we also didn't. We were from very different worlds, and as I sat across the table from Rik, it wasn't lost on me that he had not only faced judgment in court, the ultimate result being two life sentences for murder (one committed on each side of the prison walls within which he had spent the majority of his life), but he also faced judgment every time someone found out that he had spent any time at all in prison, let alone thirty plus years for two murders. Given the chance to speak, Rik was certainly much more than the sum of those labels—"prisoner," "con," "lifer," "murderer"—that led to snap judgments and that, ultimately, having been appended to him, tended to speak in his place. Labels silence, and that silencing can have a determining effect on one's life.

All too often, Canadian penal history is narrated as a history of commission reports and policy reforms enacted against a backdrop of perpetual crisis. The poetry, letters, grievance forms, and interviews collected in this book instead constitute a personal, documentary history of a long incarceration that lasted from the mid-1970s through to the late 2000s. It is in the face of that "official" history—the reports and reforms that might be read as a history of progress in thinking and a push for progressive reforms—that Rik endures and ultimately emerges from three and a half decades of incarceration both physically and psychologically broken. Where the late-twentieth-century history of the Canadian prison is concerned, the insider's story is a crucial reminder of the disjuncture between official narratives and lived experience. For that reason, prisoner accounts don't simply add to what we already know about the prison system—they provide a completely different perspective.

≡ ❋ ≡

AS IS THE case with many people who come from troubled homes, Rik was deemed "incorrigible" from very early on.[2] I knew Rik for a long time before learning anything but anecdotes about his childhood. He spoke openly, frequently, and fondly about skipping school as a second grader: he found school boring, and he'd decided that catching frogs by the neighbourhood creek was a better way to spend his days. (Judging by the way his face lit up every time he reminisced about his frog-catching days—he obviously continued to derive joy from the experience nearly sixty years later—it was hard not to agree with him.)

Rik also spoke matter-of-factly about how he was a serial runaway. Beginning in third grade, he would run away for days, even weeks on end, living on the streets, sleeping in parked cars, parks, and laundromats, scrounging for food outside of bakeries and restaurants, and occasionally breaking into homes to raid the cupboards. Rik barely completed grade 3 due to the frequency of his truancy. All of this, however, was bundled into a kind of self-fashioned caricature: Rik the incorrigible, always up for an adventure.

When Rik talked about running away, he never discussed what he was running away from. Just as he had the air of a mischievous child when reminiscing about the escapades of his early youth, when pressed to dig deeper into his childhood, Rik embodied this past in his demeanour: he slumped down in his chair, his eyes became vacant, and his voice lost all of its expressiveness. On the spectrum of childhood normalcy, Rik found his place among the firecrackers; the problem was, his stepfather had no patience for his spark. Rik was frequently spanked and beaten with a belt, and when he was caught sneaking a cigarette, he was forced to eat an entire pack. Rik's mother was of no help in these situations because she was herself subject to horrific abuse at her husband's hands, and she couldn't leave due to financial dependency. As a young child, Rik tended to run away because of the powerlessness he experienced as a child confronted by adult violence. His stepfather's violently enforced intransigence, fuelled by alcoholism, had a determining effect on the path that his life would take. Rik found his stepfather's gun and decided that the only way to stop this big and violent man from beating his mother was to kill him. All Rik needed was bullets, which he was caught trying to steal from a hardware store. Rather than reflecting upon and changing his own ways, Rik's stepfather sent Rik away to be corrected by the state. As a result of trying to save his beloved mom from his ferocious stepdad, Rik began his life of incarceration at the provincially run Brookside School at the age of nine.

≡ **#** ≡

ON RIK'S FIRST night at the reform school, he received a beating at the hands of a staff member, replete with full-on punches to his face, that was more severe than anything he had endured at home. Rik remained at the Brookside School until he was thirteen, and even then he wasn't returned home, but instead was transferred to the Hillcrest School because he was proving to be too much for the Cobourg staff to handle. Rik was perpetually belligerent and, as was the case when he lived at home, was always running away. These escape attempts weren't simply a part of who he was, of course. Like at home, there was a reason why he was running away from reform school: a staff member had been sexually assaulting him and beating him when he wouldn't comply. The first time he ran away he was picked up by the police. When he told them what was happening to him, they refused to believe him and returned him to the school.

Brookside and Hillcrest are two of thirteen training schools named in a certified class action lawsuit against the Province of Ontario stemming from allegations of rampant and horrific physical, sexual, and psychological abuse. Two months after Rik passed away, in March 2019, CTV's *W5* ran a segment on the schools. It centres on Brookside, and includes interviews with Rick Brown and Phil Mynott, two survivors who were physically and sexually abused by staff during the 1960s. Brown's tenure at the school overlaps with Rik's.[3] Shortly before the lawsuit was certified, Brookside was in the spotlight when Brown sparked a police investigation, more than half a century later, into the possible murder of James Forbes, another student at the school.[4] Rik would have witnessed Forbes being torn from his bed and beaten to a pulp by a staff member after Forbes refused the latter's request to get out of his bunkbed. Police eventually located Forbes, and he explained what had happened to him all those years ago. He was beaten so severely that he lost consciousness for three days and suffered a ruptured nerve near his spine. After he was released from the hospital, he spent thirty days in solitary confinement. Brown never saw him again because he had been sent to another part of the facility.[5]

According to the statement of claim filed on behalf of former students, staff at the training schools were unskilled and lacked proper training to have children in their care,[6] and children at the schools were not allowed to visit or be in contact with their families. Because sentences were indeterminate, " 'bad behaviour,' including the reporting of physical, sexual, or psychological abuse," served to lengthen children's sentences. The schools lacked any mechanism to report or safeguard against such abuse.[7] Children were made to hit other children, they were covered with blankets and beaten, and they were placed in solitary confinement while their feet were shackled and their hands were cuffed.[8]

Rik claimed that he enjoyed his classes, but he refused to submit to authority; he regularly lashed out at staff, smashed his cell, and filled his cell's lock with glue. His behaviour led to perpetual conflict with school authorities, and eventually discipline. Almost immediately after leaving the training school at the age of sixteen, he stole a car, got in an accident, and received his first adult sentence of eighteen months. For the next four years, Rik was in and out of BC correctional institutes, mostly due to property crime, until he was involved in a murder in 1974—a drug deal gone bad—when he was twenty-three.

Rik's pathway to Canada's penitentiary system was not unique. In a 2016 article in the *National Post*, lawyer Loretta Merritt, who has taken on hundreds of training school survivors as clients, notes that many are now housed in Canada's prisons, and some have violent and lengthy criminal histories.[9] Labelling the legacy of Ontario's training schools a tragedy, clinical psychologist Catherine Classen notes that "if we actually would address the impact of trauma in childhood, of abuse in childhood, we would empty our prisons."[10]

≡ ✿ ≡

A crisis exists in the Canadian penitentiary system. It can be met only by the immediate implementation of large-scale reforms. It is imperative that the Solicitor General act immediately on this report as a matter of utmost urgency. —*Report to Parliament by the Subcommittee on the Penitentiary System in Canada*[11]

Prison hostage taking, knifing, rape, suicide—
these occur with a regularity that is as frightening as the conditions which generate them. Put
anyone in a depraved environment and deprav-
ity will follow, since reactions are violent when
there are no other alternatives. Concrete and
steel will be demolished, and self-mutilations
will increase. —CLAIRE CULHANE, *Barred
from Prison*[12]

IT IS OFTEN said that Canada's "modern" penitentiary system was articulated in the 1938 report of the
Archambault Commission. The report was critical of
dirty and poorly ventilated penitentiaries that kept prisoners locked up for as much as sixteen hours a day with
little in the way of educational or rehabilitative programming.[13] With recidivism rates rapidly on the rise,[14]
the report criticized the continued use of corporal punishment, noting that Canada lagged behind the United
States and most of Europe in this regard.[15] To rehabilitate
offenders, the commission argued, emphasis needed
to be placed on education, work programming, and
increased recreational activity.[16] To counterbalance the
debilitatingly depressing conditions of confinement,
the report advocated for more yard time on weekends, the
development of sports leagues, the organization of con-
certs, and the encouragement of hobbies.[17] While the
report is notable in its concern for mental and physical
well-being, its paternalistic emphasis on discipline as
distinct from punishment is unaccompanied by any

consideration of how the increased prison population might be linked to the depressed economy of the 1930s.

The Archambault Commission never would have been formed if not for a high-profile uprising at Kingston Penitentiary in 1932, a disturbance that followed on the heels of uprisings at Stony Mountain, Saint-Vincent-de-Paul, and Dorchester Penitentiaries. The unrest at Kingston was directly tied to conditions in the penitentiary; the hope was to make the injustice of those conditions visible to the public in order to provoke reform.[18] A dozen more disturbances took place within federal penitentiaries between 1933 and 1937. Alongside front-page coverage of the trials that took place in the wake of the Kingston uprising, persistent unrest ensured that prisons remained in the news cycle.[19]

When Rik entered the federal penitentiary system in the mid-1970s, tensions surrounding the implementation of reforms had hit a fever pitch. The gravity of the situation is quantified in the 1977 *Report to Parliament by the Subcommittee on the Penitentiary System in Canada* (the so-called MacGuigan report). After a seven-year stretch of relative peace, uprisings grew in size and frequency between 1970 and 1976, by which time they were a more or less constant affair. While there had been sixty-five major incidents in the federal penitentiary system between 1932 and 1974, in 1975–6 alone there were sixty-nine.[20] The MacGuigan report notes that prison reform at this juncture had only "reached the surface of the system" and not "the attitudes of the people within it."[21] After nearly four decades of struggle and negotiation over working and living conditions, the penitentiary system reached a point, in the 1970s, where often open warfare had become the status quo. While guards preferred to keep prisoners in perpetual lock-up—veteran guards in particular were vocal in their desire to return to the old code of enforced silence, corporal punishment, shaved heads, and prison stripes[22]—prisoners understood that prison directors were under pressure from Ottawa to introduce programs, and to open things up.

Rik landed in the British Columbia Penitentiary in 1974; by that time, disturbances in the prison had become a constant. A major issue was the punitive use of solitary confinement, a practice whose brutality was being challenged in the BC Federal Court on behalf of a number of incarcerated plaintiffs in 1974–5. In June 1975, while the case was still before the court, three men refused to return to solitary confinement. The men took fifteen hostages and became engaged in a forty-one-hour standoff that ended with an emergency response team storming the hostage-takers. While retaking the prison, the team shot one of the hostage-takers through the jaw and shot and killed one of the hostages, thirty-two-year-old classification officer Mary Steinhauser.[23]

Solitary confinement was not the only issue plaguing the prison. Prisoners were concerned about plumbing problems that restricted access to both hot and cold water; there was a lack of outdoor recreation, and no TV room; segregated prisoners were having difficulty accessing lawyers while the case against segregation was being built; and as tensions mounted between prisoners and guards, prisoners began to express concern

with meal service: guards were serving meal trays lit-
tered with broken glass and cigarette butts, so prisoners
wanted kitchen staff to serve their meals in place of
the guards.[24]

Tensions in the 1970s were in part attributable to
large-scale organizational shifts—namely, the introduction of a new regional hierarchy that followed the
regionalization of the Canadian penitentiary system in
1961, and the formation of a staff union in 1967.[25] In the
context of these changes, prisoners found themselves
"trapped between antagonistic guards and an arbitrary
bureaucracy."[26] Although then director of the BC Penitentiary, Dragan Cernetic, did not explicitly encounter
interference from the prison's newly minted regional
director, pressing concerns about the operation of the
facility were routinely ignored for lengthy periods
as they were routed through a bureaucracy that had
quickly bloated (120 staff took up two full floors of the
Pacific Centre office tower in downtown Vancouver).[27]
Exacerbating the situation, the guards' union was pres-
suring the administration to address its demands by
employing strategies meant to provoke unrest.

The union had been using overtime bans since 1974 to
address various concerns, including an overabundance
of overtime and a lack of staff training. To address the
staffing shortages that an overtime ban would produce,
the union proposed scaling back prisoner recreation
time, which involved locking up cells at an earlier hour
(even though BC Pen already had the earliest lock-up
time in the federal system).[28] Director Cernetic was
sympathetic to many of the demands presented to

him by the union—aging infrastructure left some cor-
ridors without lights, and the telephone system had
stopped working—but unmet demands often amounted
to promises he had only unwittingly broken because
they were tangled in the red tape of the regional or
federal bureaucracy. To make matters worse, BC Pen
was being wilfully neglected; indeed, since 1948, there
had been no less than twenty-six declarations that the
aging prison would be replaced, and yet not once had
those promises been kept.[29]

Manipulation of the prison environment wasn't just
a useful negotiating chip in the union's direct dealings
with management, it also enabled guards to garner
public attention and sympathy. As Citizen's Advisory
Committee member Claire Culhane put it, "the public
could be called upon to support [the guards], as they
could then point to still another 'riot' which 'hard-
pressed,' 'over-worked,' 'under-paid' guards must cope
with."[30] Such negotiation tactics weren't restricted to
BC Pen either. As Gérard McNeil and Sharon Vance
pointed out after touring the country's federal penitentiaries with the MacGuigan inquiry of 1976–7,
"throughout the land, prisoners were being taunted,
almost urged to violence."[31] Indeed, the tactics being
used to provoke unrest had already been identified
as predictable catalysts for unrest at the beginning
of the 1970s. A commission of inquiry into an infamous 1971 uprising at Kingston Penitentiary warned
that five years of cuts to programs and privileges in
the name of security had resulted in an environment
of extreme tension based in policies and practices of

mass deprivation. That inquiry concluded that "the depressing and dehumanizing life of [Kingston Penitentiary] was the soil within which the violent seed" of the 1971 uprising had been "planted to grow."[32] Echoing recommendations found in the Archambault Report of 1938, the resulting report argued that unrest could be averted with increased recreation and programming, and by minimizing the hours during which incarcerated people are forcibly confined to their cells.[33]

Tensions in B C Pen came to a head once again in late September 1976, while the guards' union was negotiating a new contract.[34] The union imposed an overtime ban that would have pushed lock-up back by an hour on weekdays and four hours on weekends. Announcement of the ban was met with an emergency order that allowed the prison's director to assign overtime. When the director went on medical leave later that month, however, prisoners feared that union-favored policies would prevail, precipitating an uprising in his absence.[35] In the summer of 1976, a Citizen's Advisory Committee as well as an Inmate Committee had been formed to help address issues and prevent tragedies such as the one that occurred in June 1975, when Mary Steinhauser was killed. At the beginning of the September 1976 uprising, prisoners were being allowed to smash up their cells without intervention. Recognizing this to be a strategic move on the part of the union, a group of prisoners took hostages in an effort to prevent what they feared would be a violent response by guards, and to bring in the Citizen's Advisory Committee so that an amicable resolution could be reached.[36]

Citizen's Advisory Committee member and professor of law Michael Jackson—one of the lawyers responsible for bringing prisoners' concerns about solitary confinement to the BC Federal Court—argued that the uprising might have been averted altogether if prisoners had been allowed to address the public about their concerns. After all, the union had been able to do so with bias and regularity. The chair of the Inmate Committee, Ivan Horvat, was eventually able to address the media at a press conference, but he did so with a prison riot as his backdrop, and his message was ultimately suppressed by the media's decision to present his crimes as context for his address.[37] Though first-hand observers from the Citizen's Advisory Committee had a solid understanding of the desperation and urgency behind Horvat's pleas for reform, as McNeil and Vance point out, "the dilemma that all prisoners face in trying to swing public opinion behind prison reform . . . is [that it is] their past that catches the public eye, not their present. Their grievances, no matter how legitimate they may be, are overlooked by the general public."[38]

The hostages' release was eventually negotiated between the administration, the prisoners, the Citizen's Advisory Committee, and a representative from the RCMP. Excepting a call for a public inquiry into conditions at BC Pen, the terms were aimed at averting reprisal. The inquiry into the Kingston uprising in 1971 had found that guards had beaten perceived ringleaders, including making them run a gauntlet upon transfer to Millhaven Penitentiary,[39] a new supermaximum-security prison where violence and abuse of perceived troublemakers—through "the use of clubs, shackles, tear gas and dogs, often in combination"—was regularized.[40] The Inmate and Citizen's Advisory Committees had reason for hope. A negotiated settlement between the prison director and the Inmate Committee at Archambault Prison in Sainte-Anne-des-Plaines, Quebec, put an end to a work stoppage and hostage-taking, leading to better living conditions and the restoration of programming.[41] This did not happen at BC Penitentiary. After the agreement was signed, 240 prisoners were warehoused in a gym the size of a basketball court for two months without access to proper food and medical care (prisoners were only moved to another wing when a bomb was set off and a fire set, but the wing they were sent to had no running water and no lights);[42] prisoners were also denied access to the outside exercise yard throughout this period (reference to staffing issues remained a legitimizing theme); and prisoners were transferred to solitary confinement units throughout the country. When transferred prisoners were returned to BC, they were placed in the hole.[43] Illustrating the creativity employed in achieving reprisal, one member of the Inmate Committee faced thirty-seven institutional charges within three months of the settlement, including three charges of walking too close to the wall; he was taken to solitary confinement by a "goon squad."[44]

≡ ＃ ≡

RIK NEVER DISCUSSED the specifics of his involvement in these struggles at BC Pen. An institutional memo indicates his involvement in the Inmate Committee in 1976, but for Rik, the mid- to late 1970s was a time of perpetual slashings and suicide attempts during which he was ferried back and forth between the general population, solitary confinement, and B C's Regional Psychiatric Centre. In 1975, the B C Federal Court handed down its decision, establishing that the regime of solitary confinement practised at the penitentiary constituted cruel and unusual punishment. Self-mutilation and suicide were well-documented symptoms of the practice. Nevertheless, even after the decision was handed down, the violence of solitary confinement continued to be used to segregate and break recalcitrant prisoners.

For the public, hostage-takings and riots were the most visible manifestations of the wars being waged behind prison walls, but these battles were often fought on behalf of imprisoned people themselves, who were subject to some of the most horrific and inescapable conditions within the Canadian penitentiary system at the time. If it was suspected that a prisoner was plotting something within the prison, they could be held in the solitary confinement unit indefinitely, without recourse, and often without any indication of why they were being segregated; they were merely handed a slip of paper on a monthly basis letting them know that their case had been reviewed.[45] There really was no way out of the unit either. Michael Jackson called the practice a "psychological treadmill put into motion and maintained by ever increasing hostility and recrimination."[46] Due to the perceived dangerousness of the men in solitary, guards felt justified in their extremely harsh treatment of them. In turn, prisoners asserted their autonomy by refusing to submit to the guards' authority. Not only was confinement to the unit indefinite, but there was no way to demonstrate progress toward one's potential release.[47] In this context, any form of resistance was used to legitimize further dissociation; resistance was never read as a challenge aimed at changing the system itself.[48]

Rik was anchored to this treadmill of recrimination for almost half of his thirty-four years in the penitentiary system. When BC Pen was decommissioned in 1980, he went to the solitary confinement unit at Kent Institution in Agassiz, BC[49]—they even moved the furniture, so Rik's environment would have been familiar despite the fact that he had been uprooted.[50] Rik would go on to experience solitary confinement and Special Handling Units in Ontario, Saskatchewan, and Alberta. Rik took responsibility for his behaviour, and especially for the violence that he enacted upon others. In spite of this, one has to imagine how different his life, and especially his behaviour, might have been had he not been subjected to a form of detention—and perpetual recrimination—that not only claimed lives in the form of suicide, but that destroyed men's minds, rendering them disaffected and dangerous in the process. Before he even entered the penitentiary system, Rik had already been primed for confrontation. Among the damages listed on the statement of claim against Ontario's physically, sexually, and psychologically abusive training school system is prisoners' "impaired ability to deal with persons in positions of authority."[51]

Solitary confinement was not the only method employed to deal with Rik's recalcitrance. As part of a "treatment" philosophy that was articulated, if never fully or uniformly implemented, during the postwar period, psychiatric hospitals were opened within the prison system, and professional staff were recruited to work with offenders deemed mentally or socially ill. The idea was that, with proper diagnosis, classification, and treatment, offenders could be cured.[52] Doctors, nurses, psychologists, and psychiatrists played a small role in the Canadian penitentiary system in the 1950s, '60s, and '70s, but the regimes they represented meant that encounters with them had the potential to leave an indelible mark on a prisoner. By and large, these types of treatment—including electroconvulsive, aversion, and drug therapies, often in combination with solitary confinement—were reserved for sex offenders and prisoners who engaged in acts of violence.[53] In lashing out against himself and others, Rik fit within the latter group.

While Rik was in solitary confinement at the Regional Psychiatric Centre in Abbotsford, BC, he was subjected to aversion therapy using Haloperidol (Haldol), a common anti-psychotic drug whose known side effects include painful, Parkinson's-like symptoms of rigidity and stiffness, particularly of the neck. Rik would be injected with the drug while he was restrained, and it would put him into painful spasm. The nurse who administered the injection would then proceed to show Rik a second syringe containing Cogentin, a drug used to treat Parkinson's, and which was commonly administered alongside Haloperidol to alleviate the drug's side effects. She told Rik that she would only give him the second needle if he promised to behave. Because Rik sustained so many head injuries while incarcerated, it is impossible to know whether the neurological problems he exhibited later in life were related to the neurotoxicity of Haloperidol, though it should be noted that neuroscientists have been documenting the harmful effects of Haloperidol on brain tissue for the last two decades.[54] As a result of this aversion therapy, combined with consistently callous treatment by medical staff when he slashed or attempted suicide (which he did often), Rik developed a strong aversion to nurses and hospitals.

⇒ ✳ ⇐

I LEARNED OF this aversion first-hand after inviting Rik to my house one evening to watch a recently aired news segment on PTSD service dogs. Rik didn't have an internet connection in his apartment, but he had heard about the segment from a friend. PTSD service dogs had lately become an obsession for him, for obvious reasons: living with PTSD was debilitating, and Rik loved animals. As we watched the segment, Rik stared blankly at my computer screen. I imagined that he was frustrated by the mediocrity of the segment, or that he was depressed by how prohibitively expensive it was to obtain a trained dog—even for middle-class people whose traumas were culturally accepted. When the documentary was over, I could barely get a word out of Rik. He said he wanted a smoke, so we went out back and sat on the steps. I monologued while he stared at the fence. He said he had a headache and asked for some Tylenol. We sat silently for another fifteen minutes before he asked to go home.

When I dropped Rik off, he struggled to get his key in the door. He jabbed it into the air on either side of the knob before settling it onto the painted steel inches above the lock; he then slid his key down and slowly, clumsily, guided it into the keyhole. I asked Rik if he was okay, if he wanted me to stick around for a bit. He said no: his head hurt and he just wanted to get to bed.

Later that night, Rik had a seizure in his room. Not only did he fall hard onto his cement floor, but he pulled a shelving unit down on top of himself while he seized. He was taken to the hospital by ambulance. Rik was having perpetual seizures, so he was admitted into the neurology unit and was given medication to stop the seizures.

I had been told that Rik wasn't good in hospitals, and that he tended to bolt before he was officially discharged. When I visited him the next day, he was happy to see me and several other friends, but, drugged and somewhat disoriented, he was indeed unhappy to find himself in a hospital bed. When the nurse came by to fill in Rik's chart, I got my first glimpse of his distrust of medical professionals; I also became worried about the harm these perpetual seizures might have done him.

"What's *that* you've got in your hand?" Rik asked the nurse in an accusatory tone. "I saw that. What's *that* you're putting behind your back. I'm onto you," he said.

"This?" the nurse said, thrusting a blue pen up into full view.

Rik's eyes shot wide open and he recoiled on the bed, getting as far away as he could, eyes locked on the pen.

"What do think you're gonna do with that?" he spat, his defiant tone belied by his terrified posture.

"This?" the nurse asked again, confused. "It's a pen." She held up the pen to show Rik, who recoiled once again. As the nurse and her pen went from one side of the bed to the other, so did Rik, but in the opposite direction. Rik was keeping as far away as he could from the perceived danger.

If the nurse couldn't convince Rik, surely he would listen to his friends. And yet Rik wasn't comforted by our assurances either. We had little experience in his world. He had learned from many years of watching his own back; he was a survivor, and he wasn't going to let his guard down now. Rik's seizures continued unabated, as did his confusion and combativeness, so hospital staff decided to restrain him in his bed.

About a week into Rik's stay, I returned home to messages from his support team, first asking for help, and then informing me that Rik had bolted while other friends and supporters tried to convince him to stay in hospital. In the hospital, Rik was confused and drifting in and out of consciousness. His decline had been so rapid that we didn't think he was ever going to make it out. The extreme neurological events and symptoms he had been experiencing over the course of that first week merited constant monitoring and care.

After learning that Rik had left the hospital, I drove
to his apartment and spoke with him for hours. He was
a bit erratic, but he was lucid; within two days, he was
himself again. The medication they had been giving
him had been causing hallucinations. He had a pharma-
ceutical encyclopedia in his apartment and he flipped
through several bookmarked pages, explaining that his
regular medication and the new meds were contraindicated. Beyond his fear of nurses with pens, he had
seen snakes; he had been visited by Morris, a bobtail
cat whom he lived with while overseeing the feral cat
population at a prison farm annex (the hospital staff
were plotting to kill Morris, Rik said); the whiteboard
on the wall across from his bed was there to keep a running tally as staff debated the death penalty (death was
winning by a landslide—he told me about this while still
hospitalized, and he was both perplexed and distressed
by the callousness of his keepers); and Rik alleged that
he was roughed up when he was taken to be cleaned
in the shower. While this last claim is entirely possible, Rik also thanked me, with a smile and tears in his
eyes, for stopping by to wash his feet—something that
did not in fact happen. The gesture reminded him of
an event from Ginsberg's biography when, during his
travels in India, the poet washed the feet of a homeless
man. (I hated to let him down, but I also thought it was
appropriate to let Rik know that washing his feet was
something I had never thought to do.)

While it's impossible to know exactly how Rik was
treated while he hallucinated—he was often without

witnesses—there's no question that he should never have been tied down to a hospital bed and treated against his will (and Rik had the Patient's Bill of Rights to prove it). This was a new trauma for him, but it was tied to old traumas that he had lived as a prisoner in the 1970s. It was only after his experience in the hospital that I learned why Rik, even after seeking out help of his own volition, would always end up trying to flee these types of institutions.

On the basis of that experience, we learned what should have been obvious: under no circumstances should Rik be restrained in a hospital bed. It was his right to seek and refuse treatment as he saw fit. This meant that Rik, who was chronically ill (PTSD, Crohn's disease, hepatitis C, intermittent seizures, tremor syndrome, anemic, malnourished), faced a host of medical problems that went undiagnosed, and treatment was restricted to pain management (he saw a pain-management specialist, whom he trusted, on a monthly basis). When members of his support team accompanied him to the hospital, we were very sensitive to irrelevant questions about the reasons for his incarceration (his incarceration inevitably came up due to his medical history of stabbings and head trauma). Hospital staff routinely assumed that he was homeless and an addict. The sad truth is that he was treated better when accompanied by people who cared about him. When he made the mistake of telling a doctor about his murder convictions before undergoing a colonoscopy, he was subject to an extremely aggressive procedure without being administered any kind of anesthetic. After the procedure was finished, a nurse who witnessed the procedure apologized to Rik with tears in his eyes, telling Rik that what he had just experienced should never have happened.

With the help of Sister RéAnne Letourneau, Rik made use of Patient Advocate Services to make his experiences at the Regina General Hospital known to the Saskatchewan Health Authority.[55] While Rik would never return to that hospital, it was his hope that staff there would learn from his testimony, just as his support team had. Not only are medical professionals, like everyone else, a product of their biases, they are also a product of a medical system that often separates symptoms, diagnoses, and treatments from the patient who is deemed irrational if he or she refuses to submit unconditionally his or her body to a team of trained professionals. In a land of white coats and scrubs, the irate man in a gown, taking off in bare-assed flight, is sure to be cast as the fool.

⇒ ♯ ⇐

RIK'S ABILITY TO identify and speak out about systemic injustices and the needs of not only prisoners but all manner of underdogs (including feral cats) made him an asset to various causes later on in his incarceration; his incapacitation within the prison system, however, led him to adopt extreme measures in order to advocate on his own behalf. When Rik was incarcerated in BC Pen in 1975, he asked another prisoner to stab him because, although he had broken his arm and was in excruciating pain, he wasn't allowed to see medical staff. The tactic worked, but Rik's hired accomplice stabbed too deep and punctured a lung. Years later, Rik would dismiss clouding on preliminary images of his lungs as scarring from this mid-seventies wound. He died less than a year later from undiagnosed lung cancer. Rik pulled a similar stunt in the mid-nineties, when his repeated requests for medical attention in the face of a Crohn's flare-up fell on deaf ears. After learning the on-duty nurse had left on supper break, he returned to his cell, slashed his stomach with a razor blade, and stabbed himself with a pen, the wounds from which were two and a half inches deep (see "Submission of Facts Surrounding Crohn's Flare-Up" in section 6). Whenever Rik spoke about these incidents, he railed passionately against the officers and medical professionals who refused to tend to his needs, and he spoke matter-of-factly about the extreme measures that he took to get the care he felt he deserved. There's no question that such reactions are extremely abnormal, but in Rik's case they were a product of life in an extremely abnormal environment.

Rik was granted parole on the basis of a number of factors, but one of the reasons for his release was that, after years of incarceration and solitary confinement, his ill health, and especially the results of a particularly brutal attack on his person, ensured that he would be sufficiently incapacitated upon release. The attack in question took place a few days after Rik embarrassed a younger prisoner by suggesting that his hotheaded approach to a collective beef in the C Unit at Saskatchewan Penitentiary would get him nowhere, and the prisoner viciously attacked Rik while he was sleeping in front of a television on a couch in the common room. Using a sock filled with c-cell batteries, the perpetrator focused his attack on Rik's head, shattering the right frontal, temporal, and parietal regions of his skull and causing bruising to his brain. Rik also sustained fractures of his orbital bone, sinus, nose, and upper jaw. Presumably left for dead by the perpetrator, Rik nevertheless regained consciousness after five or ten minutes and was able to stagger to a nearby cell for help. His injuries required reconstructive surgery, the insertion of metal plates into his jaw and sinus area, and left him blind in one eye and deaf in one ear. Though he subsequently learned the identity of his assailant, and that of an accomplice who stood watch while he was attacked, Rik never showed any interest in retaliation. At this juncture, the prison was proving to be ill-equipped to deal with Rik's Crohn's, and the attack on him showed that he was no longer safe within the prison environment (though, scanning the many scars left on Rik's body and brain via physical and psychological trauma, the argument must be made that no one is ever equipped for life within this environment). Rik was not rehabilitated or corrected by the prison system—he was worn down and ultimately destroyed by it.

When Rik was singled out and called upon to react to a public screening of *The Cows Come Home*, a documentary about the shuttering of prison farm annexes in Ontario (presumably on account of his prison tats and general demeanour), he grumpily argued that he didn't understand all the talk about rehabilitation when so many of the people he had been caged with for so much of his life hadn't even been *habilitated* in the first place.[56] I was surprised by his reaction because we had spent many hours, including just before the documentary, reminiscing about how positive his experience of a prison farm annex had been, and how his first day at the annex marked the first time in almost three decades that he had felt the warmth of an animal in his arms. But Rik was right. Caring for animals may bring joy and teach empathy and responsibility—important pre-release lessons, especially for those returning to children—but why is such a program housed within the context of a prison, and bracketed off as part of the step-down process at the end of one's sentence? Rik was often frustrated at these sorts of things, and his insights were invaluable, because his experiences meant that he saw quite plainly what many others could not. Empathy is too often a virtue in short supply, and Rik's example shows that we have a lot to learn from the lives of others.

In the end, it's bizarre that we think prisons will systematically correct individuals who deviate from society's expectations, when we can plainly see that those individuals who are swept into that system, generally speaking, represent a rather narrow range of class, ethnic, and experiential backgrounds. When we look at this pattern, the logical target for correction becomes society itself. And the prison institution, for all the expense it incurs trying (and so often failing) to address the societal problems it inherits, has in fact proven itself adept at producing a range of new problems: it breaks up families; it harbours and breeds extreme prejudice, resentment, and violence; its environment and methods are often responsible for doing permanent physical and psychological damage to people; and one of its by-products is intergenerational distrust and resentment toward a justice system that is, for those families that are broken and disproportionately surveilled and scrutinized by it, patently unjust. We rightly condemn the violent acts of individuals while—without recognizing the contradiction—condoning and even applauding the systemic violence being done within and against poor and often racialized communities in the name of justice.

=⋕=

RIK PASSED AWAY peacefully in the palliative care unit of Regina's Pasqua Hospital in late January 2019. In his final hours, he was flanked by two nuns, very dear friends of his, who joked at his funeral that they never, in their wildest dreams, thought that they'd be spending the night together with a man between them. Rik spent his last days surrounded by the family who had adopted him. He was never alone, and nurses managed his pain with care and precision. A volunteer who worked in the unit learned that he was an animal lover and arranged to have a dog and cat cozy up with Rik on his bed.

Rik passed in the middle of a brutally cold Regina winter, and as it happens, wintering of the many bins of books and files he left behind in an unheated garage was necessary to kill off any of the bedbugs that remained after the three fumigations that punctuated Rik's final months in Waterston House, the Salvation Army building where he spent his final years. In late 2018, Rik had been systematically cancelling my visits with him due to illness. He had been battling severe Crohn's and PTSD-related insomnia since I met him, so the last-minute cancellations were routine, but I found out through another source that he was too embarrassed to share news of the infestation with anyone, and he absolutely didn't want to pass on the bedbugs to my young children. He had a particularly close bond with my oldest daughter, who was the first baby he met and held after thirty-four years of federal incarceration and almost a decade of parole. During his last week in palliative care, she insisted on accompanying me on my daily visits. His death has hit her hard. Her relationship with Rik is unclouded by knowledge of his convictions, or anything about his past. I sometimes think that it is she who knows Rik best.

About two years after we met, Rik began asking me for help publishing his poetry. As we discussed the project, we decided that his life was part of the larger story that his poetry was trying to tell. This was very much in line with what Rik had been hearing for years; indeed, friends and the many audience members he met at the restorative justice talks he gave all across small-town Saskatchewan had long been telling him that he needed to put his story to paper. An old laptop given to him by his sister might have served as a vehicle to this end, but Rik never took to computers, and the thing either sat enclosed within a store-bought clear plastic cake box on the desk in his room, or at a pawn shop up the street, where it was used as collateral for cigarette money. It was readily apparent that continued coaxing would do no good, so Rik and I sat with a tape recorder between us and talked through elements of his incarceration while he smoked. Parts of those conversations appear in this book. Conversations move organically, rather than in some linear fashion. Through our many hours of recorded conversation, there were a great many topics that we never discussed, but those topics that we did address, combined with the trove of materials that Rik left behind when he passed, determined the book's division into its various sections.

The book begins with "Initiations," composed of a single poem in which Rik narrates his fall from birth to institutionalization. This is followed by a longer section, "Solitary Confinement and Special Handling Units," exploring Rik's many years of experience with these particularly cruel forms of punishment. These are the prison environments that Rik quickly came to inhabit when he entered the federal penitentiary system; solitary confinement is where he spent nearly half of his time while incarcerated, and it's the region of the prison system that had the most indelible impact on him.

While the book begins with solitude, the next three sections explore the interpersonal dynamics of living with people inside. "Advocacy and (a) Prison(er's) Politics" collects some of Rik's political interventions—including letters, speeches, and a transcript of his intervention in a televised debate on the reinstatement of the death penalty while he was in Edmonton Max—as well as some poetry that captures his political orientations. "Prison Culture in the Time of the Code" considers the politics of living in an enclosed space over-coded with rules prescribing the interactions between prisoners. In this section, Rik discusses why abiding by the "con code" was crucial to his survival, how and why it was policed, and the long-term effects of living by rules that are particular to the institution of the prison. Finally, in "The Keepers and the Kept," Rik discusses a corresponding "guard code," and he devotes a great deal of attention, both in his poetry and the various grievance forms included—many of which are dripping with irony—to the transgressions of keepers with respect to the stringent expectations imposed upon the kept.

The next two sections explore the effects of incarceration on an incarcerated person's body and mind. That the fundamental fact of prison is confinement means that we sometimes overlook the way in which incarcerated people's bodies are treated with indignity. The section "The Bodies of the Condemned" examines how Rik was transferred from coast to coast irrespective of the location of loved ones, how his body was left to deteriorate and flare as he was denied access to proper health care, and his experience and witness of the routine violence that was done to bodies via non-consensual treatments and acts of retaliation. The short section "Posttraumatic Stress Disorder" includes a poem in which Rik takes stock of his state of mind post-incarceration, and a conversation between Rik and me on the cumulative psychological effects of his long incarceration.

The final section of the book, "Opportunities and Restorations," is somewhat hopeful—and perhaps all the more so because it sees Rik maintaining a principled stance of resistance. In grievance letters and a letter to Senator Earl Hastings, Rik is unwavering in his determination not to participate in programming if it is coerced. Also collected in this section are examples and discussion of his work as a peer counsellor and as a certified animal welfare specialist, showing that he thrived when provided with the opportunity to forge his own path. This is precisely what was denied Rik since his childhood.

While this book contains a number of one-on-one conversations about Rik's long incarceration, it is fundamentally a book of prison writing. Bob Gaucher, co-founder and former long-time editor of the *Journal of Prisoners on Prisons*, argues that the writing of prisoners is a kind of "counter inscription." In the late twentieth and early twenty-first centuries, he points out, prisoners have been writing against the grain of carceral expansion and the discourses that legitimize it; their representations of incarceration necessarily differ in content and register from what we find in academic studies, state reports, mass media, and public discourse.[57] While an increasingly robust tradition in the United States has helped the public to think its way out of certain entrenched ideas about the prison, Canada is still in the process of finding its incarcerated writers.

This book comprises many different types of documents. In addition to Rik's poetry, it collects letters that Rik wrote to politicians, advocates, loved ones, and charitable organizations; some of Rik's grievances against institutional procedures and personnel; a report on a "Cat Club" Rik started as a way to tend to the feral cat population at the Rockwood farm annex; the transcript of an interview he gave on CBC Radio; and Rik's interventions into a televised debate on the death penalty at Edmonton Max. Taken together, these documents provide a historical record of an incarcerated individual's voice over the course of a long incarceration, documenting daily life inside, as well as a perpetual struggle to connect with life outside prison walls. As an editor, one of my investments is to expand our understanding of what constitutes "prison writing." As the incarcerated person is inaccessible to society, the experience of incarceration, and therefore the administration of justice, is obscured from social view. As such, it is my contention that any document that gives voice to this experience should be considered prison writing.[58]

To think about the writing of incarcerated people is not only to consider the nature and function of various types of texts, but also to consider the relationship of those texts to the texts that constitute the prison itself. In his work on prison writing, Ioan Davies explores the "motifs, forms, continuities, metaphors, engagements [and] displacements which characterize the incarcerated imagination."[59] In his view, if texts constitute institutions—from the constituent ideas that bring institutions into being to the policy documents that drive their day-to-day operation—then "countertexts" can help us to map our way out of them.[60] Although we might look to the incarcerated writer for escape, it's a stubborn and entrenched set of metaphors that structures life inside the prison. Rik's poetry, prose, grievances, good works, and speech most definitely constitute a set of countertexts, but Rik was quite adamant about the fact that he never left the prison, even after he was paroled. To demand wholesale escape from someone who was incarcerated from the time he was a child is to demand the impossible.

If we want to understand the fundamental purpose of prison writing, which is communicative, we have to understand that escape doesn't come from the act of writing itself—even if, in the act of writing, one is trying to write themselves out of confinement. Time and time again, prisoners have risen up to protest the conditions of their confinement. Not unlike Rik, with his writings and his speech, this is because they are in search of an audience. While the incarcerated imagination might provide some form of escape within the prison's walls, to find an audience is to circulate outside of them.

Some Notes on the Text

UNLESS PUBLICLY AVAILABLE, the names of the incarcerated people Rik mentioned in our conversations are given here as a fabricated first name. I have employed this approach to allow for the humanization of incarcerated people while at the same time protecting their identities. Due to the way the names of correctional personnel routinely appear in official documents—first initial and last name—the names of individuals employed by Correctional Service Canada, unless they are public figures, have been obscured by way of fabricated initials where they appear. Rik's indictment is of the penitentiary system, and not of those individuals employed by it.

While I could not review or confirm the accuracy of all of Rik's statements, based on the way in which information was revealed during our interviews—information that is in every verifiable case consistent with Rik's personal documentary history, as well as various government reports—I have no reason to doubt the accuracy of his accounts.

1) Initiations

The dance of birth
  to breathing cries
    with startled looks
      at a sterilized world
        of rubber gloves & bacteria masks
       it has started
Bars of captivity
  thrown up for safety's sake
   while everything is tasted
    to appease puzzled sight
First words a diamond song
  which fell on possessive ears
    first steps the body's discovery
      to fall on possessive floors
        where bruises of the great game
       are first realized
The beauty of personal worlds
  played from dawn to dusk
    the ability to change with no loss
     while voices instructed
     there must be growth
First days in the great halls of learning
  play was a recess & laughing joy
    that knew no boundaries
      transcending rules of discipline
      with a refusal of recognition

To rebel against all that exists
  refusing homage to the leader
    who carried a big book & pencil
      taking notes of inquisition
        to preserve the social injustice
          of the situation
Scrambles for lineups to the mould-pouring ceremony
  callous words by ruthless authorities
    where competition for success was stifled
      until it blinded many & made them forget
        so one walked away
Battles for strength testing oneself
  with first-blood christenings in human rings
    the victor a hero to all while the vanquished
      the unknown lesser who sits alone
        left to ponder present values & future possibilities
The struggle for independence amid the blend of conformity
  While marching to a different drummer
    only to smash the drum & abandon the march
      keeping step with one's own wild abandon
Dragged through the detritus of life's failed promises
  where freedom hearts crashed & burned in the crucible of prison
    fugitive whispers rewarded with solitary confinement
      slashing open arms legs eyes & throats
        until gaping wounds bled out

11) Solitary Confinement and Special Handling Units

Introduction

JUST AS RIK WAS ENTERING BC PENITENTIARY
to begin his first federal sentence for a non–capital
murder conviction in 1974, a number of prisoners who
had spent extended periods in solitary confinement at
the prison enlisted the help of lawyer Michael Jackson
to mount a case in federal court over their conditions of
confinement. In *McCann v. The Queen*, plaintiffs Jack
Emmett McCann, Walter Alan Dudoward, Ralph Co-
chrane, Jake Quiring, Donald Oag, Keith Curtis Baker,
Andrew Bruce, and Melvin Miller sought declaration
that their experience of solitary confinement was cruel
and unusual, and they argued that the lack of hearings
and reviews regarding their placement in segregation
meant that Penitentiary Service regulations that allowed for inmate dissociation also ran counter to the
Canadian Bill of Rights. While Mr. Justice Heald ruled
that the conditions of confinement in BC Penitentiary's solitary confinement unit constituted cruel and
unusual punishment, and were therefore unlawful, he

refused to subject administrative decisions regarding segregation to judicial review. A loophole allowing for the continued use of "administrative segregation" was intentionally incorporated into the judgment. While BC Pen was decommissioned within five years of the decision, as Rik notes in our conversation below, it only took four months for the solitary confinement unit to reopen with a fresh coat of paint and a name change: it was now the supermaximum unit.

Rik spent sixteen years of his sentence in solitary, and his earliest experiences of this type of confinement were in BC's notorious "penthouse." While confined to his cell, Rik slashed and attempted suicide alongside a large number of men who did the same, and many succeeded in their suicide attempts. Rik describes his experiences in the penthouse both in the conversation transcribed here, and in his poem "Slash Solitary." "Telegram from Solitary," written in the penthouse in 1974, is one of Rik's earliest poems.

Comparing the psychological harm of solitary confinement to the harms of physical punishment for the *McCann* case, Dr. Richard Korn testified that

> It is worse, there is no physical punishment which can approach this. . . . There is simply no fear for these people of physical death, it is easier than the time. It is simply termination of your life. That is not painful, it is over, it is done, but to cling to your life in this morass of continuous torture is a much, much heavier thing to do than physical death. . . . It is easier to

die than to undergo the pain. . . . Most of them prefer to die, they hang themselves rather than sustain it. That's what the suicides are about.

The evidence is that if you keep people long enough, they will engage in self-torture, simply to focus the pain. So obviously if the inmates choose the infliction of punishment, physical punishment, they have indicated the answer to that question. Physical pain which is definite, which they can control . . . is much more bearable than the torment they can neither understand nor control.[1]

While Korn's testimony provides explanation for the self-inflicted violence that Rik witnessed and enacted while in solitarily, Jack McCann discusses the generally inadequate medical care that prisoners were provided: "Persons mutilating would not even get stitched up by a doctor, just bandaged by nurses and then brought back. . . . All you live in the scu [solitary confinement unit] is bitterness and hatred."[2] This is the "routine of unconcern" that Rik employs as a refrain in his poem "Slash Solitary."

This section ends with the poem "Force Majeure," which describes a mounting wave of fury—and the inevitable and destructive crashing of that wave—as the ultimate result of solitary confinement. In testimony he provided for *McCann v. The Queen*, Dr. Stephen Fox explained what it means to psychologically break down prisoners by way of solitary confinement: "When a person comes to have no dignity, and no self respect, no identity, you are faced with the most violent, the most dangerous possible human being. You can't reduce men to that, you risk your life to reduce them to that. . . . This desire, the good intentioned desire to create compliance . . . forgets that there is a place beyond which you don't want to go."[3] It is impossible to separate the sometimes brutal and inhuman behaviour of those in isolation from the brutal and inhumane conditions of their confinement.

In conversation, Rik also provides an account of his experiences as an early resident of the Special Handling Unit (SHU) at Millhaven. Though there was more freedom of movement in the SHU than there was in solitary, life in the former nevertheless remained violent and hopeless. Rik describes the routine yet unpredictable violence that often erupted among the men who were incarcerated at Millhaven, many of whom were destined, as a result of the duration of their sentences, to live the remainder of their lives inside, and therefore had no incentive but survival.

While prisoners often resorted to violence as a way to manage their sentences, guards often used violence to manage the prison population. Millhaven Penitentiary opened while it was still under construction to admit prisoners who had engaged in an uprising at Kingston Penitentiary in 1971, an uprising that was linked, in part, to prisoners' discomfort with the new technologies and techniques rumored to be in development at Millhaven.[4] Upon transfer, eighty-six incarcerated persons were injured at the hands of correctional staff;[5] twelve prisoners who had erroneously been labelled ringleaders of the Kingston uprising were made to run through a gauntlet of ten to twelve correctional officers armed with riot sticks.[6] Subsequent investigations revealed the use of German shepherds to attack prisoners in their cells, the hog-tying and beating of shackled prisoners, abuse by tear gas, and chaining prisoners out of reach of toilets and water taps in their cells.[7] In contradistinction to the routine unconcern at the nurses' station at BC Pen, we read about a cell extraction at the Millhaven SHU in Rik's "Untitled" poem ("They geared up").

The story of Rik's individual experience of solitary confinement and confinement within a SHU (pronounced "shoe") is a harrowing one. Rik lived the effects of these forms of incarceration via his battles with PTSD for the remainder of his life. And yet, for all their cruelty, Rik's experiences were not exceptional. As Rik explains in conversation, conditions within solitary units have changed over the years, but the practice and its dire effects on those subjected to it continues.

In 2019, while decisions on the practice of administrative segregation were pending in the BC and Ontario Courts of Appeal, the Canadian government drafted and subsequently passed legislation creating Structured Intervention Units (SIUs). The court decisions found that administrative segregation constituted solitary confinement as defined by the Nelson Mandela Rules (the United Nations Standard Minimum Rules for the Treatment of Prisoners), and that the practice was in violation of sections 7 and 12 of the *Canadian Charter of Rights and Freedoms*.[8] Reminiscent of the new coat of paint and name change at BC Pen in 1975, SIUs present something of a cosmetic response to the court decision. Whereas the Mandela Rules define solitary confinement as the practice of keeping prisoners confined for twenty-two or more hours a day without meaningful contact, for example, prisoners in SIUS would henceforth be allowed out of their cells for four hours each day, and they would have two hours of meaningful contact—thereby skirting the established definition of solitary confinement. As Anthony Doob and Jane B. Sprott found in their study of SIU implementation, 79 percent of prisoners being kept in the units were not being provided with the required four hours outside of their cells, and less than half were being provided with two hours of meaningful contact time.[9] In response to the report, Correctional Service Canada said that practices had been adversely affected by the COVID-19 pandemic, but Doob and Sprott were able to prove that the pattern they identified in fact predated the pandemic.[10] Mere months after the SIUS were opened, the independent oversight board that was struck to monitor their implementation was dissolved.[11]

SLASH SOLITARY

From his slashed arms the veins are torn,
Ripped out like so much thread,
Amid lakes of blood, the floor is worn
By the rivers that ran red.

The doctor with his morbid charm,
The nurse looks stiff and stern,
In great haste sew up his arms
In a routine of unconcern.

Will he be released, no one knows,
As he paces off that old cell floor,
So his anger and resentment grows
As Tommy pounds on that steel door.

To live in bleakest solitude
In those cells all filled with hate,
Where violent little thoughts intrude,
To which only prisoners can relate.

He cannot sleep, but he has dreams,
But of those dreams he is so wary,
Amid the cries and tortured screams
Exist the nightmares he must carry.

He could not accept their evil lies,
For his release, which they forbade,
In two quick strokes slashed out his eyes
With that piece of rusted blade.

The doctor with his morbid charm,
The nurse looks stiff and stern,
Said the loss of sight presents no harm,
In a routine of unconcern.

A year and more of time drags by,
Of madness he can take no more,
Amid the screams and tortured cries
As Tommy pounds on that steel door.

He has grown so weary of keys and locks,
So in his mind a plan is born,
Deep within that concrete box,
He braids a shirt he has worn.

His desperation plants the seed,
So carefully times the guard's last walk,
Time has come to perform the deed
And finally leave that old cell block.

Within that cell he lost all hope,
Yet free to choose his fate,
Around his throat, that braid of rope
        —as pre-arranged, the guard is late.

The doctor with his morbid charm,
The nurse looks stiff and stern,
Pronounce him dead with no alarm,
In a routine of unconcern.

His isolation after many years,
Amid the screams and tortured calls,
Played on his mind and fed his fears,
To be crushed alive by those walls.

Of those long days and sleepless nights,
For relief he vows to trade his soul
For just one hour of no damn lights,
To burn his eyes in that concrete hole.

To be denied the sunny skies,
In solitary, he could take no more,
Amid the screams and tortured cries,
As Tommy pounds on that steel door.

A concrete bed that's called a floor,
The guard walks by and cracks a joke
About his bed and back that's sore,
Then taunts him with a pre-rolled smoke.

The guard displays an evil laugh,
The prisoner's rage is so provoked,
So vows to smash his face in half
Before he gets that weed half smoked.

So charged for threats that he uttered,
Dragged in chains to warden's court,
"Thirty days on diet," the warden muttered,
"And be glad your sentence is so short."

With deliberation the court did rule,
Upon the practice of solitary,
That its design and application cruel
So its condition and state must vary.

The judge's comments were sharp and terse,
Upon the damage and its relation,
So that harmful policy must reverse
To end the suffering of isolation.

Resulting from the court's decree,
The warden devised a plan,
From horrors of the past to flee,
An ancient torture revised for man.

The warden quickly did arrange
For that unit's notorious name
To be included in cosmetic change,
While the results remained the same.

To rename a practice of ill-gotten fame
Is but a pseudo-transformation,
Yet cause and effect remain the same,
Denies not death nor mutilation.

Back in same cold cell
Where possibility closes the final door &
The great void remains . . .

Stop twenty-four-hour blinding light, dirt, spit, &
blood on walls
Stop brutal beatings & broken hand knuckles
scraped raw in protest
Stop depressing suicides
What reason forced monastic existence
Stop cruel & unusual
Screams of anger penetrate
Stop solitary confinement
The vortex of this rage & shock
of consciousness.
[Stop.]

Don't think I can continue
   living an absurd existence
     upon a foundation of
       failed promises
         and
           diminishing returns.

The realization
   that time is linear—
   and biodegradable.

Despite the paradox, history repeats itself.
       Upon our collective memory, plagued with doubt—
       a plague of doubt has entered my consciousness.

In Conversation I

DEMERS: What was your experience of solitary confinement?

MCWHINNEY: Totally destructive. It's designed and implemented to break a person—mentally, emotionally, and in many cases physically too, and often involves people taking their own lives.

A friend of mine, George, slashed both his eyes out with a piece of X-acto blade in solitary confinement. That had a tremendous impact on me. I had seen other guys hang themselves or kill themselves in various ways—it was something you heard about a lot. I've got a list buried deep somewhere in my files—page upon page of just names of guys that have died in prison, and many of these deaths were by suicide.[12] Some were by overdose, so it's hard to determine which of these were by accident or by design. But the one that had the most impact on me was George when he slashed both his eyes out.

DEMERS: You wrote about that incident.

MCWHINNEY: "He could not accept their evil lies, / For his release, which they forbade, / In two quick strokes slashed out his eyes / With that piece of rusted blade."

Yeah, George. He was living about five cells down from me in solitary, and there were fifteen cells to a range. When the guards were taking him away, he was making these deep, almost guttural sobs, like he had just committed the irrevocable act. Who knows how painful it was for him—I don't mean in a physical sense, but, he's ruined himself, you know? I had the feeling that these weren't sobs of physical pain. Far from it. This wasn't anything like that. This was emotion. Like I say, he had just stepped across that line and committed this irrevocable act. I never saw him again after that day. The last I heard they took him to RPC, the Regional Psychiatric Centre, and I never heard what happened to him after that. I don't even know if he's still alive. He'd be in his sixties or seventies if he was still alive. But blind, you know.

DEMERS: What George did is visceral, and it's an image that I know has stuck with you. But if we think about the effects of solitary confinement, was it entirely abnormal? Is it more like an extreme manifestation of normal symptoms?

MCWHINNEY: Solitary affects everybody who's subject to that type of treatment. But even the slashing of the eyes—George wasn't the only one who took his eyes out. There was another guy, he was from the States, but he got pinched up here in Canada for a bank robbery. I can't remember his name, but he was in the Special Handling Unit in Millhaven shortly after it first opened—this was the first SHU in Canada. He dug his eyes out—well, one eye—with a spoon. I don't know what happened to him because I was on the other side of the country, in BC, at the time. I read about it in the newspaper—not in a regular newspaper from outside prison, but in a newspaper that was being published inside. Guys also used to write to other guys in other prisons. They may have a brother, relative, or good friend doing time in another prison, so we'd exchange information. I may be writing to a guy in Dorchester Penitentiary while I'm out in BC Penitentiary: he'd share some things going on down in his end, and I'd share some things going down on mine. So news like this would travel. When I went to Millhaven a couple of years later, people still talked about how this guy dug an eye out with a spoon. These instances stood out, but in general, there was a lot of slashing. I slashed repeatedly. I swallowed things—pieces of wire, a bent nail—just to get out of that cell, so they'd take me to the hospital and X-ray me. Things like that.

DEMERS: And this is because it was unbearable to—

MCWHINNEY: You go nuts! You're locked in a cell that's approximately six paces long—I guess they're about eight feet long, and I think they're five feet wide, if I remember the correct dimensions of the solitary cells.[13] And they're all cement. Everything is cement except for your door, where you've got that little four-inch judas window. All you can see is straight and maybe a periphery of six to eight feet on either side. You can see down if you *really* try to look, but you can't see the cells next to you—all you can see is the hallway out in front of your cell.

It's just cement. It's a tomb. That's all it is—it's a tomb. You're in there twenty-three and a half hours a day and it just drives you nuts! And this goes on for months. Years even. I know guys that have done years like that. Andy Bruce did seven years solid. It's designed to break you, and it *does* break you. It's only sheer willpower, the strength of determination, and I guess stubbornness, that keeps you alive. But you come close. I came close many times. I slashed my neck. I slashed my arms. My arms are all scarred up. You see all those lines there? I slashed the vein there, and there. And there. I slashed my throat, there. Guys would tie themselves up with towels and just choke themselves off.

One guy slashed his femoral artery wide open, and he just bled out. I saw him when he went by the cell. He was white like that paper. There wasn't a bit of blood left in his body. A lot of guys go psychotic. They just lose all grasp of reality. They go right off the deep end—they start seeing things, and hearing things, and they just go nuts. They go insane.

I remember in 1975, Justice Heald, the chief justice in BC, ruled that solitary confinement as it was practised in the BC Penitentiary constituted cruel and unusual punishment. So what'd they do? They shut it down, paint it, and call it a different name. I forget what they called it—the SMU, Special Management Unit, or something like that. In the end, it's just an acronym. A euphemism, really. It was basically the same thing. Nothing had changed. And the deaths and the suicides continued. Claire Culhane wrote extensively about that—about the fact that nothing changed. The deaths and the mutilations were still going to happen, and they did. That's what solitary confinement does to a person. It just breaks you down. It's very debilitating. You're fortunate if you survive it. I guess how long you're in there makes a difference: the longer you're subjected to it, the worse it becomes. You deteriorate. You're left alone with your own thoughts, which become very, very bitter, and you feed off of that in order to survive. You use the anger and the bitterness—in many cases, just outright rage—in order to survive. It's like it feeds you, and you feed it, and that's what basically keeps you going. That's how you're able to withstand the deprivations.

DEMERS: You spent a lot of time in solitary over the course of many years. How did it change over that time?

MCWHINNEY: Yeah—a lot of my time was spent in solitary. It changed quite a bit over the years. It used to be just a concrete tomb. Now you have a television in most units, you have a bed, and you have a light you can control. Prior to that, the light used to burn twenty-four hours a day.

DEMERS: And there wasn't a window. So basically, there was no way of telling time?

MCWHINNEY: No. Absolutely not. Except if you had a window across the hall that faced the outside, you could see a little patch of blue, which prisoners called the sky. Other than that, you had no way of telling.

DEMERS: You mentioned beds as a more recent development. What did you have to sleep on before?

MCWHINNEY: You had a floor. You had a floor with a four-inch slab of cement raised off the floor, and you had two woollen blankets for bedding. Now you have a bed—a steel bed, mind you, but a bed, and a mattress, and sheets, and blankets. In the 1970s, you had none of that, you just had a cement floor, one blanket to lay on, and one blanket to cover yourself up. That was it. That was hard on the bones. For reading material you had a Bible, which some guys read, but most guys used them for pillows because you had no pillow. So the Bible was something to rest your head on. Bible paper also makes great cigarette papers. You try and stay away from the ink. You find an edge or a margin of the page that has no ink on it, and then you get some cigarette butts, whatever you can find, and roll up a cigarette.

DEMERS: The Bible—was that the only reading material you had access to while in solitary?

MCWHINNEY: Once every two weeks the librarian would come around with a cart for book exchange. You were allowed two books. You'd pick out two books, and two weeks later you had to turn them in to exchange them for two others. But the choice . . . [*laughs*]. Maybe you'd get Zane Grey or Louis L'Amour. Westerns. Things like that, you know? You'd be very, very lucky if you could find a book that had any merit to it. Like *The Grapes of Wrath*: you wouldn't find that in solitary confinement. Sometimes you could make a request and ask the librarian to bring you a particular book, and if he felt inclined to do so, he might. You might luck out that way. And that book would maybe last a couple weeks before it would be in pieces because you'd made sure everybody got to read it. Those books were like gold. "Wow, a book to read!" you know? A *good* book. You wanted to share that with others, with your friends in solitary, and just through prolonged use, that book would be read and reread and reread until it was a hopeless pulp [*laughs*]. Shredded and—

DEMERS: So you made pulp fiction out of literature.

MCWHINNEY: Yeah [*laughs*]. But it would really get read well. Sometimes, some guy who was inconsiderate toward others might write in it. But that's all you had for literature—two books and a Bible.

DEMERS: So how did you spend twenty-three and a half hours? How does one get through the day?

MCWHINNEY: From my experience, you're just left with your own thoughts. Self-reflection. A lot of imagination. You go on these imaginary explorations within your own mind. You think about what you're going to do twenty years from now. I was consumed by a deep, deep bitterness toward the system. They were subjecting me to that form of treatment, so I spent the better parts of my day—like a lot of guys did—reflecting on how to get even, what I'd like to do to them. That's not especially redemptive—of course, it's just the opposite—but you go right off the deep end because it's a very adversarial system. You've got two sides that are totally opposed, and in many respects, you're victimized by that system: you're locked up for twenty-three and a half hours a day with nothing to do, nothing to see, nothing to stimulate your senses. You're left to your own thoughts, which could take you in any direction. A lot depends on your own mindset, or your own state of mental health at the time.

For myself, to get through, I fed off my anger and my bitterness. I did that a lot. I spent a lot of my time just figuring out ways to get even, ways to pay them back. That sort of thing. Other than that, I would just philosophize in my own head. I did a lot of thinking. I played a lot of word games in my head, I wrote a lot of poetry—stuff that wasn't even poetry, just rambling. In a creative sense, writing would distract me from the more negative aspects of my situation, so writing was productive. But sooner or later something would interrupt that. Something would be going on down the range and then your train of thought would be interrupted, so you'd move on to something else.

It's very hard to describe the changes and transitions that a person goes through mentally and emotionally under those circumstances. It's very destructive. Man, it's destructive. There is nothing more frightening, stultifying, or soul-destructive as being left alone with one's own thoughts. And that's entirely it. There's nothing else. There's nothing to stimulate the senses. There's four walls, and that's it.

I mean, you can yell down the range to another prisoner and have a conversation with him, yelling back and forth, but that's not [*laughs*] . . . it doesn't prove advantageous to either of you because sooner or later it just breaks down into rants. He'll be voicing his discontent with the system while I'll be voicing mine—they converge. We feed off of and support each other—but it's all discontentment. This isn't healthy for a human being. In a different context, this type of camaraderie could be of some benefit—it could provide some insight into a situation. But it's not a healthy way of living through solitary confinement. It's emotionally devastating, which is exactly how it's designed and applied. It breaks you down.

DEMERS: A number of your poems were written in solitary, or about solitary.

MCWHINNEY: Yes, that's where all that morbidity comes in. It had such a profound effect on me that it keeps creeping into my writing. The majority of my poems were about solitary confinement. In fact, I remember when I was first putting my poetry together, I was looking at the titles and they all had "solitary" in the title. I thought, *Well, this is too much*—solitary, solitary, solitary—*I've got to change a few of these titles around, at least!*

DEMERS: When Ginsberg was corresponding with you,[14] he said that you should write about what you know, what you're experiencing, and what you're seeing. Solitary confinement was a large part of your existence—sixteen or seventeen years of your life, all told. It seems quite natural that this is something that you'd be writing about, and trying to work through in your poetry.

MCWHINNEY: We touched briefly on the courts—how Chief Justice Heald ruled that solitary confinement as it was practised in the BC Penitentiary constituted a cruel and usual punishment and he ordered it closed down, and how they just painted it and gave it a different name. I also talk about a fellow by the name of Tommy McCaulley.[15] Tommy was up there for seventeen months. He went insane—all he did was hit that door. His knuckles were like golf balls. They were huge. They were callused and swollen and built up from the constant pounding. Man, this guy could hit a cement wall and probably go right through it! His hands were so built up from all that pounding on that door. He would just punch that steel door constantly, and it would drive everybody nuts because at three o'clock in the morning, guys were sleeping—or trying to sleep—and all of a sudden: Bang! Bang! Bang! Bang! You knew it was Tommy. Tommy McCaulley. And I told you about George.

DEMERS: George—yes. And these things kind of fused together as nightmares, right?

MCWHINNEY: Yes, not just about George. Nightmares about everything. Every night you'd have nightmares. Everybody had them. Maybe not immediately, but after some prolonged time spent in there, they would start to creep in, and then you'd start experiencing them. Your first night there, it may not affect you, but after eleven nights, or twenty nights, they start to creep in.

DEMERS: And this is what you're experiencing, what you're writing through—it's all of these traumatic things that you're witnessing and, just like the pounding on the steel door, it's all routine.

MCWHINNEY: That's the routine.

DEMERS: And not being able to tell time—this different kind of rhythm.

MCWHINNEY: Yeah, the routine of tortured cries and screams and hollering and swearing and threatening and banging, you know, it's just like a madhouse and then there's "The doctor with his morbid charm, / The nurse looks stiff and stern," this "routine of unconcern."

DEMERS: It sounds like a living nightmare.

MCWHINNEY: Yes—in twenty-four-hour light, you know? Bright light too. Bright fluorescent light. It just drives you nuts. "To be denied the sunny skies, / In solitary, he could take no more."

DEMERS: And the six-inch concrete riser.

MCWHINNEY: Yeah, "A concrete bed that's called a floor, / the guard walks by and cracks a joke / About his bed and back that's sore, / Then taunts him with a pre-rolled smoke." You weren't allowed to smoke in solitary. Some guards would just walk by, they'd take a drag, and they'd blow it in through your little window and keep walking. So that's where this anger comes from. Wanting to smash someone's face in—it's just complete deprivation.

DEMERS: And what does this mean, "Thirty days on diet"?

MCWHINNEY: That's restricted diet. That's bread and water.

DEMERS: So this is additional punishment on top of solitary.

MCWHINNEY: Yes. If they wanted to increase the punishment, ratchet it up, they would put you on what they called a "special diet," which is just bread and water, but they could only do three on and one off and then then three off and one on. So they give you bread and water for three days, and then one day they give you a meal.

DEMERS: And they'd do that for a thirty-day stretch?

MCWHINNEY: Thirty days, yeah. You'd lose weight, boy, I'm telling you.

DEMERS: And you talk about a pre-arranged guard—the guard coming late, "as pre-arranged."

MCWHINNEY: Yes—it's pre-arranged. The guard comes late.

DEMERS: So the guard knows someone in the solitary unit is going to commit suicide?

MCWHINNEY: The guard knows some guy is going to hang himself because he hears him talking to his friends. He knows how he's going to do it. Somebody yells down to him, "Hey, Jimmy, what are you doing?" you know? "I'm cutting my shirt up." "Why are you cutting your shirt up—what are you cutting your shirt up for?" "You know how it is. You know how this place fucking gets to you." The guard knows what's going on, so instead of coming by every half-hour, he comes by a little late, to make sure this guy is hanging.

DEMERS: And there were lots of suicides inside?

MCWHINNEY: A lot of them, yes. PA [Saskatchewan Penitentiary in Prince Albert] was the worst. I think there were thirteen in one year—I think it was 1968 or 1969. There were thirteen suicides in Prince Albert in solitary. There were quite a few in the BC Pen too, but not like PA, where all of these suicides happened in a year—that's one a month, you know?

DEMERS: And this is your context, if you're in solitary. Every month, another suicide.

MCWHINNEY: Yes—they're dragging another body out, you know?

DEMERS: And then there was the self-harm, and the "routine of unconcern" that followed—the uncon-cern from nurses after a prisoner had engaged in slashing. Was slashing what people did to escape from themselves—the race of thoughts—to just get out of their cell, or for human contact?

MCWHINNEY: Just to get out of that cell. Maybe not even to talk to the doctors, because the doctors didn't even want to talk, but just to get out of that cell. A change—to get away from that range,

where everybody's smashing doors and yelling and screaming and crying and threatening
and—it's just a madhouse. It's crazy. I would do
almost anything just to get away from that for a
while, you know?

DEMERS: You talk about "his release, which they forbade." Is that about George?

MCWHINNEY: That was George. Every thirty days you
go in front of the Segregation Review Board, and
they make a decision about whether to keep you
in solitary or let you out. George would go in
front of the board and they would just say, "No,
we're not letting you out." And he'd say, "Why?"
And they'd just make up some bogus lie, like,
"Well, you're a threat to the good order of the
institution." "Well, how so? Explain." And they
wouldn't. They'd just say, "Well, we think you
know what we mean." That sort of thing. "Back
to your cell," you know? So he'd go back to his
cell. In solitary. After six to eight months of that,
a guy gets a little weary.

DEMERS: On the one hand, you can talk about acts
of resistance, but on the other, you have to be
pretty far gone and resigned—you can't have
much of yourself left when you decide to slash
your eyes out.

MCWHINNEY: Yes, that really affected me. It affected everybody. George was a friend of mine, so naturally it would affect me a little deeper, with more intensity than other guys who barely knew him, but people felt like they could relate to it. They felt his pain. I had trouble coming to terms with it, naturally. The suicides and the slashing of arms and necks and things like that—that's pretty much routine. You become desensitized to that after a while. But the eyes—that was a new one at the time. Several years later, when that guy in Millhaven dug an eye out with a spoon in the SHU, I didn't know him. I wasn't there. It didn't affect me as much as it did with George.

DEMERS: What was your experience of the SHU? How was it different from solitary?

MCWHINNEY: Yeah. The SHU is . . . Wow. That was quite a bit different from the solitary confinement that I experienced in the seventies. The SHU was where you had more access to your peers—to other prisoners. You were given more opportunity for social interaction, and it was more open in terms of recreation. You were given an hour for exercise in the morning, an hour in the afternoon. And you could spend this time outside if you wanted, or you could be inside in the gym. The place they called a gym was basically converted cells with a couple of weight machines, and that was it. But that was a big change from solitary. [16]

But the SHU had its problems too. There was a lot of mutilation going on in there; not as much as there was in solitary confinement, but it still happened. And there were suicides. That's where Leslie sliced his femoral artery open—the guy who bled out I was telling you about. There were hangings. Things like that would happen there, just not as frequently as in solitary confinement. I suspect that's because you were given more freedom to socially interact, and that made you feel a little more human. So it was a little bit more humane in that sense. But in spite of all of that, there were a lot of problems in the Millhaven SHU. There were more than a couple of murders in there, because what you're dealing with—you're dealing with the worst of the worst, you know? Or what they claim is the worst of the worst. These are guys that are put there because they either took guards as hostages, or they killed guards, or they killed other prisoners. I was there for my second murder beef, because I killed a prisoner in BC Pen.

So you're dealing with prisoners in the SHU who, for the most part—the overwhelming majority of them—are already doing life for murder, and now they're in the SHU because they committed another murder while in prison. So now you're living among a group of men who are considered the worst of the worst—and some of them are. You've got guys that are doing five life sentences, you know? They're never getting out and they know that. They're resigned to just living out the rest of their life in prison because they know that's their fate. At the same time, they're trying to survive in prison for as long as they can. In order to do that, they become predators among their own. That's why they're doing five life bits. They may have killed somebody on the outside, went into prison on a life sentence, and then ended up killing four or five other guys while they were in prison. Some of these guys have their faces all tattooed up and everything. They don't care what they look like. They don't care about anything or anybody. They know their situation is hopeless and the only way to survive for their remaining days is to become as bad as they can, you know?[17]

DEMERS: This doesn't sound like a very safe environment to throw people into. It sounds like there's people who need a particular type of attention, but people are just being thrown into this dangerous mix.

MCWHINNEY: Some of these men are stone cold psychopaths. If you just look at them the wrong way, you've got a situation on your hands. These are people with very limited social skills. These are also people who subscribe to the subculture—how they see it, or how they interpret it—and they're mean, vindictive, dangerous people. You don't want to mess with them. But you do have to learn how to get along with them, or work around them. In order to survive, you've got to get rid of them somehow; some agree to disagree, but some people get rid of their problems, the imped- iments to their own survival, by killing them. Or they beat people up so bad that they don't want to cross paths anymore.

So that's how crazy that place was. Guys were killing themselves out in the yard. It was like sharks in a feeding frenzy. I was there for three years. I didn't think I'd make it out of there alive. I had a few serious beefs in there myself, but I was much younger and much stronger then. I was in good shape. There was only one incident where there were weapons involved: there was a knife involved and I got stabbed in the leg down here, but . . . yeah. Three years. I'd had enough of that place, man.

DEMERS: Was that in Millhaven?

MCWHINNEY: Yeah. That was in Millhaven. Three years—I was sick of it after three days, you know [*laughs*]. I seriously doubted I was ever going to get out of there alive.

DEMERS: What was it like to rejoin the general pop- ulation after?

MCWHINNEY: It's okay in terms of surviving because you're looked up to with a great deal of respect. Anybody that comes from the SHU is looked up to with a great deal of respect, for various reasons. Number one being, I guess, that you were able to survive that, you know? The fact that you're in there in the first place proves that you're a badass, and the badder you are, the better you are, right?

So guys that are released from the SHU into population, they're usually looked up to with a great deal of reverence and respect, you know? "He survived the SHU, so he's nobody to mess with."[18] Guys did respect you, and they did like you—you had a lot of friends, but you're always constantly aware of your enemies too. When you put a group of men together in an enclosed space, there's certainly going to be disagreements, or differences of opinion. Not everybody's always going to get along, so you've always got to be navigating those waters with some degree of finesse.

But that transition, like you say, it's very challenging to make. You're dealing with PTSD, but you don't recognize it as such. You know, I didn't even hear the term "PTSD" until the mid-nineties. I'd never heard of it. But, like I say, it's been with us for countless years. I mean, look at what Holocaust survivors must have gone through, and World War I victims, and veterans. You don't recognize it as such in prison—you think that what's going on, the way that people act and react, is all just a part of the dysfunction of living in that environment. It's part and parcel of the whole thing. It's what I've got to deal with, you know? There's the dreams. A certain amount of paranoia. You try and keep that in check, because if you don't it can destroy you too. You don't become a victim of that. You do want to maintain a healthy dose of it in order to survive, though. Like, how close should I get to this person? Is he trustworthy? Can I turn my back on him? Or, he says he's got my back, but does he? Things like that.

And then on top of that, you've got to deal with the guards who you know are the enemy. There's absolutely no paranoia there—at least to our way of thinking, that's just fact.

So it's a difficult transition to make from the SHU back to the general population. Most people survive it quite well. They get through it. Those who don't, who aren't able to cope, they end up back in the SHU. I have a friend—I don't know if he's still alive; last I heard of him was about ten years ago, and he was still in the SHU. He had been in there for seventeen years. I don't think he can cope in a normal prison population. I think he's been so traumatized by seventeen years solid in a Special Handling Unit that he's just totally incapable, and he's given up all desire to go back to general population. I talked to him one day, and I asked him, "Aren't you getting a little tired of this?" I think he had eleven years in at this point.

I said, "Isn't this weighing you down a bit, man?" He says, "You know, Rik, I got my job, and I got my birds, and I'm happy. That's all I care about. I don't care as long as I got my job, and I got my birds, and nobody fucks with me." So he's pretty much resigned himself to that fate. And what he meant by that, "his job": once a day they let him outside to sweep the yard with a steel push broom. I mean, the yard is all cement, but he can go out there and sweep it and feed the birds. The crows. A lot of crows. He had names for them all. He did that for years. I know that he wouldn't make it in a population setting now. He's old school. He was quite the character—a real character. The guards were deathly afraid of him. He'd stand out at the middle of the range and challenge the guards to come up and fight him. They'd be screaming at him over the loudspeaker to get back in his cell and he'd refuse. "You want me in that cell? You come up here and put me in that cell, you creeps." He'd call them names. Finally, they'd come up, all geared up with big boots, shin guards, brass plates, elbow pads, gloves, helmets with face shields, and then shields and riot sticks, pepper spray—and boy, they'd have a hard time with him. They just hated him [*laughs*]. We loved it! We'd all be in support of Jack, you know? We'd all be up at our doors, banging. We'd be banging our doors and that and yelling to leave him alone, and taunting the guards. So in some sense, that had the ability to pull us together as a group. You know, as a solid, solid group—

DEMERS: And to also further entrench that division between the keepers and the kept.

MCWHINNEY: Yeah, very much so.

DEMERS: —especially considering the equipment. I mean—

MCWHINNEY: Yeah.

DEMERS: —the guards are no longer even human in that respect.

MCWHINNEY: Yeah. No.

DEMERS: They're almost like robots—

MCWHINNEY: Yeah.

DEMERS: —wearing—

MCWHINNEY: Yeah, exactly.

DEMERS: —this stuff. A hard shell and—

MCWHINNEY: Yeah. Yeah—actual skeletons. They're like aliens or something, you know?

DEMERS: But then the prisoner, for them, is like a rabid dog—an inhuman animal that has to be subdued.

MCWHINNEY: Very much so. And it does nothing, like you say, to lessen that divide between these two opposing groups. It strengthens it, and deepens it. It's a bad situation, that SHU. But that was copied from the United States. It's from Marion.[19] I don't know how they're run today because it's been so long since I've experienced a SHU, but from the last I heard, they're not that much different from what they were when I was in there.

UNTITLED

They geared up

They geared all up

They gathered around all suited up & rushed his cell en masse

They gathered around & counted down

They stood around & counted down then rushed his cell

They stood around & counted down then rushed

They stood around & counted down then rushed his cell

They stood.

They gathered around.

They counted down before they rushed his cell en masse.

FORCE MAJEURE

The cells are hot of summer sun
That sears and burns like hell,
After many years he's done
Inside that tomb-like cell.

So endures the pain of no gain
Of his release from solitary,
His tears of rage fall like rain
No respite from his own fury.

To fix with cold and piercing eye
All those who bend and kneel,
To embrace the challenge to defy
Who chains him with the steel.

He never strayed from the path
Of which he chose to walk,
Of those despised he vent his wrath
As well-prepared to mock.

Who lived his life in agony
Under constant key and lock,
May be compared a simile
Of that vulture, chain and rock.

III) Advocacy and (a) Prison(er's) Politics

Introduction

RIK'S COMING OF AGE COINCIDED WITH THE
radicalization of the counterculture of the late 1960s,
a process that saw youth band together to dismantle
"the establishment" in the hopes of erecting a more
open and equitable culture in its place. This work was
conducted by various liberation movements, including a prisoner liberation movement spurred in part by
the confinement of movement participants and sym-
pathizers. The icons of the revolutionary Left whom
Rik and other politicized prisoners celebrated may
lack universal appeal, but they were ultimately adopted as symbols of resistance against, and with the
hope of liberation from, medical experimentation on
prisoners, solitary confinement, and the creation of
Special Handling Units in the 1970s, a high-tech and
notoriously violent prisoner-management solution for
the problems that existed within the Canadian penitentiary system.

While Rik's "The Revolutionary's Prayer" and "Che" constitute a sort of prisoner's creed, his Prison Justice Day interventions stand as testament to the larger struggle for recognition of the prisoner's humanity. The aggressive response on the part of correctional authorities to all manner of problems within the penitentiary system resulted in the deaths of many and, in turn, prompted the creation of Prison Justice Day, a day of fasting and inside-outside solidarity in commemoration of the growing number of prison casualties. The event first took place on August 10, 1975, at Millhaven Penitentiary to commemorate the first anniversary of Eddie Nalon's death by suicide while in solitary confinement. In addition to being a day of tribute, it was also an occasion on which to demand a greater recognition of prisoners' rights. Collected in this section is a Prison Justice Day interview Rik conducted with a reporter from CBC Radio Edmonton while he was incarcerated in Edmonton Max, as well as a short speech and a poem. After his release in 2007, Rik recited both of these in front of a small audience every Prison Justice Day in Regina. At these events he would also read out a partial list of prison casualties, copied from a publication that he kept among his files, and reproduced in this section. Clearly, Rik was intimately aware of many of the deaths that occurred within the penitentiary system.

Though Rik was inspired in large part by late-sixties radicalism, his federal incarceration coincided with the forceful suppression, during the mid-seventies, of these resistance movements, a process that accompanied the turn to neoliberalism during the 1980s. In this context, crime and crime control meant a sharp turn away from the welfare state and a renewed emphasis on individual responsibility, punitive sanctions, expressive justice, and populist sloganeering about "zero tolerance," being "tough on crime," and confinement as risk management. The perniciousness of such penal populism is evident in the episode of CBC Television's *Crossfire* filmed at Edmonton Max as political leaders debated, in front of an audience of lifers, whether the country should return to the retributive practice of capital punishment less than a decade after its official abolition in Canada. The debate preceded an open vote to reinstate the death penalty in the House of Commons; the vote, which failed by a slim margin, was the result of aggressive lobbying efforts on the part of Conservative MP Bill Domm, one of the participants in the debate at Edmonton Max. Rik's participation in a Q&A at the end of the debate is collected here. Against Domm's assessment that Rik has lost his right to life, we might read Rik's letter to the solicitor general, written several years prior, in which he asks him to intervene so that a lifer being kept in segregation—due in large part to his illiteracy— be able to continue participating in the University of Victoria's post-secondary educational programming in the Kent Institution. In his case management files, Rik is identified as a champion for underdogs within the penitentiary system.

As a whole, the poems, letters, and transcriptions collected in this section represent Rik's concern for those condemned to punishment by Canadian law. Incarcerated people are marked by their crimes and are profoundly affected by the institutions within which they are kept. Following Rik's example here, we must resist the temptation to reduce incarcerated people to a label, or to understand them solely by way of their most harrowing moments.

Our Marx, who art in the dialectic,
Hallowed be thy dogma.
Thy revolution come;
Thy process will be done in Kanada,
As it was in Cuba.
Give us this day our proletarian victory.
And forgive us our bourgeois tendencies,
As we forgive our comrades'.
And lead us not into exploitation,
but deliver us from capitalism.
For thine is the thesis,
the antithesis, and the synthesis,
For ever and ever.
Che Guevara.

Prisoners who took on the role of leadership in the struggle
       for prison reform embraced Che as an exemplar for
       self-determination & a paradigm of self-sacrifice for the
       greater social good.

We quoted Chairman Mao & discussed the revolution of our
       rising expectations while keeping six for a comrade
       tattooing Che's image on the back of his hand in a cell
       down the range.

When asked about Che I respond: He was the Marxist Saint,
       the Red Robin Hood & to prisoners prior to & during
       the 1976 riots the St. Ernest de la Carnaval Reforma.

We had no television stereos computers.

Today when I am asked whose name belongs to the image
       on my T-shirt that stares back at them with the
       unwavering stare of accusation I sometimes reply:
       Are you asking me who he is, or who he was?

This response usually elicits a slack-jawed, glazed-eye
       response of: *Hah.*
       Which can only be described as vacuous.

Who he was.

Agitation Propaganda

THE BIG LIE: NAZI PROPAGANDISTS OPERATED on the theory that any lie—if stated authoritatively, repeated incessantly, and guarded from critical analysis—will eventually be accepted by most people.

As you are probably aware, there was a smash-up at Kent on the twenty-eighth of October. Subsequently, J.S., spokesman for the penitentiary service for the Pacific Region, released a statement to CKWX radio that the incident was sparked by the movie *One Flew Over the Cuckoo's Nest*. This is a clear example of agitation propaganda. Prisoners resent comments of this nature in the sense that we, as prisoners, *are not* a group of mindless robots that are easily influenced by television programs to the point of going on a rampage of self-destruction. It is quite evident from the nature of J.B.'s press release that it is his intention to portray us as such. It was a deliberate and cowardly act on the part of J.B. to discredit and slight us in the minds of the public! This leads us to the question: What is the CAC[1] doing to rectify this situation? To prisoners in general, the question leaves three distinct possibilities:

1. The CAC is unaware of this comment and has no knowledge of its propagation throughout the penitentiary system, from the CX-1[2] security guard right up to the higher echelons of the system.

2. The CAC is fully aware of the comment, but is mentally incapacitated to the point that it fails to grasp the ramifications of this propaganda tactic practised by the penitentiary service.

3. The CAC is aware of the comment and of agitation propaganda, but it does not view either as a problem. In fact, the CAC condones this type of behaviour and helps to perpetrate these vicious rumours.

In terms of the first possibility, it is hard to believe that the CAC is unaware of the comment because I have personally discussed it with individual members. It would therefore be ludicrous of them to plead ignorance on this matter.

As to the second possibility, it is highly unlikely that the CAC will admit that they are stupid.

So we are therefore left with the third possibility, which has more credence to it than the other two, and therefore leaves no doubt that the CAC has lent itself to becoming an instrument of hate directed against a select group of prisoners. There is no question that the CAC is collaborating with the penitentiary service to undermine prisoners and eviscerate the last vestiges of their pride and moral standards.

By the use of agitation propaganda, the penitentiary service, along with the CAC and various other committees, have proven that they do not care about prison reform and are preoccupied with the idea of subjecting us to the measure of selective genocide. What purpose does a CX-1 have in mind when he whispers to inmate X that inmate Y is an informer, knowing full well in advance that the stigma of "stool pigeon" being attached to a prisoner is tantamount to a death sentence?

Such tactics are totally immoral and are practised by purveyors of administrative terrorism against prisoners who have no recourse but to resort to physical violence as a reflex action to express our resentment against all forms of agitation propaganda!

As long as this problem exists, there can be no reconciliation between prisoners and the prison administration for the advancement of prison reform.

Letter to Solicitor General

Dear Robert Kaplan:

Enclosed please find a copy of a memo sent to Warden H.K. concerning the continued incarceration of one of our Lifers' Group members, Trevor, in the segregation/ punishment unit of Kent Institution.

As of this date, during a meeting with the acting head of Social Development, T.F., we have been informed that this issue does not concern us and that we should desist in making such appeals for Trevor's freedom.

We have no intention of ceasing our efforts to have this man released from the punishment unit. Whatever the reasons for his primary incarceration there, we feel that the eight months he has spent in there more than makes up for any institutional charges he had incurred.

Warden K. advances the reason of Trevor's illiteracy as the most important for not releasing him. However, this particular affliction does not seem too important when one realizes that there is at least one other person confined in this institution who is also illiterate. If this constitutes criteria for punishment status, the other prisoner would also be confined there (and Canada would also appear to be one of the worst offenders in the area of contravention of human rights and dignity).

As with the objection of his release on the grounds of imminent transfer to RPC [the Regional Psychiatric Centre], we have overcome any objections on the grounds of illiteracy by offering to have another prisoner, who teaches English in the UVic program, help Trevor to learn to read and write.

Any and all objections can and have been logically overcome. Yet, Trevor remains in solitary. We ask that you look into this matter at the earliest possible time so that a fair resolution can be found.

We thank you for your indulgence at this time.

Rik McWhinney
Chairman, Kent Lifers' Organization

Prison Justice Day Speech

AUGUST 10 IS THE COMMEMORATION OF NA-
tional Prison Justice Day. It is a day to recall to memory all the men and women who have died in prison,
either by design or by neglect. Although we mourn
their absence, we also celebrate the reforms that have
been won by their sacrifice: A victory to the end of the
common prison practices of starvation diets of bread
and water, drug research, aversion therapy, electric
convulsive therapy, and the indefinite imposition of
solitary confinement—stretching from months into
years. It is a soul-killing story of the human condition, of the inexorable crush of time testing its slender
underpinnings. It is a story of bitterness, tears, and
insanity. Of slashed flesh and hanging bodies. Of broken dreams and broken men, reduced to the shrunken
world of madness and despair—three paces long, and
an arm stretch wide. Many prisoners fast on this day,
as do their outside supporters, to remind ourselves of
deprivations previously imposed.

CBC Radio Interview:
Prison Justice Day[3]

UNNAMED NEWS REPORTER: Twenty-one minutes after seven. For prisoners at Edmonton's maximum-security prison, today is a very quiet day. The inmates will stay in their cells; many of them will fast. For prisoners, this is National Prison Justice Day. It's a time for prison inmates to remember their friends who have died within prison walls. Yesterday, Donald Kumpf visited the Edmonton Institution.

[*Clanging of cell doors*]

GUARD: Rik is available.

KUMPF: Okay.

GUARD: So, you can lead with him first . . .

KUMPF: Okay.

GUARD: ... and then if you have any questions for me ...

MCWHINNEY: My name's Rik McWhinney. I'm a prisoner in Edmonton Penitentiary. I'm serving a life sentence—actually, two life sentences for murder.

KUMPF: Can you tell me what Prison Justice Day is?

MCWHINNEY: It's a day that started in 1976 upon the deaths of two prisoners in Millhaven Penitentiary—Bobby Landers and Eddie Nalon. And prisoners as a rule across the country were just fed up with the—what they saw as needless or unnecessary deaths that occur in prison. And so, we embarked on a protest—it started out as a protest—more or less to commemorate the memory of all those who have died in prison.

　　I have a lot of feelings about it, since I've seen a lot of friends die over the years in prison, and a lot of people I didn't even know die. I had a fairly close friend in solitary confinement who was kicked to death by the guards in 1968, and this happened two cells down from me. I always think back to that incident on August 10, and more so, you know, throughout the year. But, on August 10, I always think of him. It has a lot of personal meaning for me because I was in prison when the very first one came about. I haven't been out of prison since then. Just three days ago I celebrated my twenty-second year in prison on a life sentence. So, I've seen a lot of them come and go.

I'm more or less resigned to the fact that I'm, you know—I'm in prison, I'm going to stay in prison, I'm never getting out of prison, and in all likelihood, I'll die in prison. So, that's my fate. I don't harbour any illusions about the future, things like that. I tend to, like a lot of us, even out in society, I tend to live in the past for the most part.

KUMPF: Is there anything you'd like to get across to people on the other side about prisoners? About why they should care?

MCWHINNEY: Why they should care? Well, I guess... I don't know it's so much if they *should* care, but why they may *want* to care. We have feelings, we have hopes, we have fears, we have aspirations. We enjoy many of the same things that ordinary people out in society enjoy: good literature, good food, a great hockey game. We all enjoy these things too, even though we're deprived of them, you know, at the present time. We can share a sense of humour; we have many of the human traits that everybody else does.

[*Clanging cell doors*]

PRISON JUSTICE DAY

Upon every Prison Justice Day,
To honour who in death did pay
For the groundwork that was laid
And sacrifices that were made.

Now the ritual has all but vanished,
And its salience slightly tarnished.
There is no code, they broke the mould,
With every shirt now bought and sold.

So the creed now not remembered,
As well its tenets all dismembered,
To pay lip service some talk the talk,
Yet lack the moxie to walk the walk.

To impress on others they have soul,
They wear a shirt to play a role,
To a level they cannot meet,
So in their drums they sit and eat.

That day's merit goes all for nought,
With each shirt that's sold and bought,
From their mien you may discern,
They bought a shirt they could not earn.

Of those too young to remember,
Or take comfort in their slumber,
Remind them not to be remiss,
That their ignorance is not bliss.

So in reverence, let's not forget,
The challenges that were met.
So that August day was born,
For those from whom life was torn.

For those who could no longer carry
The oppressive weight of solitary,
Who took their lives or went mad,
Under cruel conditions so very bad.

For the legal and outside support,
Who took our struggle to federal court,
Who spoke for us, until out of breath
Of prison suicide and suspicious death.

Let's not forget them, and their pain,
Nor our incessant voice in Claire Culhane.
On some park bench they placed her mark;
They should name for her the entire park.

For all who acted in prison riots,
To end those damn restricted diets,
Who said no more to bread and water,
And for those that time did slaughter.

To remember all who would not sell,
And their spirit they could not quell.
Now most of them are sadly gone,
As well their eyes once brightly shone.

For their trouble they were gassed,
While night and day as well harassed,
So for the record it must be said,
We owe a debt to those now dead.

For all who dared to risk their neck,
For our freedoms they wrote the cheque.
To honour them in graves amassed,
We vowed that cheque will not be cashed.

Now dead and buried deep in dirt,
Their history drawn upon a shirt,
For all who sadly did depart,
Their memory lives within the heart.

In Remembrance[4]

SOME OF THE PEOPLE WE REMEMBER ON AUGUST 10:

Eddie Nalon, Bobbie Landers, Steven Abbot, Mark Anthony Acera, Clarence Francis Adams, Terry Roy Adams, Rocky Albert, Timothy Albert, Gary Allan, Bruce Allen, Michel Amyot, H.J. Andrews, Randall Andrews, Maxwell Ansah, Bruce Archer, Herbert Archer, Pitseolak Arnaquq, Allan Edward Aronson, Dollard Arsenault, Andre Arsenault, Gilles Arsenault, Garth Robert Ashick, Robert Assogna, Mary Astaforoff, Marcel Aubin, Raynald Auclair, Moses Aupaluktuk, John George Auxi, Bryan-Adams Awasish, Ray Babcock, Robert Babin, Paul Bachynski, Thomas James Bailey, P. Baker, Mark Neil Baker, Osama Mohamed Baky, Abdel Baky, J.A. Barnett, Wayne Douglas Barrick, George Barron, Louis Bartley, Bobby Barton, Henry Baum, Pat Bear, Wally Bear, Johny Bear, Phillip Elliot Bearshirt, Alain Beaule, Arthur Beauvais, Jacques Bedard, Paul Belliveau, Claude Benard, Joseph Thomas

Bendell, Constance Berard, Bernard Larry Bergeson, Michel Bernard, Corey Allen Bertrand, Gordon William Bidnell, Donald Philip Bigg, Charles Billings, Fernand Bilodeau, Terrold Black, Jerry Blair, Farnand Blais, Donald Walter Bleaney, Erwin Blight, Leon Boily, Gerry Blouin, James Boland, James Bolyantu, Leanore Leon Bonneville, Robert A. Bonogofski, Guylain Bordeleau, Robert George Bottineau, Christian Bouchard, Roger Joseph Bouchard, Irenee Bouchard, Gaetan Bouchard, William Boucher, Rene Boudreau, Jacques Boulay, Jacques Boule, James Walter Bradley, Donald Richard Bragan, Solomon Brass Jr., Walton Brass, Earla Stephanie Brass, Denis Bratford, Byron Bray, Denis Breard, Byron Brett, Peter Brideau, Kennith Craig Briggs, Spencer Briltz, Michael Brnjac, David Nathan Brockman, Donald Broken, Daniel Brouillard, Robert Brown, Glenn Brown, Robert Brown, Godfrey Paul Brown, Paul Earl Brown, Jean Buissiere, J. Bybyk, Ross Arnold Byers, David Cabana, William Charles Cadioux, Jarod Wayne Calder, James Callus, Dwayne Cameron, Peter Campbell, Gerald Robert Campbell, Petronilo Candelaria, Dennis Ralph Cardinal, Richard Irving Cargyle, Ronald Carlson, John Carmichael, Joseph Augustus Caron, Paul Anthony Carson, Betty Case, Leslie Casey, Robert Castillo, Gerard Castilloux, Cecil Ellwood Caverley, Guy Chapdelaine, Andre Charbonneau, Richard Charest, Roger Charron, Raymond Chartrand, Ellis Ford Chase, Joe Chester, Bernice Eva Chief, Robert Choquette, Marvin Blair Christensen, Frederick R. Christie, Grant Clark, John Clifford, Gordon Coe, Cory Cole, Fred Bradford Cole, Meredith Coleman, Denis Colic, Frank

Collins, Tyrone Conn, Robert Consey, James Edward Conway, John Edward Conway, Roddy Cook, James Bentley Cook, David Copeland, Richard Copenale, Calvin Corbiere, Marc Corbin, Gunthier Cordes, Frederick Corey, Earl Cote, Victorien Cote, Arlene Cote, Claude Cote, Jacques Coulombe, Normand Courteau, Noel Franci Courtoreille, Andre Couture, Glen Alan Creasey, Jean Croteau, Raymond Crowe, Roger Miles Cumpstone, Gordon Robert Currence, Donald J. Currie, Careen Daigneault, Raymond W. Daniels, Michael Danielson, Daniel Daniluck, Paul Daoust, Viateur Daraiche, Guy Davis, Wayne Dazz, Feroz Kotub Dean, Alex de Jesus, Steven Leo Deforge, Martin Deresti, Sylvain Desforges, Napoleon Desrosches, Randolph Lyle Dewan, James Deyoung, Gordon Didnell, Guy Diotte, Andre Dixon, Benjamin Dixon, Ray Doiron, Pierre Dollard, Brenda Donovan, John Doria, Bradley Doughty, Gregory Ducharme, Fernand Duchaussoy, David Joseph Dufour, Ron Dulmage, Jean Dumont, James Edward Duncan, Myles Keith Dunkley, James Robert Dunlop, James Allen Dunn, Trung Ky Duong, Jacques Dupras, Gerald Dupuis, Karnel Singh Dusanj, Regis D'amour, Ross Earle, Shawn Earle, Kenneth Edwards, Samuel Sidney El Safaidi, Thomas Edward Elley, Robert A. Ellis, Ross Elworthy, Walter Emkeit, William Engel, Leonard John Engell, James Oliver Erdman, Kevin Ethier, Anthony Ezzo, Mefus Fastugnak, Denise Fayant, Michael Fazekas, Philip Joseph Ferguson, Francois Talon Ferland, Doug Fetterley, Joseph Fiddler, Alex Finlay, David A. Fisher, Larry Brian Fisher, Robin Cacey Fisher, Alexander Fitzpatrick, Terry Fitzsimmons,

G. Forsythe, Barry Forsythe, Clyde Jeffrey Fortier, Phillipe Fortin, Ernest Edwin Fortt, Patrick Stanley Fountain, Robert Fraser, Charles Fraser, Joseph Fredericks, Denis Frenette, Robert William D. Frisbee, Serena Fry, Irving Donald Funk, Robert Gagne, Regis Gagnon, Jean-Claude Galland, Keith Mansel Gallop, Janise Gamble, Marilyn Gardener, Gordy Garghty, Gary Garnett, Patrich Michael Garve, Peter Gattola, Yvon Gaudreau, Dennis Gauthier, Gerry Gavin, James Gay, Edward Geddes, Michel Gendron, Yves Gendron, Robert Gentiles, Vincent Michael George, Norman Gerrard, Ralph Ernest Gervais, Ian Gibbs, Carl Edward Gibson, Donald Gordon Gillard, Lucien Gerald Girard, Marcel Girard, Jeffrey Alfred Gladeau, William Goakery, Michel Godbout, Brian Gary Godfrey, Alan Gonzalez, Christopher Good, Gerald Gosselin, Roger Gosselin, Armand Albert Goyette, Jason Christopher Graham, Terrence Graw, Harry Hall Green, Simon Grenier, Paul Yvon Grenier, Christian Grenier, John Griffiths, Daniel Grimard, Jacques Grosso, Chris Grulinsky, John Guitar, Robert Gulash, Roy Thomas Gunderson, Michael Lorne Gwilt, Donat Hachery, Kamikar Singh Haer, Dennis Hailles, William George Haley, Marc Halle, Richard Hamilton, Robert Hanson, Lorne Hanson, James L. Harris, Michael Harris, James Hugh Harris, James Harvey, Robert Hassim, Benard Hebert, Allen Doug Henderson, Clarence Hennebury, Bonnie Henry, Francois Herbert, Peter Herney, Francois Heroux, Keith Roy Hess, Larry Douglas Hill, Gordon Hill, Steve Hill, Carl Hines, Kenneth Hiscox, Robert Histed, William Holden, Barry Lynn Holm, Edward Holnessy, Tom Holtom, Christopher

Hood, Doug Hooey, Robert Norman Horning, John Horseman, Ivan Horvath, Michael R. Horwood, Eugene Truman Hough, Earl Houle, Louis Houle, Thomas Samuel Houston, Charles Allan Hughes, Robert Gary Hume, Doug Hutton, Clarence Jace, James Patrick Jacobson, Roy John Jenkins, John Brady Jenkins, Oliver Jinkerson, Lauren Jodoin, Devender Johal, Kelly Johns, Ralph S. Johnson, Ambroise Johnston, Roger Allan Johnston, Alain Joly, Gary Jones, Lorna Jones, Wally Joseph, Laszlo Katona, Terrance Keeler, Rodney Keepins, Teddy Keg, Elmer Kennins, Bradley Kerswell, Riaz Khanzada, Joseph Batiste Kilroy, Charles H. King, Harry Kitch, Walter Koltucky, August Komac, Darwin Michael Koo, Helmut Kraemer, Winnifred Olive Krill, Roy Kully, James Labarge, Michel Labonte, Jean Lachappele, Michel Lafleur, Vincent Everett Laird, Glendon Laking, Raymond Laliberte, Jacques Lalonde, Katherine Francine Lamb, Del Lambert, Diallo Mamadou Lamine, Glen Thomas Landers, Robert Wilfred Landry, Dean Thomas Langford, Rollan Lapointe, Michel Laporte, Jocelyn Larochelle, Percy Larocque, Julien Larocque, M. Laronde, Henry William Laronde, Daniel Larose, Kevin Laurila, Jacques Lavasseur, David Walter Lazarawich, Dong Le, Donald Leblanc, Randy Leblanc, Wilfrid Leclerc, Ernest Albery Ledoux, Marie Ledouxe, Douglas Harold Lee, Andre Lefebre, Normand Lefebvre, Jean-Guy Legault, Romeo Legault, Eric Leigh, Jean Leonard, Jacques Lepage, Dennis Endel Lepik, Lucien Leroux, Andre Levesque, Vernon Levy, Louise Ann Lewickie, John Lewis, Harry Lewis, Earl Lewis, Douglas Littlejohn, George Locke, Michael Joseph Long,

George Longman, Louis Longpre, James Lonnee, Keith Lawrence Lotsberg, Gary Low, Roy Armstrong Lowther, Harold J. Loyer, **Ricky Luo**, **Ian Stewart Macaskill**, Jody Macaulley, Hector Daniel Macdonald, Kenneth Allan Macdonald, Vince Macdonald, Janice Lynn Macdonald, James Machum, Joseph Mackenzie, Bob Mackenzie, William Douglas Majury, Larry Mallat, Pierre Maltais, Thomas Manual, Real Marceau, Serge Marcouiller, Jacques Mareoux, John Marlow, Mario Marquis, Alfie Martin, R. Martin, Yvon Martin, John Mason, Louis Masse, Jacques Massey, Herman Mathaes, Martin Russell Mather, Charles Mathew, Robert Matice, Steven Matice, Michael Matthys, Dennis Maze, George McAteer, George McBride, Edward McCave, **Barry William McClurg**, **Shaun McCord**, Paul Andrew McDonald, Gerald McDonald, **David Sidney McDonald**, A.J. McDonald, Steven D. McDonald, Joseph McDonald, Wayne James McDougall, John Manley McDowell, Shane McEachern, Shawn McEwan, John Alexander McGarry, Leonard James McKay, Hugh David McKinnon, Rob McKinnon, George McLean, Michael McLellan, Stu Geoffrey McLeod, Donald McMillan, Allen Wentworth McMullen, Todd McMullen, Ronald Merasty, Joseph Mercier, Pierre Messier, Dana Metosos, Lorie Miles, Harold Miller, Guy Millete, James Mills, Timothy Milne, Leonard Miville, John Clement Moiny, Sergio Mokino, Vaughn Mondou, Juan Francisco Monterrosa, Marlene Moore, Wilmore Moore, Thomas Morden, Paul Morden, Philippe Morin, Germain Morin, Hubert E. Morris, Richard Morrison, Andy Morziak, Francois Mousseau, John Mrozinski, Allan

III) *Advocacy and (a) Prison(er's) Politics*

Phillip Muckle, David Muir, Derek Murphy, Harry Alexander Myer, Bertrand Myran, Renald Nadeau, Edwin Najera, John Frederick Neilson, A. Nelligan, Gary Neufeld, David William Nicholls, Kim Nielson, Robert Doan Niven, Jimmy Noade, Gary John Nussio, Kuwant Singh Oberoi, Donald Obrey, Isabella Fay Ogima, Richard Oimette, Robert Harry Oimette, E. M. Olson, Gregory Obstinik, Donald O'Brey, Robert O'Dell, John Henry O'Hara, Tommy O'Keefe, Eban Jan Page, Joseph Pahpasay, Dwight Arthur Palendat, Larry Parney, Serge Pasgagne, Joey Passalelpi, Marc Patenaude, Robert Pattison, John Francis Pauze, G. Paynter, Lars Pederson, Debra Pelletier, **Robbie Pellettier**, Dominico Pellicano, Claude Peloquin, Giles Raymon Perrault, Christian Perrault, Jean Perron, Archie Pete, Edward Peters, Seymour Peters, Barry Phillips, Louis Pichette, Sylvain Pichette, Carlson Piercey, Joe Pitt, Michael Wayne Platko, Donald Poore, Steven Poutsoungas, Leonard Prescott, William Prest, Clement Prevost, Richard Pribag, Daniel Probe, Ernst Prophete, Arnold Pruner, Leslie Purvis, Michel Quesnel, Normand Quinn, Don Raaflaub, Abdul Rasoul Rahemi, Bikash Rai, Andrews Randall Arnold Thane Raphael, Larry Rathgaber, Douglas Rattray, Pasquale A. Redavid, Ronald Redcrow, Robert William Reid, Paul Edward Reid, Peter Martin Reilley, Richard Reynolds, Lucien Richard, Maureen Shirley Richard, Joseph Richard, Normand Richer, Wilson Rideout, Niki Rivard, Andre Robichaud, Serge Robidauz, Richard Roche, Raymond Rochefort, Conrad Rochette, Germain Rochette, Camilla Rochon, Paul Aurelio Rodrigues, Donald Cormack Roger, Aubrey Rolfe, Allan Roska,

Tony Ross, Clarence Ross, Donald Joseph Rossetti, Robert Charles Rowles, Richard Thomas Ruby, Daniel Ruel, Gerald Rushton, David Sabourin, Paul Sabourin, William R. Sackville, Roy Howard Sam, Jean Guy Sansoucy, Helio Santos, Robert Satiacum, John Henry Saunders, Antonio Sauro, Sandra Sayer, Leslie Scott, Joseph David Segal, George Seggie, Jean Senecal, Randall Sexsmith, Shaun Shannon, Mark Shannon, Patrick Sean Shea, Robert Shepherd, Gary Shields, **Dick Schiere**, James Shoemaker, Gilles Simard, Ranjodh Singh, Steven Trevor Siple, Norman Skedden, Bronko Skerl, Garry Sloboda, Barry Henderson Smith, Florence Smith, Frank Smith, Francis Smith, Michael Clifford Smith, John Christopher Smith, Gaston Souce, Murray B. Spark, Crawford Sparvier, Daniel Spilchuk, Donald St. Germaine, Randall Stadnyk, Darren Stapleton, Jan Jerze Steinke, Fred C. Stephens, David Edward Stevenson, Gerald Stewardson, Robert William Stewart, Glen Stewart, Jimmy Stewart, Charles Benjamin Stiltz, Carl Stonechild, Marcel Thomas Strand, Dennis Stratychuk, Mathew Strukel, David William Sykes, Andre Talbot, Gordon Henry Taylor, Paulette Taypotat, David Teed, Kristopher Thaler, Gaston Theriault, Leonard Theriault, Earl Howard Thomas, Wayne Maurice Thompson, Robert Joseph Thompson, Agnes Thompson, Gerry Tilley, Renaud Toulouse, Michael William Tran, Roger Tremblay, Bruno Tremblay, Pierre Tremblay, William Tuer, William Richard Turcotte, Roberto Enrique Turjillo, Anthony Turner, Mark Clayton Tyler, Larry Unger, Kennith Guy Vanzyp, Johnathon James Vardy, Darren Varley, Richard Vienotte, Sando Viola, Paul Violet,

Bimbo Votour, Lynn Wabasso, Ralph William Waboose, Arther Gerald Wadlow, Michael William Walker, Robert Wall, Lyle Wambadiska, Kenny Warren, **David Warriner**, Arnold Watcheston, Larry Waters, James Watters, Joe Wazuk, Robert Lee Weatherbee, Ronald Welsh, Corey Wenger, Hudson West, Brian Whiffen, Walter Whipple, James Leland White, Robert Wayne Williams, Rick Williams, Stanley Williams, Scott Williams, Ralph Williams, John Willington, Robert William Wilton, J. Wiltshire, Noel Winters, Lucas Wojtowicz, Wolfhead, John Woltucky, W.G. Wood, James Elmer Woodside, Brian Orville, Dean Wyatt, Shoji Yamazaki, Vincent Yellowhorn, Robert Yemen, Paul Dwight Young, Donzel Young, Troy Darrell Young, Jan Zaborek, Vaclav Zavadil, Michael Zima, Michael Zubresky, Walter Zurbilo . . .

This list includes deaths in federal and provincial prisons, remand, lock-up and prisoners on parole.

— THIS LIST IS NOT COMPLETE —

There are almost 200 prisoner deaths nationwide every year. Please send us names we have missed for next year's issue.*

....

* The names in bold were highlighted in Rik's personal copy for reasons unknown.

Televised Debate on the Death Penalty, CBC's *Crossfire* at Edmonton Max[5]

RIK MCWHINNEY: Given Mr. Domm's religious background and his use of the word "justice" in relation to capital punishment, do you use that term synonymously with "an eye for an eye" out of the Bible? And if so, what about the people who have already lost an eye through virtue of social injustice?

BILL DOMM: Well, you brought up the Bible, and I'm not a theologian—I'm just the son of a minister. But I can tell you that there are a lot of theologians across Canada—two thousand church congregations whose leaders support a return of the death sentence. So, I don't wish to get into a debate with them, nor do I wish to get into a debate with the Council of Church's theologians. All I'm telling you is that the Bible without question, the whole of the Old Testament, supports the death sentence for taking another person's life; and the New Testament—nowhere, anywhere in the New Testament does Jesus Christ refute the laws of the land for the right of the state to take another person's life.

RON COLLISTER: No teaching in the Bible teaches to turn a blind eye to social injustice.

WARREN ALLMAND: It also says "turn the other cheek." It doesn't say "an eye for an eye." As a matter of fact, I'm not well schooled in the Bible either, but I know Christ did say, "it's not an eye for an eye or a tooth for a tooth, but when your brother does something, you should try and be merciful towards them." That's what he says—something like that.

COLLISTER: None of us are theologians, so let's get back to it.

GEORGE OAKE: The whole tone of the Bible is on redemption and forgiveness, gentlemen. [. . .] Something interesting happened here: these men who are locked up have hope for the betterment of mankind. They think that man will get better and can rehabilitate himself, and you, Mr. Domm, were a legislator—you don't have any hope for the betterment of mankind because you want to murder some people.

DOMM: I'll say one thing, Ron. In following his profession of being the devil's advocate, because I'm sure when he analyzes what he said—what he said is that I am preaching that there's no hope for mankind and that there's no possibility of rehabilitation. I'm talking about *planned, deliberate*, repeated in many cases, murder—the intent of taking innocent lives. You're talking about people, probably some of them in this room, that have [a] life [sentence], who are not here because they planned and deliberately murdered someone with a first-degree offence under today's legislation.

OAKE: So, you're sitting there saying that you can rehabilitate *some* murderers, but not all.

DOMM: Certainly! Certainly! All kinds of murderers. We only had last year two hundred first-degree murderers in Canada.

ALLMAND: But who is so wise today to determine . . . who are those who can't be rehabilitated and those who can? Sometimes the guy who looks the worst today is the guy that, after a certain period of time, may turn around and be a great contributor to society.

COLLISTER: Okay, let's ask our questioner. Who makes those kinds of decisions? Our panel can't agree

on it. Who makes decisions on who can be rehabilitated and who can't?

MCWHINNEY: I think the individual makes that decision himself over a period of time. And Mr.
Domm's made reference to repeat murderers
or repeat offenders—I'm here to tell you, Mr.
Domm, *I'm* a repeat offender. I'm in for two life
bits for two murders, one of which is prison
related. Now, given the fact that I'm probably
never going to get out of prison, and the chances
of my repeating murder again are probably ten
times more likely than the average man out in
the street, how do you propose to deal with that?

DOMM: I think you made the choice when you committed not only that first, planned, deliberate,
premeditated murder, but then on parole, or for
whatever reason, in jail, as you stated, to take
another person's life, you made that choice.
When I say that you made that choice to do that,
then you lose your right to your life.

ALLMAND: The challenge for a civilized society is to
continually look for ways of dealing with these
difficult situations, and not to sweep it under the
rug and bring back capital punishment.

MCWHINNEY: It seems to me that Mr. Domm is stating
that those convicted of second degree, or less of
a charge, are redeemable, and those who fall over

the fine line of a court's interpretation of what constitutes first degree are not redeemable, and therefore should face the noose or the electric chair or whatever.

COLLISTER: Can I ask what you would substitute for the death penalty or the twenty-five-year term? What is the proper penalty for, we'll call it first-degree murder? How would you treat it if you were a judge and a jury—how would you deal with it?

MCWHINNEY: I would deal with it in the same that my colleague answered that question. I see that there are no redeemable factors within the human being after a certain amount of time being warehoused in a prison. As I say again— that choice is up to the individual himself. But I say a review after seven years, and if a parole or immediate release is not forthcoming, then an additional review. And lots of supervision. If a release is considered, I would recommend lots of [supervision].

COLLISTER: Does this place rehabilitate you or not? This place you're in, does it rehabilitate you and the others?

MCWHINNEY: It doesn't rehabilitate me, no.

COLLISTER: What's missing?

MCWHINNEY: Programs. Facilities.

COLLISTER: Hope?

MCWHINNEY: For the most part, yeah.

COLLISTER: What does the twenty-five-year term do for your sense of hope or hopelessness?

MCWHINNEY: What does it do? Well, it increases [your hopelessness] somewhat.

COLLISTER: Is it more inhumane than the death penalty itself?

MCWHINNEY: No. No, it's not. I'll do twenty-five years if I have to. And if I can. You understand? But I'm not going to passively walk to some gallows so some redneck can string me up. You know what I mean?

[*Applause from the crowd.*]

Throw a stone, throw another
Bind a wound, help a brother
Raise your fist, raise your voice
Don't be passive, make the choice
Wear a mask, shout a slogan
Go underground, build a hogan
Claim your history, claim the streets
Know the enemy, accept no defeats
Break a window, break a sweat
Man the barricades, have no regret
Sew a suture, sow a seed
Build a network, prop the deed
Steal the files, steel your heart
Be committed, from the start
Strike a blow, strike a chord
Take no prisoners, nor reward
Feed the homeless, join a cell
Help the workers to rebel
Learn a kata, talk in code
Use diversion, block the road
Bait the traps, bait the hooks
Wreck the tracks, take second looks
Walk a picket, pick a lock
Be as solid as a rock
Hold your ground, hold your tongue
Respect the Elders, help raise the young
Take to rooftops, pull a caper
Be proficient, change a diaper
Distribute leaflets, trick the man

Pack a knapsack, devise a plan
Deliver the goods, wrapped so neat
Go the distance, evade the heat
Check your ego, watch the sky
Let your fear go, always try
Use a safe house, aid a fugitive
Rely on few, be intuitive
Test a theory, have a meeting
Take the weight, take a beating
Expose the traitor, silence the snitch
Supply the shovels, dig the ditch
Challenge a dogma, wipe your prints
Leave no trail, give no hints
Un-tap a phone, cut the wires
Destroy the evidence, light the fires
Take the lead, don't forsake
Mourn the dead at their wake
Plant a garden, grow some weed
Give back to nature, fulfill one's need
Share your empathy, lend an ear
Embrace those you love, cherish a tear

IV) Prison Culture
in the Time
of the Code

Introduction

IN HIS CLASSIC 1940 STUDY, *THE PRISON COM-
munity*, Donald Clemmer coins the term "prisonization" to describe how the adoption of values and
practices particular to life inside prison makes reintegration difficult.[1] Where those values come from—
whether they are "imported," or whether they are the
product of the "deprivations" that characterize prison
life—has been a source of division and debate.[2] In the
Canadian context, the Ouimet report of 1969—the major report that directly preceded McWhinney's federal
incarceration in 1974—falls on the side of deprivation.
Echoing the Archambault Commission's unrequited
1938 call for or a rehabilitative rather than a punitive
approach to incarceration,[3] the authors of the Ouimet
report explain how prison staff "become the symbols
of repression and the enemy,"[4] and they suggest that
becoming part of a prison subculture is necessary for
prisoners to preserve a sense of self-worth. The report
describes the following narrative arc:

Adaptation to prison life follows a progression from "I am a failure" to "I don't care" to "I am a success on the basis of a new value system which I share with most of the others here who were also failures by the old standards." Thus the offender institutionalizes his socially unacceptable behaviour. He is no longer an isolated misfit in society but has become a part of his own society, the prison subculture, which in turn supports his resistance to the demands of conventional society.[5]

Rik repeats this line of logic almost verbatim in our conversation below. Putting it succinctly, Rik points out that becoming nothing is something that nobody wants. If prisoners are "scum," nobody wants to be "scum within scum."

Based on conversations with former prisoners, Rose Ricciardelli narrows the code down to a set of five themes, all of which are recognizable in Rik's accounts. In prison, the following code applies: "(a) never rat on a con and don't get friendly with the staff; (b) be dependable (not loyal); (c) follow daily behaviour rules or else!; (d) I won't see you, don't see me, and shut up already; and (e) be fearless or at least act tough."[6] Where the Ouimet report links assimilation of the code to the existence of an oppositional group dynamic that is reparative with respect to self-esteem, Ricciardelli notes that concern for individual safety is just as fundamental. While Rik often describes the code in ways that resonate with this sentiment (for example, you don't play your music too loud because the person in the cell next to you might be doing something they shouldn't and they need to be listening for the footsteps of an approaching guard), Ricciardelli's overemphasis on the individualistic elements of prison culture obscures the respect and compassion that accompany the rule in this case (others on the range might be studying or mourning in private), and it certainly disregards the ways in which the prison has, since its inception, been a site of collective struggle. It is worth noting that Ricciardelli's ultimate assessment of the code—that "these norms emerged in response to risk . . . and presented a strategy that uses violence to decrease future violence"[7]—reads as a mirror of prison administrative logic in the context of neoliberalism. Though the concern for personal safety is profound, the inmate code shouldn't be read in isolation from larger institutional and interpersonal dynamics, many of which emphasize the importance of friendship and camaraderie to everyday life, survival, and advocacy for change.

Just as penal philosophies are fluid, so, too, are attitudes toward the inmate code. Rik, for example, discusses a lack of respect for those who fought for the improved conditions that younger generations of prisoners now enjoy. In Rik's poetry, we witness his and others' frustration with a changing inmate culture and anything that demonstrates a lack of respect, from disdain for prisoners spitting on a shared floor (with a nod to Gwendolyn Brooks) in "A Lamentation on Salivation," to Rik's adoption of a terrifying persona in "Romantic

Slumming," a murder fantasy poem targeting a "gangsta" wannabe "middle-class white boy." Rik railed against insubordinate youth for their lack of respect for rules that allow for the maintenance of a kind of prisoner equilibrium, and he often blamed this shift on the influx of gangs into the prison environment. As is generally the case with trends in the criminal justice context, the emergence of gangs is the product of complicated social forces and protracted social histories (e.g., the intergenerational trauma, born out of the residential school experience, that has destroyed Indigenous families and led to the creation of surrogate families on the street).[8]

Rik's writings give us insight into the culture of Canadian prisons in the late twentieth and early twenty-first centuries, in this case from somebody who not only abided by, but who was also subject to, the codes that structure prison life. The con code that he describes was conceived, and is policed, for the purpose of instilling pro-social behaviours in the context of the prison. As his experiences and observations attest, the inculcation of such values, particularly among those forced to navigate the prison system over the course of long sentences, amounts to a type of institutionalization that isn't conducive to reintegration. While one might have expected progress since Donald Clemmer identified prisonization as a fundamental problem of incarceration in his 1940 study, Rik's experience is instead a perfect illustration of its persistence decades later.

A LAMENTATION ON SALIVATION

There are some in jail who never fail
  From doing other people's time
Just like a snail they leave a trail
  Of little pools of slime

So there they sit to hack and spit
  Compelling others to walk in it
They revel in their own expulsions
  To most others' shared revulsions

Perhaps they sit to ponder fate
  Pausing only to expectorate
Perhaps they dream of a future bit
  To go to jail to sit and spit

Between each spit they trade dull wit
  As quick as feeble minds permit
Through a bacterial-viral bog they trod
  While salivating like Pavlov's dog

Yeah, they're real cool as they play the fool
  And sit surrounded by their own drool
It's a shame that they just don't get it
  As a shared space they should not wet it

ROMANTIC SLUMMING

A rude awakening
white noise infrasonic
grating on nerves
so raw autonomic
tracking to source
that relentless bass beat
not hard to find
some middle-class white boy
a study in caricature
ballcap flipped sideways
pants jailing off hips
He be locking & popping
to the beat of the rap
talking shit about busting a cap
yea he be killin all dem snitches
as he be pimpin all his bitches
Someone inquires of all the noise
gangsta boy loses all poise
says people been dissin him
says he wants respect
that he deserves it
that he needs it
then demands it
at least that's the shit he was talking
before they found him
stabbed three times to the chest

In Conversation II

DEMERS: Can you tell me a little bit about the "con code"? How did it work and why was it important to you and other prisoners throughout your time in prison?

MCWHINNEY: The code was basically a system for survival. When I first went into the penitentiary on a life bit, the code was a form of survival because it was us against them—the prisoner against the system. It was a very brutal and dehumanizing system, and in order to survive that you had to collectively resist it. In order to do that, there had to be certain rules and guidelines. We imposed these guidelines upon ourselves and others in order to survive, you know? For instance, informants. Of course you couldn't survive if you had informants around. It was just like the groups out on the street, like the Panthers, where you're infiltrated by agents provocateurs and things like that. We had to constantly guard ourselves against these types of people, and we had to weed them out. In order to do that, there had to be a code in place—the con code, or the prison code, as we called it, and so we'd abide by that. We would enforce it, and we would enforce it quite rigidly, even to the point of murder, you know? That's how we felt we had to survive, so that's how that operated. Informants were at the very bottom of the pecking order, along with other undesirables, people that we felt were undesirables, like child molesters, rapists—people of that sort. Informants were a big enemy. [...] You couldn't survive if you were infiltrated by agents provocateurs. You just couldn't. You needed that code in place in order to survive and stay solid. That's how that worked.

DEMERS: The code was pretty specific around matters of etiquette. I remember you talking about things like playing your music loud without putting on headphones. That was in the code for a reason. What were some of those other aspects of the code?

MCWHINNEY: Yeah, here's how that worked. Of course prison is a lawless place. There's crimes going on in prison every day, every moment in prison, throughout the day, and even through the night, there's things going on in prison that are illegal, and you couldn't participate in these types of activities if people were informing on you or drawing undue attention—drawing the guard's attention to you. The code was rigidly enforced against playing your radio too loud primarily because the guard might be coming. How can you hear the guard coming if the guy next door is playing his radio too loud, you know? Next thing you know, you're locked up. For what? Because the guard came by and he saw you down on your floor sharpening a blade on the cement or something, and you didn't hear him.

Why didn't you hear that guard? Because some careless person, insensitive or whatever, didn't care. He was selfish and he just wanted to listen to his music, and he wanted other people to listen to it too. The code was in place—it was strictly enforced in that respect—to prevent any undue attention from the authorities, from the guards. And we used numbers. One guy couldn't tell three guys to turn their radios down because he's a loner. He's one against three, or it's two against seven. "Hey, dummy up—you're playing that music too loud." You had to have numbers. That's why the code was enforced, and it was adhered to by a majority.

So, for instance, if I hear somebody's radio, I would yell loud down the range, "Hey, dummy that music!" You know? And the guy may yell back, well, "Fuck you!" You know? "I'll play whatever I want." But the next thing you know you hear four other guys screaming out, "Hey, dummy that fucking music, you goof. You were told once, and we're telling you now, for the last time, you dummy that music. We're not going to tell you again. Or next thing you won't have any music. We'll guarantee it."

The code was enforced with numbers as well. There was also a large degree of pride within the code because nobody wanted to be outside of it, because that meant that you didn't belong. You weren't part of the—not the elite, I don't want to use that word, but it was sort of elitist, I guess, in a manner of speaking. But, people wanted to belong, you see? In order to belong, you had to go *with* the grain. You had to accept the code. And you had to enforce it as well. Once you accepted and enforced it, then you see the reason behind it; it made perfect sense. Why can't I play my radio loud? Because I may be drowning out the approach of a guard, and the guy next door to me may be doing something illegal in his cell, and he may get caught because of me.

So, in a manner of speaking I'm almost like a rat. It's what we call "dry ratting." It's not right out, overtly putting the finger on somebody, but you're doing it by indirect means. So, people came to understand how the code worked, and why it was enforced—and it made perfect sense.

You also didn't play your radio too loud because the guy next door—this is the time when they had post-secondary education—he might be studying for mid-term exams. Because you respected that guy—or you feared him, one or the other, or maybe both—you didn't want to run afoul of him. You respect his privacy, and you don't play your radio loud because he needs quiet to study.

Or maybe the guy on the other side of you— maybe his family just got wiped out in a car accident and he needs time to grieve. He's not feeling good. He's a good guy and he's well respected, and people have empathy for him, so why upset the guy even further? Why torment the guy? Let him have his space. Let him have his privacy. Let him have that moment of silence so he can grieve for his family or his loved ones that got wiped out in a car accident. Or maybe his girlfriend dumped him, you know? Wrote him a "Dear John" and said "that's it, I've had it," you know? And now he's shaking rough time, you know? Because that person is well respected—or maybe even feared, or both—you don't want to run afoul of him.

Or maybe he's sleeping. You don't want to wake the guy up next to you because your radio is loud. That guy might be in for two murder beefs. I swear people really don't understand the magnitude of some of the problems they create for themselves when they're in prison, because half the time they don't know who they're dealing with. They may start mouthing off to a guy, and they have no idea who that guy is, what his background is, what his reputation is, what his past consists of—and they might be walking into a hornet's nest. So there's that consideration as well.

You had to respect people. It was about respect. Now, that word has lost its meaning over the years, and it doesn't really mean much anymore, but at one time it did, and it was very important. In order to gain respect—to attain it and retain it—you had to give it as well, and you can't do that if you're inconsiderate toward others. If you have no respect for others, ultimately, you have no respect for yourself either, you know?

It's better to belong to a group that decides that they're going to follow the code. Therefore, there's no loud music, there's no undue noise, or things that will upset your neighbour, or upset somebody else, or draw unwanted attention to him, where he may find himself in trouble because he didn't hear the guard coming because you were making too much noise.

DEMERS: So it's a social system in that respect, with laws and codes that very much mirror and mimic society outside of prison, where you have all these different codes that you have to abide by, and if not, there's going to be consequences. In society, you have different institutions that teach you these codes—the education system, your parents, and the family as an institution that teaches you what morals and manners are supposed to be, or you might be religious, so there's the church. These are the various institutions that socialize an individual, in combination and to varying degrees, outside of prison. How do you become either socialized into the code, or institutionalized into prison, and learn how to be a part of that majority?

MCWHINNEY: Well, here's how it works. We're thrust out of society by the system—the legal system, the judicial system, the law—and as our punishment we're placed in prison. So we look at it in terms of, well—I've been rejected. Nobody wants me. I'm unfit to live among others in society, so therefore, in turn, I reject them. Once you're thrown into prison, your identity is taken away from you. Your sense of self-worth and all that—you become a nothing, or a nobody, which nobody wants. Nobody wants that, you know? They all want to be somebody, or at least to be recognized as a human being. Even though we broke the law, that doesn't diminish our value as a human being, as a person—even though we don't follow the straight and narrow. Our ideas may differ from society at large, but nevertheless, we're still a person—a human being. So we don't want to become a nothing or a nobody. So our reaction, once we're thrust out of society and rejected, we, in turn—to salvage what little self-worth we feel we've got left—we're, like, "Oh, I'm a prisoner. I'm scum. In society's eyes, I'm scum. So I've got to search around for meaning. For an identity. Where can I find that? Only among my peers—other scum within the system." But nobody wants to be scum—scum within scum, you know? So they strive to raise themselves a little higher.

That's where the code comes in, you see? It helps reinforce your new identity. Now you're somebody because you belong to somebody. You belong to the code. You're respected because you follow the code in prison, you know? And now, in order to survive from becoming a nobody and totally disenfranchised, you search around, and you say, "Well, here's a group of people that will accept me. My own kind. Provided I abide by the rules. Their code. I don't understand their code. This is all new to me. I've never been in prison before. Why can't I play my radio loud, or mouth off to this guy? Well, if I don't abide, then I don't belong. I'm a nobody." So in order to become somebody, or to become accepted, you have to grasp something, you see?

DEMERS: Yeah.

MCWHINNEY: And so therefore you have to go along with the mainstream and accept the code. And sooner or later, after you accept it, you come to realize—"Hey, this isn't such a bad thing. This thing makes sense." It's no different from people out on the street, in society, who make their own laws, and who abide by rules and codes—in schools, in the workplace. You need a cohesive group in order to survive, and to get along. So that's how that comes about.

Now, there's people that are constantly running afoul of the code. Some people don't care about it. Some people are too dense to even grasp it, or they're just too selfish and self-centred to embrace it—it's about them, you know?

"I don't care if this guy next door to me—I don't care if his whole family got wiped out in a car accident and he needs quiet time to grieve. I like my music loud and the louder it is, the better. Forget him. I'm turning it up. I don't care about this guy on this side of me," you know? "He's studying. He's cramming for mid-term exams or something," you know? "He's got a test coming up or whatever. Forget him. I like my music loud. And I'm bigger than him. I'm tougher than him. If he says something, I'll cave his head in," you know? But he can't have that attitude if there's twenty guys behind him who are grieving as well or who are studying for mid-terms. Now he's got to abide and say, "Hey, I better turn this music down. In fact, I think I'll even get rid of this radio just so I can survive," you know?

DEMERS: It's interesting, too, because, the way that you talk about it, not only does it mimic society in the sense that there's a set of codes within the institution that determines how it operates, but there's also a system of punishments, and a way of dealing with people who don't fit or who decide not to conform: people that abide by the code punish individuals who don't, it really does mimic—

MCWHINNEY: It does—although it goes a little to the extreme. For instance, if somebody in society is out cutting their grass at three o'clock in the morning and keeping their neighbours awake, what do you do? You phone the police or something, I don't know. You know, he's violating a code—a bylaw or something.

DEMERS: And he'll get a warning—

MCWHINNEY: Yeah, or he'll get talked to or something. In prison it goes to the extreme. First it's a warning. Sometimes there isn't even a warning. You've got to be careful with some people. Typically, though, first it's a warning—sometimes an extreme warning, and it may even be followed up by another warning, by other people. There may be a second warning, but generally there's not three. That's it. There's where the extreme lies. Unlike society, I've seen people killed in prison, just over a term like—which people out here use every day, practically—"goof."* The word "goof." You call somebody a goof in prison, boy, you better be well armed and you better be prepared

---

* This term can insinuate that someone is a child molester, and it can also mean "get out or fight."

to battle, because it may cost you your life. I've seen guys killed just over that one word. I've seen guys killed because they played their guitar too loud. If a guy's playing his guitar a little too loud, he's warned. Everybody's locked up, you know, but it's all open cells. It's bars—this is before the solid-door prisons came in. With the cell bars, noise carried, and I saw a guy killed over a guitar, because he'd play his guitar a little too loud. He was warned and he got a little mouthy. He disregarded the warning and responded in an inappropriate manner—he should've known better, but he didn't really know who he was dealing with, or what he was dealing with, and the next morning, at breakfast time, as soon as the doors opened, the guards opened the doors for breakfast and this guy didn't make it to breakfast. They found him underneath his bed, full of holes, lying in a pool of blood. Over what? A guitar.

Well, it started over a guitar but then it escalated to worse, because one thing leads to another. People in prison feel that they have to be identified as tough for some reason. This is even more prevalent today, with the gangs and that, than it was back in my time. Back in my time, it was very gentlemanly, you know—very respectful. But, at the same time, it was very dangerous, because these guys—although they were gentlemen and very respectful—you did not want to cross them, boy, because they were dangerous people, you know? And they may not even be—they may be in for a bank robbery, you know? They may be doing seven years for a bank robbery. It's not like they're in for murder, but because of their situation, because of what's going on within the system, they'll kill you. So someone might start out doing seven years for a bank robbery and then they'll run that up to a life bit. I've seen guys starting out with three years and end up doing three life bits, you know? And they're never getting out of prison. In part that's because of the code, but ultimately it's what people impose upon themselves. People dig holes for themselves. Prison is a very fearful place.

There's a lot of people that come into prison and they become very introverted in order to survive. They say, "Hey, this is a dangerous place, and in order to survive this place I better not run afoul of the code," you know? "And I better respect people. And I better be quiet"—and they are. And that's how they survive. There's other guys that come in who recognize the situation that they're in, and it's a very scary situation, very fearful, and they say, "Well, how am I going to survive this? The only way I can get through this is to become a part of it and prove myself." And so what they do is they talk themselves into graves. They dig graves for themselves. A guy will come in, and upon entering the system he'll try and impress upon others how tough he is, how mean he is, how rugged he is—until he's put to the test. And somebody's going to test him. And now he realizes that he's not as tough as he was bragging he was. Now he's in trouble and he realizes that. So what's he got to do? He's got to kill somebody. So that's what he does. He kills somebody. Because in order to live up to the reputation that he built around himself, with his own mouth, in order to live up to that reputation, he's got to prove it. And how does he prove it? He goes and grabs a weapon and he uses that weapon, you see? So he becomes a victim of his own grandiosity or whatever. He talked himself into a situation that he couldn't really get himself out of. He dug a hole for himself, and somebody tested him, put him to the test, and now he has to prove himself. In order to prove himself, he turns violent. As a result, he's charged for murder within the system. He started out doing maybe three years and now he's doing life. Why? Because he talked himself into a situation that he couldn't extricate himself from. I've seen that quite a few times. It's sad, but that's the way it goes.

That's what prison does to these guys. They feel that in order to survive, they've got to become tough. Make no mistake about it, some of them are tough—I've done time with guys who scared me. Stone cold psychopaths. They don't care. They're doing five, six, seven life sentences already. They don't care. They've got their face all tattooed up and everything, you know? They don't care. They're never getting out and they realize that, so they'll do whatever they please.

Don't mess with them because they'll bury you just as soon as look at you.

DEMERS: So, on the one hand the code ensures that there's smooth operation inside, and that particular rules aren't transgressed.

MCWHINNEY: Exactly.

DEMERS: But then, on the other hand, it also produces and encourages people who feel the need to show that they can work within that system to the extent that they're the masters of it?

MCWHINNEY: Yeah, there's some guys who believe so strongly in the code that they'll enforce it to their own detriment. They'll even run the risk of doing another life sentence or end up doing a life sentence just to enforce that code.

DEMERS: Is there a code for the enforcement of the code?

MCWHINNEY: That's interesting. How do you mean that?

DEMERS: Are certain "sentences" attached to certain transgressions? The code is for the larger collective—but then is it left to individuals to ultimately police the code on an individual basis, or is there a kind of code for how to police it?

MCWHINNEY: Yeah, it's funny how that works. It depends on the individual, or the individuals that are interacting with one another—the guy with the guitar and the guy that's studying—they're clashing. The guy that's studying may just give that guy a warning, or he may have his friends give that guy a warning. Depending on his mindset, he may give no warning at all. He may not even tell that guy to turn down his radio, or to lay his guitar down. He may just come up, find the cell the next morning, and just punch that guy full of holes, and the guy doesn't even know what he did wrong. "What did I do?" He has no idea.

And then there's people who just can't survive in prison because of the nature of their offence. Guys who are in for child molestation, they can't survive in the general population. We just kill them, you know? Pretty much. Either that or terrible beatings are laid on them to the point that they're almost dead. They can jump the gun and realize that the nature of their offence is against the con code and that they've got no hope of surviving within the system, and therefore, in order to live, they've got to check into protective custody, and they do so.

DEMERS: Do you think that child molestation is considered to be so vile, or such a horrible transgression, that it's punished in that way because so many in the penitentiary system—so many that are considered to be some of the worst inmates, serving some of the longest sentences—were themselves abused as children? I remember you pointed me to an article where someone said something to this effect, about people graduating through the system—and you corroborated that. Scores of people who you knew in the penitentiary system went to the same training schools as you did when you were a kid, and people in that system were sexually abusing children.

MCWHINNEY: That plays a role in it. The overwhelming majority of guys in the penitentiary were abused when they were children, so it's not a stretch to understand how they would come to abhor that type of behaviour years later, once they came of age, because of their own experience as a child. I was abused when I was a child, in reform school. Physically, sexually, and emotionally, verbally—you name it. Everything, you know? And the overwhelming majority of guys in the penitentiary system were abused themselves, as children—physically, sexually, verbally, emotionally—the whole gambit.

In turn, there is a form of payback. "Hey, see that guy down the range there? He just moved on the range. You know what he's in for? Oh, is that right? Well, I'll take care of him then. Because I remember when I was three years old, or maybe seven or nine, or maybe thirteen, I was raped and abused—so I'm going to take care of this guy. I'm going to let him know," you know? So it's a form of payback. There's that aspect of it. There's also the aspect that we look at that crime as so repugnant that we just can't deal with it. We don't want to deal with it, you know? The only way we choose to deal with it is to exact some type of vengeance, personal vengeance on a guy, and so a beating's laid on him, or worse, but—but, yeah, you're right.

That plays a role into it—our own personal experience. But it's also what defies the norm. Preying on children. A guy that goes into a bank and presents a note to the teller—you can't do that in banks today, it's all automated, but years ago you could go into a bank and slip a note to the teller saying, "I'm armed, I have a loaded weapon, hand over all the money," and walk out, you know? No violence. And that's it. He may get away with it or he may get caught, but we understand that. You know what I mean? A guy's broke, he needs money. He's got no job. He's got no skills, so he's got no hope of ever getting a job. Or maybe he's got a drug habit to feed—whatever the case may be. He needs money so he robs a bank. We may not necessarily agree with that, but at least we understand it. A guy who lurks around the corner of a building or in the bushes of a park or a public schoolyard or something like that and grabs some innocent child and sexually abuses that child, physically harms or kills that child?

We don't understand that. That's not within the realm of the code, you know? It's repugnant.

I had a warden once ask me, "What's your kick against sex offenders?" I say, "Well, I find it repugnant." He says, "Yeah, so do I, and that's normal. That's a normal response," he says, "because so am I. I'm repulsed by that behaviour, as well. But my concern, Rik, is what you do to these guys. Because as a director of this institution I have to make sure that it's running smoothly and operating on an even keel. I don't want to have to come to work and have homicide detectives here investigating a murder because you happen to take your dislike out on a sex offender," you know, "because you objected to his crime." I says, "Well, let's put it this way. I'll make you a deal, warden. I'll leave them alone providing they leave me alone. How's that?" "Good enough," he says. That's what that's about. There's something repulsive about that whole thing, you know? And it reaches the point where we're so incensed by it that we cannot control ourselves, and we act out in the most violent manner, you know? And prison, being a lawless place—you don't ever want to go to prison on a sex beef, man.

DEMERS: I seem to remember, in your files, that one of the issues stopping you from having a transfer go through was that you were violent toward sex offenders. Was that what got you into solitary that time? Was that something that was a part of your life in prison?

MCWHINNEY: I used to hunt them down. I used to actively seek them out, you know, in prison; although I didn't have to try too hard, because there's very few of them, because they don't last long. They understand the gravity of their offence and in order to save themselves, they generally go to protection right away, or ask for protection right away, or the guards tell them, "Hey, you're in for this. You want to live? You're doing ten years for a rape? If you want to live those ten years, you better check into protective." The last thing the guards want is police investigations into murders in their prisons, you know? They want smooth-operating prisons. They don't want bodies lying on the floor. And they swear an oath to protect people. When you become a prison guard you swear an oath—you take an oath to the system, that you're there to protect the life not only of your peers, fellow guards and that, or civilians, but even prisoners, you know?

But that's how that works with sex offenders. Basically, it's because we feel that revulsion very deeply. We feel that very deeply because of our own past, or just through a natural revulsion toward that type of offence.

DEMERS: To kind of wrap up with your experience of the code, if you think about prison in a sense as a form of social experiment where you're throwing a bunch of men in, some wearing one type of uniform, others wearing another, and both groups are abiding by a particular code that encourages those values to become entrenched—what does that do to somebody who is then supposed to be released back into the community?

MCWHINNEY: Some carry that out into society with them and they end up back in prison—or some end up dead.

DEMERS: What's the value of prison when the end result is that you're put into a system whereby, in order to survive within that system, you have to adopt a code that in effect makes your life functional within prison but—

MCWHINNEY: Dysfunctional outside.

DEMERS: Yes—dysfunctional outside because automatically you've internalized all of these values that put you in absolutely entrenched opposition to the law and to authority?

MCWHINNEY: What's required is that the individual has to shed those values, and that lifestyle, and adapt to the pre-existing values that are set in place outside of prison, you know? You have to shed the old life and adapt to the new one. Some are able to do it quite well and succeed.

Some are marginally co-opted back into the society's norms, but not completely, and so they're still on the borderline. And some are still fully entrenched in the prison code, and they bring it back out to the street with them and they end up back in prison or dead.

There are certain words, phrases, or names that are used in prison that can't be described as anything other than a pejorative term. Like the word "goof." Guys have been killed over that word in prison. Out here in society, people use that term every day and think nothing of it. "Ah, you're a goof," or, "You're acting like a goof," or, "You look like a goof with that orange toque on," or something like that. In prison, that word in and of itself is a death sentence. You use that word in prison, you better be prepared to kill over its usage, because that guy who you directed that term toward is coming after you.

There was this one guy, Bobby, who got out of the SHU [Special Handling Unit] and he went to a halfway house in Prince George. His second day out he went downtown and got drunk. He's been in jail for nine years, with three years in the SHU. Of course he wants to let loose, so he goes downtown and gets drunk. Finally, he realizes that he's got to report back to the halfway house. He's past his curfew, but he figures he can slide by. So he calls a cab. "Where you want to go?" He gives the cab driver the name of the halfway house, but he doesn't know the address—he's never lived in Prince George in his life. He's never even been in BC before, other than in prison.

So the cab driver is driving around at one o'clock in the morning trying to find this place and Bobby doesn't know where it is. Finally, the cab driver gets fed up and calls Bobby a goof. "What, don't you know where you live? What are you, some kind of goof or something?" That was his death sentence. Bobby beat him to death. He beat him to death and ended up doing a life sentence. Why? Because he wasn't adequately equipped to deal with the way people live, think, and behave out on the street, as opposed to in prison. Bobby had been in prison most of his adult life. He's only been out of prison a little better than a day. Now he's drunk, and you know, as a result of that, he's also somewhat mentally incapacitated. He doesn't know the directions to where he is supposed to go, he can't convey that to the cab driver, the cab driver gets fed up, and Bobby doesn't know how to deal with this. He deals with it in the sense of prison, how he would deal with it in prison, because in his mind he's still in prison, you know, and you use that word in prison, you better be prepared to kill somebody. You cannot call somebody a goof in prison and expect to get away with it. You just cannot.

If you can shed those old values. Basically, all they are is a coping mechanism to survive in a situation that's horrendous, but then once you're released, you have to shed all those values and then you can become—as much as possible—a useful, contributing member of society.

DEMERS: And the problem is that if it *is* possible, if you go through the process of shedding those values, that personality, that code that was necessary in order to survive within prison, then successful reintegration is *in spite of*, and not because of, your incarceration.

MCWHINNEY: Very much so.

FOREVER LOST

Hello my friend of times long past
Do you recall of memories now
So seldom since I saw you last
Do you rue that broken vow?

Yes, I'm the friend you once sought
For that friendship dearly rendered
Never once to be sold or bought
My good name that you surrendered

Now I gaze upon your face
I detect a certain sorrow
You freely chose to run that race
As if absent of tomorrow

Now your eyes show great regret
You have nothing left to say
Your casuistry did beget
A moral compass gone astray

You took a risk on Fortune's wheel
Now you walk forever lost
Your disenchantments now reveal
That it was not worth the cost

v) The Keepers
and the Kept

Introduction

RIK'S FAVOURITE MOVIE WAS *RUNAWAY TRAIN*, a prison escape story penned by Eddie Bunker.[1] More than just a high-octane action film about a train that has lost both its brakes and its conductor, the highly meta-phorical film takes place in a tech-driven, morally bank-rupt present in which escaped convict Manny plays the anti-hero monster to Ranken, the Dr. Frankenstein–like prison warden, a maker of monsters. The film opens with the announcement that Manny has won a court battle and is set to be released from his prison-with-in-the-prison, a solitary cell that has been welded shut for three years. The warden scolds the media for hu-manizing brutish Manny; in Ranken's opinion, Manny is only celebrated by other inmates because they're all animals. The film ends with Manny sacrificing himself while saving others, choosing death over recapture while ensuring that others won't be harmed. Dialogue from Shakespeare's *Richard III* closes the film as an epilogue: "No beast so fierce but knows some touch

of pity. / But I know none, and therefore am no beast."
We might imagine that the first line of the epilogue describes Manny, who saves others while choosing death
as the only manner of freedom left to him—he would
rather die than return to his cell. Ranken, however,
has shown no pity throughout the film—he has been
merciless to Manny and all the other prisoners—and
is therefore, like Richard III, the pitiless ruler who is
only beyond reproach because that is what he declares
himself to be. As warden, Ranken is in the position,
vis-à-vis the incarcerated, to make authoritative declarations, and it doesn't matter if they are senseless,
contradictory, and logically unacceptable.

This section explores the antagonistic divide between
the keepers and the kept, and it is largely composed of
instances where Rik wishes to call the purported irre-
proachability of keepers into question. While general-
izations about either the keepers or the kept are equally
unhelpful, for an incarcerated person, witnessing the
unequal application of absolute standards on either side
of this divide calls the very system in which they are
kept into question. While insubordination and revolt
were go-to responses at home, in training school, and
during the earlier years of his incarceration, Rik would
subsequently come to use his writing as a vehicle for
expressing his irreverence toward authority figures.

With "Fear & Loathing in Bowden," Rik wears his
influences on his sleeve. The title of the poem is a nod
to Hunter S. Thompson; it points to what Rik identifies
as a moral degeneracy at the hypocritical heart of the
carceral system. The poem itself, however—an exposé

of the everyday corruption he witnessed at Bowden, a medium/minimum-security penitentiary in Alberta—is modelled after Allen Ginsberg's "America." Rik met Ginsberg when he was young, free-spirited, selling and smoking cannabis, and drifting between cities and provincial correctional centres in British Columbia. Rik admired the Beats, and he maintained a correspondence with Ginsberg while he was incarcerated.

While the poem is, like much of Thompson's and Ginsberg's writing, notable for its sense of humour, the subject matter is nevertheless serious. As we read below, while incarcerated at Bowden, Rik alleges he was assigned to, and subsequently removed from, a bookkeeping position in which he witnessed and documented the widespread theft of thousands of dollars of farm equipment, feed, and bovine growth hormone. Rik alleges that the farm equipment was reappropriated for personal use by staff who owned farms, and that prison shops were used to do free, off-the-book work for the warden (prisoners produced furniture for the warden's house, for example, and they detailed his car). While staff misappropriated the spoils of the prison, programs were chronically underfunded, and living conditions were dire. Rik later discovered that the prison doctor, Dr. Aubrey Levin, was a South African–born Canadian with false credentials who used electroshock therapy, drugs, and sex-reassignment surgery to treat gay conscripts and conscientious objectors in South Africa during the apartheid era.[2] (In 2013, Levin was given a five-year prison sentence after more than fifty men came forward to testify against him for inappropriate sexual advances while he was practising medicine in Alberta.[3]) In the face of these disturbing events, Rik attacked the status quo with a biting sense of humour.

One can see from Rik's faux grievance concerning "The Purloined Chairs," or from his suggestion that a correctional officer be forced to work for four weeks at the Edmonton Food Bank for wasting meals ("Lockdown Meals: Grievance"), that the grievance system was a source of both comedy and critique for Rik. The carbon copies and paper trails left behind in Rik's files, however, demonstrate that he navigated these channels often, and with very limited success.[4] While sense of humour and irony were common tools, in poems like "The Blatant Beast" and "Nolo Corrigendum," Rik demonstrates how language can serve as a pressure release valve; indeed, in several of the pieces gathered in this section, the writers of life-determining reports are cut down to size in articulate and eloquent—even if sometimes sesquipedalian—rants.

Bowden you've taken all but the brutality of my insightful
    observations & the spirit of my endurance
Bowden three dollars & sixteen cents.
I won't write my poem until my muse has moved me.
I don't feel good don't bother me.
Bowden when will you confess your sins?
When will you follow your own directives?
Bowden why is the library always closed?
Bowden your victims need closure not the library.
Bowden stop withholding the mail.
Bowden your arrogance is too much for me.
I refuse to give up my obsession.
I'm obsessed with my obsession.
Bowden your flower gardens are sinister.
Bowden I'm sentimental about the feral cat prowling
    your prison.
I go to the dining hall get fed up & leave.
Bowden if you can't stand the meat get out of the kitchen.
Bowden I fill out grievance forms every chance I get.
Bowden how can I write a holy litany of your transgressions?
Bowden there aren't enough trees!!!
Bowden why have you declared war on single cell
    accommodation?
When will you come to terms with your own self-loathing?
Bowden why are so many dying in health care?
When will you become unworthy of your South African war
    criminals?
Bowden when will you reveal where you have buried all
    the bodies?

Bowden when will your farm annex submit to a forensic audit?
Why are you pumping bovine growth hormone into all
    the cattle?
The warden is obsessed with bovine growth hormone.
He self-medicates with it every morning before succumbing to
    his own udder madness.
Bowden it's about your parole officers.
Your parole officers your parole officers your war criminals and
    your parole officers.
Your parole officers are power hungry.
They want the clothes off our backs.
They want us all in orange jumpsuits.
They've abolished our cigarette lighters.
Our tobacco is next to go.
They want us all rehabilitated.
The non-habilitated in pursuit of the rehabilitated.
Bowden is this politically correct?
Where was the correctness as I struggled with Trotsky's theory
    & my own revolution of rising expectations while chained
        to the sink of my cell in solitary confinement in B.C.
            Penitentiary 1975?
Bowden you are totally clueless.
Your work board is clueless, your schoolteachers are clueless,
    your doctors, nurses, kitchen stewards & grievance
        coordinators are all clueless.
Everyone is clueless except the prisoners & the majority of
    them don't have a clue.
It occurs to me that I am the clue.
I am the clue that holds the glue together.
My clues are more individual than Japan's automobiles.
And much more radical in their design.

It's true that I don't want to work in the cabinet shop producing
    custom furniture for the warden's private residence.
I'm chronically depressed & suicidal anyway.
This is the impression I get from doing time in Bowden.
I better get right to work on the problem.
Bowden I need more grievance forms!

The Purloined Chairs

Complaint:

OVER THE COURSE OF THE PAST YEAR, THERE has been a protracted diminution of dining room chairs at the Stan Daniels Centre. This situation raises a serious problem in terms of consuming one's meals. In an attempt to discover where these items are going, or why they are disappearing, one is left to ponder the whole gamut of possibilities as to their whereabouts. The rumour mill has it that D.W. is loading them into his vehicle along with kitchen whites from the premises every Wednesday afternoon. It remains uncertain what he actually does with the chairs in question. I personally do not believe that D.W. could obtain any amount of cocaine for institutional chairs. However, the exchange of these chairs for vast quantities of tainted elk meat is not beyond the realm of possibility. But, then again, these are unsubstantiated allegations that have yet to be confirmed. Either way, the fact remains that there exists a serious seating problem at Stan Daniels.

CORRECTIVE ACTION REQUESTED:

- That a full investigation be conducted into the pur-loined chairs and that they be replaced immediately.

Lockdown Meals: Grievance

Complaint:

ON 95/03/16, B UNIT WAS PLACED ON LOCK-
down. Lunch-time meals were prepared & placed on
food carts to be delivered to the unit when correctional supervisor C.R. radioed the kitchen & told the se-
nior food officer R.K. that B Unit will not be fed.

When R.K. responded that the carts were already
loaded & ready to go, C.R. responded by ordering him
to throw the food out & subsequently twenty-four meals
were thrown in the garbage. This action is in direct
violation of Commissioner's Directive 880, Section 4,
& Standing Order 880 Section 6, Subsection B.

CORRECTIVE ACTION REQUESTED:

- That correctional supervisor C.R. pay for these
  meals that were wasted.

- That prisoners who are being forced to pay room & board expenses be reimbursed for the loss of this meal in question.

- That correctional supervisor C.R. be required to work a minimum of four weeks at the Edmonton Food Bank so that he may learn & appreciate the value of food.

- That C.R. be demoted from correctional supervisor until he familiarizes himself with the Commissioner's Directives.[5]

#274991A

R. McWhinney

Denial of Transfer: Grievance

Complaint:

ON 24/04/96, I RECEIVED A DENIAL OF MY transfer application to Bowden Farm Annex. I submitted the application on 20/09/95, fully anticipating an answer within the time frame documented in the Commissioner's Directive, as well as the Case Management Manual that specifically states: "For intra-regional transfers, the decision-makers shall, within sixty days of the inmate's request being submitted, respond with an answer."

Given the excessive amount of time it took to respond to my application (seven months), I, and others, have not failed to notice that the decision-maker did not use that time to properly examine my case. Instead, he appeared to rely upon outdated and, in some respects, false information when making his decision.

Warden J.R. cites that I have "exemplified a lengthy and serious institutional history of violence and disruptive behaviour." I believe the key word in that statement is "history," and nothing more relevant than that. As a consequence, it is quite apparent that he has made a snap judgment based upon who I was rather than who I am.

While I freely admit that my file documentation of the past can be shocking to the reader, it does not reflect my recent or current situation. For the past three years I have held an executive position with the Lifers' Group while serving on a mental health committee that was responsible for establishing a mental health unit in the institution. This unit has subsequently received much favourable attention within Correctional Service Canada.

In addition, I currently hold the position of inmate redress coordinator and peer counsellor, where we mediate disputes and/or complaints in a proactive fashion so that both parties (inmates and staff) are satisfied. This program has reduced the number of formal grievances by 80 percent within the past seven months. I have held this position for approximately fourteen months while retaining a medium-security status since December 1994. This demonstrates that I behave in a mature and responsible fashion, and it can be supported by reviewing my preventive security files and speaking to my work supervisors.

I would like to address the misleading statement entered onto the decision sheet by Warden J.R.: "Finally, you have listed incompatible inmates at Bowden Institution." I want it to be known that at no time have I compiled a list or identified incompatibles at Bowden Institution.

First and foremost, I applied to transfer to Bowden Farm Annex, so it is of no concern to me if incompatibles exist at Bowden Institution or not. Secondly, I resent the manner in which Warden J.R. has attempted to place the onus upon me for denying my transfer. As if I would go to the trouble of applying for a transfer to Bowden Farm Annex only to nullify it by stating somewhat as an afterthought: oh, by the way, should you decide to approve my application, I have a complete list of incompatibles at Bowden Institution.

I made the application to transfer to Bowden Farm Annex based upon the recommendation of the National Parole Board in 1995. One of the motivating reasons that I applied for this transfer, as stated on my application, is that I suffer from a chronic and debilitating disease (Crohn's). Stress plays a critical role in enabling symptom control and preventing remission. I currently possess a body weight of 127 pounds and find my physical health deteriorating with each passing day in an institution that is not conducive to relieving stress levels associated with managing the disease and its inherent deficits.

Finally, in closing, I wish to state that there exists no active or passive evidence that I currently display any overt or covert manifestations of violence or anger, nor have I for several years.

I believe the logical conclusion at this point is to move on, and not to dwell upon the past. "Quantum mutatus ab illo."*

....

*   Latin for "How changed from what he once was."

CORRECTIVE ACTION REQUESTED:

• That Warden K.'s letter of April 4, 1996, be stricken from all of my Correctional Service Canada files.[6]

#274991A
R. McWhinney

On False File Information: Letter to the District Director of Parole

Dear J.,

Greetings from the gulag. Contrary to the community assessment attached, I write this letter to address an issue. An issue, albeit not initially mine, has been thrust upon me. However, I believe the solution may rest within your domain, and I therefore appeal to you for assistance in this matter.

On 07/08/06, I submitted a release plan as requested by the National Parole Board, and this in turn resulted in my rejection by all of the CRFS [Community Residential Facilities] in the Edmonton area. These rejections are based upon the nebulous assertion that I am "unwilling to address my issues." Whatever these issues may be remains unclear as they are not stated or identified. As well, my "failure to change my entrenched pro-criminal values and behaviours" is in doubt, and how these values & behaviours are manifest or demonstrated is equally unclear. What is abundantly apparent is that there exists within the system, as well in positions marginally related to it, individuals that have become habituated by the powers vested in them to making unfounded & injurious written reports. They perform this ploy from the position of authoritarian officialdom with the arrogant belief that their skills are magical, unimpeachable, incommunicable, & hidden within directives.

How dare anyone question their motive, abilities, or the veracity that they project as being beyond reproach. This most often represents the prevailing attitude the prisoner encounters upon confronting the author of false reports. Unable to sublimate his frustration with the writer's doctrinaire attitude, he now becomes further frustrated to the point of anger, and understandably so. This in turn is met with the writer's dysfunctional response of denial, blame transference, non sequiturs, implausible error, and non-related recriminations, followed by retaliatory recommendations for anger management & emotions programming. The whole process and sequence of events are best described as Goebbelsian & Byzantine in nature. For the prisoner, the results are very frustrating, Kafkaesque, and polarizing.

The writer's denial is analogous to the response of a prisoner with a positive drug urinalysis. He becomes rigid in his denial and blames his girlfriend by saying that she put cocaine in his spaghetti while he watched the hockey game on television, or that his friends put heroin in his beer while he was in the washroom. Notwithstanding, he has an alcohol abstinence restriction on his parole conditions. This is not dissimilar to many of the absurd responses one encounters when confronting some writers of false and misleading file reports.

However, I digress & wish to bring your attention back to the community assessment. You may notice E.S.'s name on pg. 2. She was my parole officer at Grierson Centre. I found a wallet in the parking lot that belonged to a woman who worked upstairs in your office, J. Upon discovering this wallet, I was overcome with a great sense of empathy for the owner. Had I lost this item, my life would have been seriously disrupted. I immediately turned it into the Grierson Centre staff, a Mr. W.C. & Mr. U.T. So I ask you, is this the behaviour of a criminal? Or, to put it another way, is this representative of the motivations of a person with "entrenched pro-criminal values & behaviours"?

I guess by E.S.'s standards, it clearly is. She is also well aware of the wallet incident as we discussed it together at my workplace in the resource library afterwards. While she was my parole officer at the Grierson Centre, I found her to be very engaging, caring, supportive, and certainly proactive. For the uninitiated, the flagrant dishonesty of her report may pose the naive question: What circumstances prompted her negative approach to this report? However, the question in and of itself remains the answer. The existence of an adversarial system, and the arbitrary relations set within it, dictate circumstances whereby some of its officials/employees have become so co-opted & vitiated that they are no longer capable of the self-discipline and moral courage to resist & rise above cynical temptations. False file information is by design, apathy, and systemic self-interest the most unacknowledged barrier to the system's stated goals and objectives. It negates the very title it carries: the Correctional Service itself, reducing it to an unambiguous misnomer and a glaring paradox. False file information sets in motion a chain of events that serve to alienate & polarize the prisoner that the system claims to assist and correct. A system both unwilling & unable to correct itself cannot assist or correct the prisoner who becomes polarized by the false file information that is used against him. These circumstances create a role reversal whereby the prisoner becomes victim, and the legal authority over him the offender—at least on a moral level.

The scenario I describe in this letter only acts to widen the schism and strengthen all of the pre-existing subcultural codes and biases that exist on both sides of the criminal justice divide. It engenders and fosters the "us versus them" mentality whereby the system, greater than the sum of its parts, and through its inherent hypocrisies, maintains this schism as well as its own credibility gap. The statement concerning pro-criminal values & behaviour is made with such a degree of authoritarian certainty that one would expect immediate police intervention & appropriate arrest and charges laid. One may ask the question: Faced with the same circumstances of the wallet incident of June 2003, would I react and behave in the same fashion? I remain flush with confidence to answer in the affirmative, even so much to say that if the wallet belonged to E.S. herself, I would follow the exact same path. For it is an intact & healthy superego that compels me to do the correct thing in all matters such as this.

Doing the correct and pro-social thing in June 2003 demonstrates that I am of a greater moral persuasion than the author of that report. I understand why it was written the way that it was, and I also expect that any subsequent reports will be written in an effort to deflect or minimize all criticism of the first. There is nothing so destructive or so savaging to the heart's core as the final confirmation of the long-held belief that one is no longer relevant as a person. It begs the question on an existential level if one ever were other than the proverbial "grist for the mill."

I anticipate your response in the hope of rectifying this matter at your earliest convenience, particularly with respect to alleged criminal behaviour.

Thanking you in advance for your attention to this matter, I remain sincerely,

Rik McWhinney

In Conversation III

DEMERS: Is there something like a guard code that corresponds to the con code?

MCWHINNEY: Guards, like prisoners, have little set remarks—con lover, for example. A guard doesn't want to be called a con lover, you know—that would mean he's out, he's a rat, he's not to be trusted. If a guard is too supportive of prisoners' rights, or is too supportive of, or empathetic toward, prisoners in any sense or form, guards don't tolerate that—and they get rid of those guards, you know. Some of them may be fortunate enough to hang on for a while, but sooner or later they burn out, and they get rid of them.

It's very similar to the con code, only on a different plane and working in a different direction. They don't like rats, they have a pecking order—the same as the con code—they don't like skinners: sex offenders. This is allied with our

thoughts and our attitudes toward these subjects as well. We don't like rats because you can't
survive if you've got agents provocateurs within
your midst.

DEMERS: So that encourages an antagonistic relationship—because it's policed on either side.

MCWHINNEY: Oh yeah, very much so.

DEMERS: In spite of those divisions, and in spite of
that policing, did you experience compassion and
good treatment from some of the guards during
your time inside?

MCWHINNEY: Yeah, but very, very few. Particularly
for the first, I'd say, twenty years.

DEMERS: Do you think it's something that has to
do with age on either side of the equation?
Aging out—

MCWHINNEY: Well that plays into it. As you become
wiser you're able to differentiate the wheat from
the chaff. You say, well, maybe I can get along
with this guard, if he understands where I'm
coming from, and I understand where he's coming from. I already know where he's coming from
for the most part because they tend to have a
one-dimensional view of us. Some are a little
more humane and empathetic toward us, but I

experienced that very, very, very seldomly, and very rarely. It was only one or two guards over a long period of time.

I told you how they gave me a parole, and took it away, you know, for no reason. I didn't reoffend—I didn't even get out on that parole. I didn't even get out—released, and they took it away. In 1993, I went up in front of the parole board, and they gave me a parole. I'm waiting for this parole to take effect, about five weeks go by, and I'm still in prison. I'm supposed to be out on parole. What's going on here?

Finally, a psychologist called me down, he was an advocate on my behalf, and he said, "Rik, it looks like there's a problem here with your parole."

I say, "No kidding. I was granted that parole five weeks ago, and I'm still here. What's going on?"

He says, "Well, it looks like they're having second thoughts about honouring it."

"Well, it's a done deal—I've got the paperwork here, they signed off on it. Parole granted. I've got their signatures on the decision sheet."

He says, "Well, they think you scammed them. They want a PCL-R test done on you." That's what they call "Psychopathy Checklist-Revised." They wanted me to do this test because they think I scammed them. And my initial reaction is, no—I'm not doing it. But this psychologist talked me into doing it. He says, "If you do it, Rik, I've been assured that they'll honour the parole—provided you pass the test. They think that you're a psychopath and you scammed them. I'll conduct the test, and I'll tell you right from the get-go that I'm going to mark you very, very hard, harder than I do most of the others, just so there's no doubt in their minds whatsoever that this is all on the up and up, that you're not scamming them, so I'm letting you know beforehand that I'm going to mark you very, very hard."

So, I guess against my better judgment, I said, yeah, okay, and I did the test. And I passed—so the board wants another hearing now. In the meantime, I'm taking them to court. I'm taking the National Parole Board to court, which is not a good idea, because they resent that. And the judge even said so when I went to court. He says, "Well, the parole board, they do what they want—and I suspect they always will. However, I do not like the way in which they cancelled this parole, this letter in the mail"—that's how they cancelled it, they just sent me a letter in the mail saying my parole has been cancelled. No hearing, or anything. Had I gotten out on that parole and reoffended, I would have had the benefit of a revocation hearing where I would have gone in front of the board and explained my case. I didn't even have that opportunity. I just got a letter in the mail saying that my parole had been cancelled. The judge didn't like the way they did that, so she ordered them to give me another hearing.

So a year from the day that they gave me that full parole, I got another parole hearing. This time it was ordered by the court, so they have to give it to me. So I go into that hearing, and believe me, I'm angry. And because all parole hearings are audiotaped, I have a copy of the tape in my back pocket, and I have a copy of the written decision in which they granted me full parole in my shirt pocket. I go in there, and because I'm a lifer, I have to have three board members, and it has to be a majority that rules in order to grant a lifer parole. Only one of those board members is from the previous hearing—nevertheless, they're all familiar with my case. They know what's going on. And none of them can make eye contact with me. They're all staring at the desk, or up at the wall. They can't look me in the eye, you know? And I'm almost daring them to look at me.

The hearing commences, and I interrupt. I say, "Listen—I was here a year ago and you granted me parole. I have the tape here." And I reached into my back pocket, I pulled out the audiotape. "I have the tape here, and I also have the written decision." And then I pulled out the written decision that said parole granted. I say, "you gave me a parole with a proviso that all leaves and passes from the Gunn Centre were in the accompaniment of an escort. That's where I was to reside, at a halfway house. Your lawyer told the court that the reason you took the parole away was that I lacked escorts. I have the escorts. You said full parole."

And this board member looked at me, and he says, "Yes, Rik—we did say that. However, that's not what we meant."

I was actually shocked by what I heard. As soon as I heard that, I got up out of my chair, I turned around, and I walked out of that hearing. That was the end of the hearing. Right in the middle of it, I just walked out. I vowed to myself never to revisit that type of abuse upon myself ever again, and never again would I go in front of the parole board, you know? That's it. I've had it with these idiots. They say things they don't mean.

There were guards that I didn't like, and who didn't like me, hard-core guards, and even them, the worst guards in the system, they were empathetic about my situation, you know? They could not believe how the parole board could do that to a man after twenty-one years. Offer him a light, only to turn the switch off, five weeks later, for nothing. I hadn't done anything.

So for the next thirteen years I never went in front of the board; even though people would try and encourage me to go in front of the board, I wouldn't. Finally, in 2007, I did go in front of the board, and they gave me parole. But I had to do another thirteen, fourteen years after that. And for nothing, you know? I could have been out in 1993 instead of 2007, but that's the way they operate. That's the way they are.

I'll tell you, Jason—I was very tempted to lock myself into the system after that experience. I could have been like those other guys, with their faces all tattooed up, and just start killing guys at random. Believe me, the thought crossed my mind. But I didn't. I continued on my way, and continued doing what I was doing, you know, in terms of animal welfare, working with battered-women's shelters, and working with all kinds of charity groups. It brought me a lot of satisfaction, even though it went unrecognized and unrewarded for the next thirteen to fourteen years. It wasn't an easy road by any means. And it was very, very difficult to accomplish those things while incarcerated.

DEMERS: You were quite critical of a lot of the processes while you were incarcerated, not just what happened with the cancellation of your parole.

MCWHINNEY: They write bogus reports on people in prison, then you can't get it corrected. They refuse to correct it for a number of reasons. First of all, they just hate to admit fault. They just can't come to terms with their own inability to lay out the facts as they are.

Case in point: At my last and final parole hearing, in which they granted me parole, I had a report—a seven-page report written by my parole officer in Bowden, with fifteen lies in it. Just outright lies.

So, the board adjourned for a moment, and as I left the hearing, my parole officer walked out with me. Now, I hadn't been talking to her for a couple of months, but as we left the hearing, she asked me if I was going to comply with the National Parole Board's request for a community assessment. My response was, "Why did you write all those lies about me?"

She responded, "They're not lies."

"Oh, they're not? Well, how would you characterize them?"

She says, "They're errors."

"Well, that's interesting," I say. "Fifteen errors in the body of a seven-page report? What does that say about your credibility and your professionalism as a parole officer?"

She lost it, and I just walked away.

This was my response to her file reports that she wrote on me [*Rik hands me the poem "Nolo Corrigendum"*].

DEMERS: "I refuse to correct"?

MCWHINNEY: If I wrote a report on you, Jason, and you questioned the veracity of it, and you confronted me with it and you say, "Rik, why did you write all those lies about me?" my response would be, "What lies are you talking about?" You know, "Identify it—what are you talking about?

What lies?" But her immediate response was, "They're not lies." Well, they're not errors either if she's aware of them.

DEMERS: If you're not lying and you're aware that there's errors, then they should actually be corrected in the record.

MCWHINNEY: Hence the title of the poem. But that's the type of thing they engage in. It's just outright lies. And they duplicate the process, because there may be an error—an honest error contained within your file, or it may be a set-up, a deliberate lie made to cast you in a negative light. They refuse to correct them. So, throughout the course of your sentence, *this just gets repeated over and over*. It's never corrected—so *it's a duplication of process*. So that lie—

DEMERS: —It has immediate effect, but then it has another effect down the road, when—

MCWHINNEY: —Yeah, that lie follows you in your file, over the course of your whole sentence, because they refuse to correct it. There was one time when they did correct the error, but only after they had achieved their goal, you know—

DEMERS: They transferred you to another facility.

MCWHINNEY: Yeah—they get a transfer and six months later they correct it, after the transfer had already been effected. It's very destructive, and as a result, you become more embittered and enraged. It just reinforces that us versus them mentality. How can you ever come to friendly terms with a person who has authority over you when they're falsifying your file? You hate that person. You despise them.

DEMERS: You're somebody who's attuned to procedure, and who tries to correct these types of mistakes, but there's a lot to navigate here—drawing attention to particular codes. There's a lot of nuance involved. Are incarcerated people generally able to navigate as easily as you are?

MCWHINNEY: No. For the most part people are apathetic, or they may be semi-literate, or they just don't have the wherewithal to navigate the codes and rules and regulations.

DEMERS: It's not like lawyers are hanging around to give you legal advice.

MCWHINNEY: There's an old term that's used in prison—jailhouse lawyers. This is used to describe people who are very adept at working the system and holding the system to account. I was often accused of being one myself. It's used by guards as a pejorative term—"Oh, McWhinney, he's a jailhouse lawyer," which means, to them, that I'm a troublemaker. In other words, "Watch him. He's going to try to draw heat on us because we're mistreating him, or we're mistreating other prisoners."

They implemented a program where you can now have legal representation for an institutional charge, but not too many guys make use of it. The grievance system is a process where you file a formal complaint against something that was done to you, or done to a group of prisoners, that you feel is wrong. It's a whole process that's long and drawn-out, and there's time frames and everything surrounding it. But, for the most part, prisoners don't bother with it. They may file a complaint, but if they don't like the answer that they receive in reply, in frustration they'll just crumple it up and throw it out. They don't go to the next grievance level. And this really upsets me, because they'd come to me with a problem, and I'd tell them to file a complaint. They say, "well, I did."

And I'd say, "what was the answer?"

"They denied it."

"On what grounds?"

"Oh, I can't remember."

"Well, where's your complaint? Let me read it."

"Oh, I don't have it."

"Well, what did you do with it?"

"Oh, I threw it away."

"Well, what did you do that for?"

"I was pissed off."

Listen—anything that they write and they put a signature to, you keep. You never, ever throw anything away. That's why I've got a whole file cabinet full of papers, because I learned at an early stage to never give them the upper hand. The minute that you destroy something in writing, that they offered, you're basically out of luck. You've got no recourse to go to the next grievance level. I used to chastise guys severely. "You never, ever do that. And don't ever come to me again complaining about a complaint that you threw away, because I can't help you, nor will I help you, because you're unwilling to help yourself."

But, like I was saying, false file information is one of the greatest barriers to the prison's stated goals and objectives, because it undermines the entire integrity of the system.

DEMERS: You said that there was a lot of corruption at Rockwood.

MCWHINNEY: Oh, there's corruption in them all, but there was corruption there—theft off the farm, mostly. A lot of cheese because they had a dairy and cheese-production operation going there. A lot of feed and things. And a lot of medications because they have a beef industry there— they raise beef cattle. They were heavy into the BGH—bovine growth hormone—antibiotics.

These drugs are very, very expensive, and they disappeared at an alarming rate. Prisoners aren't taking them. What use does a prisoner have for bovine growth hormones? A lot of medication went missing out of that place—antibiotics and hormones, which are not cheap.

A lot of that was going on in Bowden too. They were getting really carried away in Bowden—gasoline, feed, livestock, medication. They had a little beef industry there too. They were raising beef cattle. Black Angus. One cow had twins—she dropped two calves—and one of the prisoners reported to work the next morning and these two calves are missing.

So, he went to the farm boss, and he says, "Hey, where did those calves go that were born last night?" He says, "Oh, they died." Now, those calves didn't die. Those were healthy twins— robust, fit, and healthy calves. There's no way those calves died. Two guards were seen hauling them into a trailer at three in the morning. This is the kind of thing that goes on. And it raises the question: Who's to be trusted here? The keepers or the kept? Bowden was a bad place. That's a place where I had to seriously question why the warden—he wasn't innocent, why he wasn't in a cell next to me, doing time? That's how corrupt he was.

They have an automotive shop there, and he brought a car in—a classic 1962 Buick Electra, a beautiful car, mint condition, cherry—he brought it into the automotive shop. He got four brand new tires all the way around, the whole interior cleaned and polished, waxed. The outside Simonized, waxed. The engine compartment power-washed, steamed. You could eat off it. A friend of mine was doing the work on this warden's car in the automotive shop, and after they do all this work on this car, this beautiful classic Buick, he goes into the office and asks the boss for the requisition slip for all this work that's done on it. And his boss says, "No, that's the warden's car. Just forget about that," you know? So that warden got all that work done on his car gratis. That warden was corrupt. He's been a warden at about four different penitentiaries. He'd go to one, burn himself out, and they'd just transfer him to another joint. He'd burn himself out there, go to another one, burn himself out there.

There's a guide for guards—I forget the name of it now, but it's a guidebook for guards, with rules and regulations and standards. No prison guard is to profit or gain from any work or gratuities received from an inmate. That's the code of conduct—the prison guards' code of conduct. So here's a warden, breaking his own guidelines, because that was all prison labour that went into that car, it was taxpayer money that went into his tires, and his wax job, and everything else. It's little wonder that prisoners resist the system. It's the ones that are on the lower rung of the ladder that pay for the crimes of higher-ups.

Born of Chimera and sired by Cerberus
Bares a countenance so vile and leprous
A grotesque appearance to assault the eyes
With innate duplicity that all despise

The calumny of mud she slings
Steeped in venom of her beastly stings
One hundred tongues with speech betray
Her appetite for truth to slay

With talons clutched to her keyboard
Her anticipation to strike false chord
A chord of lies so meretricious
Reveal a nature so avaricious

With false memory records the crimes
Both imagined and absent of the times
To laugh at reputations torn
Now display them such for all to scorn

Of such low character, so diabolic
Her typed reports so Bellerophontic
Of reputations she will strive to blot
To infect them with her contagious rot

Will not relent until they bleed
To suck them dry as maggots feed
Of mean self-interest her ambition clear
The need for power & to coerce with fear

Performs this task with benediction
The wardens blessing & love of fiction
Her speech betrays the bigot's tongue
Of which none are safe, neither old nor young

With profane disdain & malice prepense
Types false reports for daily dispense
Despite a verdict of the highest court
Toward her guilt to file false report

Upon the evidence of clearest proof
Will deny & cry then stomp her hoof
Then shriek out loud as last resort
As she is found in contempt of court

NOLO CORRIGENDUM

For what purpose one may ask
Why her motives wear the mask
The Janus complex unconstrained
For the record goes not unstained

Lured by the evil of the lie
Her wretched presence cannot deny
Lacks bright occasion of dispensing good
How seldom used or understood

To nurse so tenderly the thriving art
Her need for slander to impart
The invective by design and scope
Inveighs the truth and search for hope

To confront the truth she'd rather die
Or deign obscure it with a lie
As one falls victim to her feign
Her serpent tongue and pen profane

While fingers itch and bleed to write
To hide the truth from the light
Buried deep within the blackest hole
Lay the thunder that she stole

The sycophant with incipient smiles
Traduced the innocent with her wiles
Beguiling all with eyes to drink
From her poison pen the toxic ink

In pursuit of self-serving scheme
Inscribed on paper ream by ream
Sowing seeds of doubt with uncommon zeal
For control and power have bold appeal

Upon the falsehoods there erected
Her most vile nature now detected
Finds great amusement to invent a lie
While tearing wings from a fly

To fulfill her need she has designed
The paper profile much maligned
Her prevarications prove not proficient
Through social skills most deficient

Her deceitful web so finely wrought
Compounded so when finally caught
Her *mea culpa* of pseudo-errors
A subterfuge of smoke and mirrors

Upon dubious waves of error tossed
Her ship of moral compass lost
Now pleads the case of incompetence
Her treachery shall know no recompense

VI) The Bodies of
the Condemned

Introduction

WHILE INCARCERATED AT THE KENT INSTITUTION in BC in 1984–5, Rik went on what was assuredly one of the longest hunger strikes in Canadian prison history. His fifty-one-day strike came just three years after Bobby Sands went on his fatal sixty-six-day hunger strike in Maze prison in Northern Ireland. *The Writings of Bobby Sands*, published in 1981, was a prized possession in Rik's cell. Although he was motivated by Sands's methods, Rik's protest was not overtly political. While Sands and nine others protested the removal of Special Category Status from members of the Irish Republican Army, which stripped them of their status as political prisoners, Rik protested his transfer to segregation while he was being investigated for the murder of another prisoner—a murder he could not have committed. The administration used the new charges to effect a transfer, adding that he would not be safe if he returned to the general population at Kent.

Although he was not fighting for an entire class of incarcerated people, his personal discontent was indicative of systemic problems. Rik was upset because his assignment to segregation, and the attempt to bring about an involuntary transfer out of the Pacific region, was antithetical to any kind of healthy correctional plan. In a letter he submitted twenty-two days into his hunger strike, Rik notes the following:

> I have spent four of the past five years in segregation and Special Handling Units. It is primarily due to my family and these four years in closed confinement that I have never taken anything for granted since my arrival here. Even the simplest pleasures of sitting or laying on real grass I considered a privilege, a privilege that is taken for granted by many others who have never experienced the concrete and asphalt of segregation and Special Handling Units.

At this juncture, Rik was managing his incarceration much better and had established a meaningful connection with his common law wife and their twelve-year-old son. Although he survived the fifty-one days of his hunger strike, these relationships did not. The ultimate result of his strike was severed relations due to the onset of paranoia as Rik grew malnourished. This was then followed by involuntary transfer to the Edmonton Institution. In his files, the head of the living unit at Edmonton Max notes that the files that implicated Rik in institutional offences contained various inconsistencies, suggesting that officials at Kent had been trying to mount a strong case in order to get an undesirable prisoner off their hands.

Within months of his hunger strike and relocation to Edmonton Max, Rik was found hanging in his cell, and was revived in hospital. He had been written up for transfer to a Special Handling Unit and a decision was pending. The following note, addressed to the coroner's inquest, was found when his cell was searched:

> I cannot live this meaningless existence. The only positive aspect of it all has been the "amelioration of the beast." I am tired of it all. 12 years of murders, animal screams & suicides. Oh my immortal soul redeem your promise. In spite of the night alone and the day of fire.

The last two sentences in the note are an approximate rendering of four lines from Arthur Rimbaud's *A Season in Hell*. In a *Maclean's* magazine article describing a week of public tours that preceded the solicitor general's shuttering of BC Penitentiary in 1980, Paul Grescoe includes the same two-sentence quote in a list of inscriptions found on a wall in the supermax unit at BC Pen.[1] As noted in the book's introduction and in section 2, "Solitary Confinement and Special Handling Units," Rik had been a mainstay in BC Pen's supermax unit during the first years of his incarceration; Rik attempted suicide several times while he was there.

Because the fundamental fact of incarceration is confinement, it is easy to overlook the extent to which confinement robs prisoners of control over their own existence—the very movements and functions of their own bodies. To confine someone is to take them away from their loved ones, and to transfer them is to make visitation impossible, and relationships strained. The MacGuigan report, which was written during the early years of Rik's federal incarceration, notes that "one of the most imperious acts of the penitentiary authorities from the inmate's perspective is an involuntary transfer to another institution," and that it was common for prisoners to be moved suddenly and without notice.[2] In the face of involuntary transfers that had become routine, the report argues that "ordinary standards of decency require that a person be conceded the dignity of being treated as something other than an object to be manipulated according to whatever appeals to the absolute power and unfettered discretion of the Canadian Penitentiary Service."[3] One can easily understand how Rik's abrupt and arbitrary separation from loved ones, combined with the end of his short-lived reprieve from the concrete tombs into which he'd been interred, would necessarily have led to the onset of extreme existential despair.

In this section, we read about Rik's hunger strike, and we see his frustration mount in written grievances as he is transferred, against his will, back and forth across the country. But transfer is far from the only indignity visited upon the bodies of the condemned. The section begins with "Footnote to Slash Solitary," a fragment severed from Rik's longer poem "Slash Solitary" that details the stomping death of Wally Brass. In conversation, Rik relates similar instances of violence and indignity bestowed upon the bodies of prisoners, and he speaks of the bodily resistances mounted by incarcerated people as they struggle to have control over their bodies and relationships. In Rik's letters to a warden and his mother, we see the importance of those relationships while incarcerated people despair in isolation.

To be incarcerated is also to have proper care of one's body rendered impossible.[4] As Rik develops Crohn's disease—a diagnosis that was withheld from him—we see him going to extreme measures to obtain pain relief. As he is systematically denied proper treatment by directors, contractors, and subcontractors, we witness the utter helplessness of someone who cannot narrate his own body without suspicion, and whose well-being is entirely within the hands of people who don't understand his condition, and don't appear to have any desire to delve beyond their suspicion of his desire for pain relief in order to learn anything about it. While Rik's experiences of prison health care were dire, as the beginnings of a complaint against the Regina General Hospital make clear, his struggles to have any form of control over his profiled body extended beyond his incarceration: Rik's prison tattoos and his demeanour— his suspicion and fear of anyone associated with the health-care profession—spoke in his place post-release, rendering him a candidate for restraint and forcible treatment. Rik's post-release experience of hospitals was not only triggering, it also constituted a repetition of traumas experienced during his incarceration.

FOOTNOTE TO SLASH SOLITARY*
(For Wally Brass)

Guards dragged him from his cell en masse
Then they stomped upon his head,
That prideful soul who we called Brass
They did not quit till he lay dead.

The doctor with his morbid charm
The nurse looked stiff and stern,
Said aneurysms did the harm
A routine death of no concern.

The coroner's inquest finally ruled
That it was a natural death,
But those who saw it were not fooled
Vowed to avenge his dying breath.

The population is in the yard
With baseball bats and some rocks,
They refuse to leave and play it hard
And decline to enter into talks.

....

*   Rik wrote many versions of "Slash Solitary." The electronic
version used for this collection saw this sequence of stan-
zas separated from the main text by one and a half pages of
hard returns. The title was chosen by the editor in homage
to the author's favourite poet, Allen Ginsberg.

Up on the wall is Reverend Speed
We want justice for our Brass,
As he reads the riot act & its creed
We tell him to blow it out his ass!

So rocks & bats begin to fly
We are committed to the cause,
As tower spotlights light the sky
We don't care about their laws.

In Conversation IV

DEMERS: The news story that you reminded me of earlier was the shooting of Walter Scott in South Carolina. He was the latest Black man to be killed by a police officer in the United States.

MCWHINNEY: Yes—he was shot eight times in the back.

DEMERS: And the officer planted his Taser beside Scott's body.

MCWHINNEY: Yeah, he drops it beside his body and he handcuffs him. Presumably, after he's shot eight times in the back—

DEMERS: —he needs assistance: first aid, as opposed to restraint.

MCWHINNEY: He shoots him eight times in the back from a distance of maybe fifteen or twenty feet, then runs up to him, handcuffs him, runs back, grabs the Taser, runs back and drops it near the guy's hand—yeah, it's . . . [*laughs*]

DEMERS: It reminds me of the case of Michael Brown. According to the police officer who shot him, Brown was grabbing for his pistol through the cruiser window, while Brown's friend says Brown was shot with his hands up in the air. That sparked the Ferguson, Missouri, "Hands Up, Don't Shoot" protests.

They left Brown's body uncovered on the ground for four hours. They didn't put him in an ambulance; it took over an hour to even cover up his body. He was given no respect, no dignity. This is similar to the treatment of Walter Scott's body—eight shots and handcuffs.

So much violence—inappropriate, unsanctioned, unprovoked—can be visited upon a body. I wonder if you could talk a bit about the treatment of prisoner's bodies.

MCWHINNEY: A particular case comes to mind. I remember one time when Barbara Schonhofer from the John Howard Society came out to PA Pen [Saskatchewan Penitentiary, located in Prince Albert] to see me after a hostage-taking took place. A friend of mine took a guard and another prisoner hostage. His name was Gerry McDonald—we'd been in the SHU [Special

Handling Unit] in Millhaven together and we knew each other for years and that.

Gerry didn't like PA. It was a terrible place, and he just couldn't do time there. I don't blame him—I hated it there too.

He put in a sheet to a psychiatrist and told the psychiatrist that he was on the verge of committing suicide if he didn't get out of there. It had gotten bad for him. The psychiatrist's response was that he had to stay there, and that if he wanted to kill himself, he should go ahead. She said it would be one less file for her caseload.

So Gerry, in his own desperation to get out of there, got together with another prisoner and they took a guard and another prisoner hostage. The prisoner was what we call a skinner—he was a sex offender who was in protective custody at the time. They were holding them for about a day in the carpentry shop, and finally the prison tactical unit shoots him. They nearly blew his head right off with a shotgun.

A couple of weeks later, I'm talking to Barbara Schonhofer, who was involved with the coroner's inquest. What I found out—what was revealed at the inquest that nobody else knew about—was that there were boot prints all the way up and down his torso. So, one starts to wonder: What really took place, you know? Did they shoot him first and then kick him to death, or did they kick him half to death and then just decide to finish him off with a shotgun blast? That wasn't fully determined at the inquest, I guess, but the fact remains—he had a mortal wound, a shotgun wound, to his body, as well as these boot prints all up and down his torso, both on his back and on his chest.

DEMERS: It reminds me of Attica[5]—the hostage-taking, and everything that came out in the commission of inquiry afterwards. A lot of torture took place because it wasn't only the National Guard that came in to retake the prison, but correctional officers, as well. News had spread that hostages had been castrated and killed—it was reported weeks later that none of this actually happened, but this is what was being reported by the *New York Times* the day before state troopers and correctional officers retook the prison. The correctional officers went in with a score to settle.

Witnesses say that incarcerated men were killed with their hands in the air. Everyone was stripped and made to run a gauntlet. They had people lying on the ground balancing shotgun shells on their knees. A prisoner testified that he was made to lie down naked while people spat on him, prodded him with sticks, and put cigarette butts out on his genitals. It was really brutal.

MCWHINNEY: There was an incident in Quebec, I think it was in Laval prison. Two guards were stabbed and killed. As a result, it was payback time for the guards. Once they regained control of the prison, they took a bunch of guys, they scattered all this pea gravel on the cement in an enclosed courtyard, and they made them run out there in their bare feet, stripped right down. They've got no clothes on, they're stripped naked, and they're turning fire hoses on them from the windows up above to make them move. They have to run on this pea gravel to get away from the fire hoses, so it's cutting their feet, digging into their heels. A couple of those guys ended up in the SHU, and they told me about this experience. They weren't involved in the stabbing or killing of those two guards; they just happened to be on that range where it happened.

I've also got a poem about Wally Brass. He lived about five cells down from me in solitary. They just went in, dragged him out of his cell by the hair, and they kicked him to death on the range.

DEMERS: For what reason?

MCWHINNEY: For mouthing off. He was screaming at the guards from his cell, threatening them, antagonizing them. He had an ongoing beef with this one guard. They come along at suppertime, and they hand you a steel tray with your food on it and two slices of bread on the side. This one guard didn't like Brass—and Brass didn't like him either. This had been going on for weeks—arguing and threatening back and forth. So one night at supper, this guard was heard telling the guard who was handing out the trays not to give Brass any bread.

So he hands Brass his tray and there's no bread on it. Brass isn't the type of guy to let things slide, so he demands his bread. The guard who initiated it, whom he had a beef with, says, "You got your fucking bread. You're just trying to get extra bread. You got your bread—so shut your mouth."

That set Brass over the top, so he started swearing at the guard, and he started threatening him. This went on for a while, and then five guards came down, opened the cell door, and they started beating him. They dragged him out in the range by his hair, they stomped on him, beat him some more, dragged him into the shower, beat on him some more—you could hear them kicking him and swearing at him.

Suddenly, you don't hear Brass anymore. The shower's turned on, and then it's turned off. That's it. They drag Brass out and he's dead.

They had a coroner's inquest, and they ruled that he died of an aneurysm—he slipped and fell in the shower and died of brain aneurysm. There was a riot over that.

DEMERS: You suffered a lot of trauma—you witnessed a lot of traumatic things while in solitary confinement in BC Pen. Did you have psychologists to speak with?

MCWHINNEY: Well, they had a psychologist there they called Odd Socks. He'd come to work wearing one blue sock and one brown sock, or one black sock and one white sock. The last I heard, his wife sent him out to get a loaf of bread and a quart of milk and he didn't come back until six months later with a Honda motorcycle [*laughs*]. They got rid of him—nobody was bothering even to go see him. They'd see him once and that was enough—he needed help more than they did.

They had another guy at BC Pen—the psychiatrist. He was doing drug experimentation. He was a piece of work.

DEMERS: What kind of experimentation?

MCWHINNEY: He liked playing with sodium pentothal, which some people refer to as truth serum—but it's not really. He'd give you an injection, which would get you so high that all your inhibitions would break down. You'd just be more relaxed and free—open-ended, so you'd just say whatever was on your mind. You wouldn't care because you were so high. You'd say whatever you felt like saying. A lot of guys went to him. They'd go up there just to get that shot so they could coast on their high until their next visit. I wasn't there then, but this is also when they were doing drug experiments with marijuana and hashish from Tunney Farms in Ottawa. That was back in the

fifties and sixties. There was a lot of drug experimentation going on at that time—I've got documentation on that—and it was sponsored by both
pharmaceuticals and government. I didn't get to
BC Pen until later. But they were administering
LSD as well, and just—

DEMERS: Taking notes?

MCWHINNEY: Taking notes about the effects. Observing and conducting interviews. I think Dorothy
Proctor's lawsuit against CSC [Correctional Service Canada] is still ongoing. They administered
LSD to her without her knowledge.[6]

DEMERS: So it was essentially human experimentation—it was just a matter of a captive population
that they could essentially experiment on.

MCWHINNEY: Yes, that's all it was. There were no
rewards for participating in the program or anything. Some people got a cheap high out of it, I
guess. But a lot of people went the other way,
because a lot of these experiments were carried
out in solitary confinement, and you're already
undergoing that torture of solitary. To have that
added—being subjected to LSD experimentation
while you're already hallucinating in solitary—

DEMERS: It's not a very good control group.

MCWHINNEY: No—it's a controlled setting, but it's not a controlled experiment. I hated that. Thirty-two months was the longest they ever kept me in solitary in one shot.

DEMERS: Almost three years. Was that in BC?

MCWHINNEY: Yeah, that was in BC Pen—the 1970s. I think it was 1975. The nurses, if you could call them that—I don't even think they were trained. Actually, I don't. They were more career-orientated rather than goal-orientated. Like, rather than having a mandate in place, and following that for treatment, for the betterment of a person's well-being, they were there primarily just to pacify people. There was aversion therapy. I was subjected to that.

Boy, that was a nightmare. They would give me a drug, haloperidol, and they have to give you another drug, as an antagonist, to counteract the side effects of this drug. If they didn't, you would go into spasms—terribly, terribly painful, painful, debilitating spasms, you know, where you would lock up and seize and you couldn't move. The best way to describe it is if you've ever woken up with a stiff neck, where you can barely turn your head because it hurts so much, because you slept on it the wrong way or something. That's similar to what I'm trying to describe here, where you would seize and lock up in a very painful position and you couldn't move. It was torture. The only way to relieve this was for a nurse, or a doctor, to come and give you an injection to counteract that. That drug was called Cogentin. But, before they would administer this, they would blackmail you. "Oh, you're not feeling too well, McWhinney? I understand you're not feeling too well. Your neck and your back are seized up and you're having trouble moving? Well, would you like some relief? I've got an injection here that'll help you. Would you like some relief? I can give it to you, providing you promise to behave and not do this, this, this." They'd lay out a whole string of demands. You've got to abide by the rules. You've got to do this, do that. And you would admit to anything, you know? It was almost like being waterboarded or something. You would admit to anything just to relieve the agony of it. So that's what they called aversion therapy. If you're a badass in prison, they would come in—four, five strong—nail you to the floor, jam a needle in your ass, and next thing you know you're seized up, and you're desperate. And you don't know what's going on. It's very painful, debilitating—and very frightening, because you don't know. You don't know what's going on. What, am I going to be like this forever, you know? And then they come along and they blackmail you.

DEMERS: So this was the mid- to late seventies this was happening?

MCWHINNEY: Yeah, this is the seventies. They did this to me in the seventies in the Regional Psychiatric Centre in Abbotsford. I was in the hole, in solitary—and in the RPC in Abbotsford, they came in and they muscled me to the floor and they injected me with that haloperidol. I just seized right up, and they left me like that.

DEMERS: They did this out of the blue? Was there anything that provoked them to do this?

MCWHINNEY: They did it because I was banging on my door. I was yelling through the door and calling them goofs and creeps and fucking idiots and, you know—whatever, just raging. I was just raging, you know, because you're locked in a cell, a stripped cell, there's no bed, nothing, and it's cold because all the windows are smashed out and it's January and it's freezing cold, and all you've got on is a pair of underwear, a little pair of underwear. That's all you've got. And there's water on the floor, piss or whatever, because you've got no toilet, just a bucket to piss in, a plastic two-gallon bucket to piss in, and that's been knocked over or smashed or whatever, or it's cracked because the guy that was in that cell before you smashed it on the wall and cracked it, so now it leaks, you know? So when it's your turn, when they put you in that cell, they don't care if that bucket's cracked.

They don't know or they don't care. So you have to take a piss, you'd piss in that bucket. Next thing you know you got all this piss all over the floor. Where's that coming from? Pretty soon it's starting to freeze. It's turning to ice because the windows are all smashed out. So you're screaming through the door. You're banging your door and screaming, "Guard, guard, guard!" You know? And they're ignoring you. And so you smash louder, and then you start hollering and calling them names. "You fucking goofs, you fascist fucking pigs!" you know? Whatever you can think of. You're just enraged.

And so finally they'd had enough of it. The next thing you know, your door is open. Four guards, five guards rush in, nail you to the floor, and a nurse comes in and jabs you in the ass with a fucking hypodermic. The next thing you know, you're seized up. And they'll leave you like that for half an hour, an hour. Some will even taunt you. "Oh, you're not feeling too good? Oh, your back's a little sore?"

Some of the things that were done to me were beyond the concept of just outright cruelty. I was diagnosed with Crohn's disease. They knew about it, because they diagnosed me, but they didn't inform me about it, and they didn't even treat me for it for two years until I was transferred to another institution.

DEMERS: Where were you when you were diagnosed?

MCWHINNEY: At Saskatchewan Penitentiary. In Prince Albert.

DEMERS: And where were you transferred?

MCWHINNEY: I went back to Edmonton Max.

DEMERS: Did you find out about all of this after you were transferred, or did you find out that they were refusing to treat you and then ask for a transfer?

MCWHINNEY: Here's what happened. I was lying on my floor in a fetal position in a SHU in PA. I thought that I was dying. I didn't know what was wrong with me. I weighed 126 pounds and I was in extreme pain. I couldn't get up, I couldn't walk—I could only lie there in agony. They eventually got me out of my cell and sent me to see the doctor in the health-care unit. He examined me and recommended that I go to an outside clinic for some testing. So three days later they shackled me up and took me to a clinic in Prince Albert. They performed a colonoscopy and, the next day, a nurse came down to my cell in the SHU and said, "McWhinney, I want you to go out and have some more tests done." I asked her what she was talking about.

She said, "Well, we think we've seen something. We want to do some more tests."

"What do you mean, you think you've seen something. What did you see?"

"Well, we're not sure," she says. "That's why we want to do some more tests."

I explained that I wanted to know the results of the first test before I agreed to undergo another test, because there was nothing so humiliating, embarrassing, and painful as that first test, and I wasn't going to go through that again unless I was provided with a little more information.

She told me that she wasn't going to tell me other than that "we think we've seen something," so I said I wasn't going to subject myself to another test.

"Well, will you sign a waiver here releasing us of any responsibility then?"

I told her that I wasn't going to sign anything. I was upset, so I was screaming at her through the door at this point.

The guard pulled her away and said, "Don't worry about him. I'll sign it for him." So he signed—and I'm screaming at him as he's walking off with the nurse.

About a week later the deputy warden comes down, they pull me out of my cell, and they put me in a cage. There's glass separating me from the deputy warden, and he says that they've agreed to let me back out into population providing I don't hurt anybody.

"Hurt anybody? I can't even hurt myself," I said. "I'm sick."

He said, "I know. That's one of the reasons we've made a decision to let you back in the population."

That clued me in right there. They knew something but they weren't telling me. Two days later they let me out of the SHU and put me in population. Three months later, they grabbed a bunch of guys and transferred them to Edmonton Max. I was the first on the list. Because this is an involuntary transfer, they want us to sign.

I said, "No. I'm volunteering. I want out of this shithouse."

He said, "You're volunteering?"

I said, "Yeah."

"That's great," he says. "That makes our job that much easier. Just sign here."

The next day I was on a bus back to Edmonton. I had been away for two years. I'm really in bad shape. I'm starving to death. I can't keep any food down, and what little food I do eat is coming out both ends. I have terrible diarrhea and I'm projectile vomiting. It's something like right out of the movie *The Exorcist*—it's just shooting out, and I'm just skin and bone. So I go to health care when I get there, and the doctor knows me. He's known me for thirteen years because that's how long I was in Edmonton Max before spending two years in PA. The doctor knew me really well. He got me up on the examining table, he examined my abdomen, and he told me right there that I had Crohn's disease.

I said, "Crohn's disease? What the hell is that?" I'd never heard of Crohn's before. I had no idea what it was. He explained it to me, and I asked him, "Well, how do you know this—how do you know I have Crohn's?"

And he said, "Rik, it's right here in your medical file."

In my file there was a diagnostic sheet from a clinic in Prince Albert. They had diagnosed me with Crohn's disease two years ago and they hadn't informed me. I had no idea. Even worse, they hadn't been treating me for it. They weren't giving me medication or a special diet. They were just ignoring it.

DEMERS: They took away your ability to understand your own health. They treated you as something less than a human being, as someone who isn't entitled to know what's happening with their own body.

MCWHINNEY: I had no rights whatsoever. And that's just one case, you know?

DEMERS: You went on a fairly lengthy hunger strike. Why did you go on that hunger strike?

MCWHINNEY: It started in Kent Maximum one evening in BC. I was in a visiting room with my common law wife, and I left after visits were over—it was about nine o'clock at night. There were two guards there—generally there's only one. I stripped down, which is par for the course, but generally after they search you, you just walk back to your unit on your own. This time, both guards escorted me. On the way to the unit, we have to pass by the gymnasium. The gymnasium is generally open at this time of night, but I could see that it was closed, the lights were dimmed, and they had police tape across the doorway.

I knew something was going on, so I asked the guard, and he said I'd find out in time. When I got back to my unit, it was locked down, and everybody was locked up, which was unusual because it was only nine o'clock at night, and lock-up isn't until ten o'clock. Once I'm in my cell, I start yelling down the range to guys trying to figure out what's going on. They said, "Colin got killed in the gym tonight—about an hour or two ago."

The next morning, four guards came to my cell and said, "Grab your cigarettes or your tobacco, McWhinney, you're going to the hole."

"What for?"

"For investigation under 231A." That means for the good order of the institution. So, for the good order of the institution, they told me I was being held in segregation under 231A, "pending investigation."

So I get to the hole and they want me to sign a piece of paper saying that—I'm not too sure what it was. Something about being placed in the segregation voluntary or involuntary, either one, pending investigation into a murder.

I said, "No I'm not signing that. I object to the whole thing. I wasn't in the gym last night. I was in a visiting room with my wife." They didn't care. They locked me up and that evening the RCMP came to talk with me. I knew that I hadn't done anything, I knew I wasn't involved in this murder, in any way, and I had so much to lose. I was going to university—this is when they still had post-secondary education—I had a family, a common law wife and a child, and I was on a year's probation from the SHU. I had just gotten out of the SHU, and generally, when you get out, you do one year of probation in general population. I had about a week to go. I figured, I'll go talk to them, get this thing cleared up, they'll let me out of segregation, and I'll go back to my unit. Things will be okay.

They asked me if I knew Colin, and I said, "Sure, I know him to say hello and goodbye—two ships passing in the night sort of thing. I'm not really involved with him." They say, "Okay well I guess that about wraps that up," but I said, "Wait a minute here—they said I was being placed down here pending investigation into a murder. I had nothing to do with this murder." They said, "We know you had nothing to do with that because it's physically impossible to be in two areas at the same time. We're satisfied that you were in the visiting room with your wife at the time in question, when Colin was killed in the gym."

I asked them why couldn't they tell these people here that, because they seem to think that I'm involved somehow, and they're keeping me locked up in segregation. They said, "Hey McWhinney, they don't tell us how to run our police force and we don't tell them how to run their prisons. You're on your own." They sort of laughed at me and kicked me out the door. That was that.

But anyway, a couple days later they pull me out of my cell, and I go up and see the head of internal security. He's basically asking me the same questions as the RCMP. He told me they had reason to believe that I was involved in this murder, and he told me I was going to remain in seg until they got to the bottom of things. I wasn't making any headway, so what do I do? My hands were basically tied.

So I yelled out to Clyde, who was also in the visiting room, and who they were also keeping in seg. I said, "I'm going to go on a hunger strike—how else am I going to call attention to the situation we're in here?" He said he couldn't. "I'm hungry right now," he said. They don't feed you that well in seg. "I can't go on a hunger strike, I need my food." So that was it. I made a commitment, and the next morning at breakfast when they came down to feed us through the slots in our doors, I just left mine there. I didn't get off the bed, I wouldn't take it. I did the same thing at lunch and supper. I was committed. I put in for a phone call and told my wife what was going on. She was upset. She couldn't understand why they were treating me like this. I continued that hunger strike for about three weeks, and then, when I went to get a drink of water out of the sink one morning, there was no water. I yelled down the range to the other guys—"Hey, any of you guys got any water?"

"Yeah we've got water."

"Well, I've got no water coming out"

Then one guy said, "Rik, last night at about two in the morning, the guards went into the duct"—the duct was what we called the little utility room nearby—"and they turned your water off."

So now I've got no water. I'm already on a hunger strike, so maybe I'll just quit drinking too. So I can't drink now. I've got no water except in my toilet—my toilet still flushes—but I ain't drinking out of the toilet. I'm not that desperate yet. A couple of days later, the nurse and the doctor came down and came into my cell. The doctor examines me and he's trying to convince me to start eating. I refused. As far as I was concerned, they were holding me down there illegally. I had nothing to do with the murder in the gym that night.

The doctor told me, "You're in serious condition, Rik. I'm a doctor. I have nothing to do with running the prison, or how they operate the prison. I'm just a doctor, and I'm very concerned about your health. You're very malnourished. Your breath smells of acetone. That's a sign that your internal organs are starting to malfunction or shut down. I'll be very honest with you, Rik. Once that happens, it's fatal. It's not like a car where you can restart it. Once an organ shuts down, you can't restart it. The acetone smell indicates to me that you're on the verge of a liver shutdown."

He did a simple test on me called tenting, where they pull your skin and if it goes back, that means it's got elasticity to it. If it just sticks up like a little tent, that means you're dehydrated. Of course mine stuck up, so he told me, "You're very dehydrated too. I know you haven't been eating, but have you been drinking?"

I said, "No. Even if I wanted to, I couldn't drink. They shut my water off."

"What do you mean they shut your water off?" He went to my sink and he pushed the buttons. Nothing came out. "When did this happen?" he asked.

I said, "I don't know. A couple of guys on the range told me they did it at about two o'clock in the morning a couple of nights ago."

He was upset. He said, "This situation is intolerable. I'm having you moved out of here to the hospital." So the doctor ordered the guards to release me and move me to the hospital they had in the prison. They got in a big argument—I could hear the doctor arguing with the security. But a couple of hours later, they escorted me to the hospital. In the hospital, they started giving me water and juice, but then I quit, and all I would drink was coffee. Coffee and cigarettes. Still no food. It's been about thirty-eight days, so my wife went to the press. I've got a radio in my room in the hospital, so I was listening to it on the radio, and I had a television, so I also saw them interviewing my wife on the local Vancouver news. She explained how they've locked me up for a murder that happened in the gymnasium while I was in the visiting room with her, and she was very upset. She got a hold of a lawyer who came out to talk with me, and he tried to convince me to start eating—which I wouldn't—so he then goes and tries to bargain with the warden. He basically said that I obviously wasn't in possession of all of my faculties since I hadn't eaten in forty days and nobody in their right mind would do that. So he says, "How about we compromise here? If you feel he's such a threat to your institution and you want him out, why don't you send him to RPC, the Regional Psychiatric Centre, and get him the help he needs so that he'll start eating?" Their answer was that they were going to ship me out to Edmonton Max. Now that really upset me because that meant that I lost everything—the educational programming I was involved in, because I was going to school, and my relationship with my wife. I'm in BC, and their plan—the moment my wife draws media attention to my situation and arranges for a visit from a lawyer—is to ship me all the way to Alberta, taking me away from my family, my support.

About a week later, they put me on a plane and flew me to Edmonton. By this time, I was fifty-one days into my hunger strike, and I was a mess. Before my hunger strike, I weighed 184 pounds, and by that point, at intake, I'd gone down to 124 pounds. As soon as I got to Edmonton, they put me in the hospital and I gave up. What was the point of continuing the hunger strike? I went on the hunger strike to protest my innocence, my involvement in a murder, and now I'd lost my family—my wife and her child—and I lost my schooling. I lost everything. So what was the point of continuing with the hunger strike?

I started eating, but I was getting sick every time I ate. I would eat, get sick, and throw it all up. And then, within a week of arriving in Edmonton, I started losing my mind. When people talked with me, I'd answer out of context, and I just wasn't making any sense at all. I was just rambling, and they could see that. So they sent me to the Regional Psychiatric Centre in Saskatoon. When I got there, they put me in a cell, in solitary confinement, but there wasn't even a bed; it was just a cement floor. There was a mattress on the floor, there was one blanket, and there was a steel combination toilet and sink.

I struck up a relationship with the psychiatrist there though. He really liked me, and I liked him. He got me out of solitary and on to a regular unit. I was there for about two weeks, and they came and kidnapped me again. They shipped me back to Edmonton and put me in segregation. By this time, I was eating, and I could keep it down, but I was still very sick. I was gaining a little bit of weight back, but very little. I'm in segregation now and they're recommending me for transfer to the Special Handling Unit. I asked why and they said it was because I was involved in a stabbing in Kent. First it was a murder, now it's a stabbing. What were they talking about?

Colin was killed with a baseball bat. There was no stabbing. So now they're accusing me of stabbing someone in Kent, and they're asking Edmonton Institution to act on their behalf by recommending that I be put in a SHU for my involvement in a stabbing that happened in Kent. This dragged on for about three months while I was in seg. I fought: I wrote letters and complaints all the way up to the commissioner of penitentiaries.

I felt like they wouldn't be satisfied until they buried me. They were just trying to hang everything that came along on me—stabbings, murders, everything. If something happened, McWhinney was guilty of it as far as they were concerned. After about three months, they denied me for the SHU. They said that Edmonton

Institution couldn't act as a proxy for Kent. If they felt I was involved in a stabbing in their institution, they should have sent me to the SHU there, not ship me out and then a couple of months later ask Edmonton to send me for something they believed I did while at Kent.

After I got out from under that, they cut me loose into the general population. I was there for a number of years, from 1984 until 1990, before they sent me to PA. I never gained my weight back. I think the highest I got was 137 or 138 pounds; I never got any heavier than that. I used to be very active in sports, so I'd go down and throw a couple baskets, hit the bag, or run laps out in the yard, but I couldn't regain any substantial weight.

They shipped me to PA because I got in a knife fight out in the yard in Edmonton, and that's when I was starting to get really sick; that's when the Crohn's came on. They figured that that's what brought the Crohn's on—that hunger strike.

I'm inclined to believe that, because when I watched the movie *Hunger* on Bobby Sands, they said that hunger strikes affect the intestines. I also had access to my medical file, and I read some reports from doctors there that said that they believe my hunger strike is what initiated my Crohn's.

DEMERS: You mentioned Bobby Sands. Hunger strikes are a common mode of protest, a common method of protest for inmates. Why is that the case?

MCWHINNEY: That's the last option you have. You have no other recourse short of killing yourself—which is basically what a hunger strike is, only it's prolonged. It's not sudden, like hanging yourself, but it's a form of suicide. That's the reason it's a form of protest—it's the last recourse short of killing yourself immediately.

It's also a vehicle for calling attention to your situation though, because sooner or later, somebody might pay attention and make your plight known to a wider audience. Other than that, you have absolutely no voice. But what I found out through my experience is that even this protest of last resort isn't a very effective vehicle.

DEMERS: In spite of the length of your hunger strike, the effects that it had on your body, they still moved you.

MCWHINNEY: Yeah—I still lost everything. It's no wonder that I had a sort of hate on for the system after that experience, because I had absolutely nothing to do with that murder. And here's the kicker: subsequently they charged and convicted someone for that murder, and my name wasn't even mentioned during the trial.

DEMERS: Lots of the injustices that happen within prison are entirely buried—if they aren't a part of public legal proceedings, if they don't make it into the newspaper, or on to the radio.

MCWHINNEY: Every day in prison—as we speak right now—there's an injustice going on. Several. It's happening all the time—somebody's getting railroaded for something, and they have very little control over it, very little recourse to address it, and they lack resources as well. You're left to your own: there's not much you can do once you're locked up in a segregation cell.

DEMERS: In the United States, for a time they called some segregation units communications management units, or CMUS. These were units that were conceived and reserved for people who were raising their voices about conditions inside and riling up the general population—this was one of the responses to prisoners organizing for better conditions in the seventies. Organizers were put into segregation—and then entire prisons were put under permanent lockdown—as a way to manage communication, which is really the heart of mass mobilization and protest.

MCWHINNEY: Isolate organizers from their power base, from the possibility of influence. Keep them quiet. Shut them down.

DEMERS: On the one hand, from the standpoint of authority, it makes complete sense, because you want to be able to control the population that you're tasked to control. On the other, the reason why these protests are occurring is because that mode of authority is entirely—I wouldn't necessarily in this instance say *corrupt*, but it's certainly—

MCWHINNEY: Well, it's highly dysfunctional.

DEMERS: Yes, it's dysfunctional and it's—

MCWHINNEY: And it is corrupt as well. But yeah, it's all those things tied in together and, yeah, it's—

DEMERS: And so you go on a hunger strike.

MCWHINNEY: Yeah. I mean, what else can you do short of killing yourself? And then—

DEMERS: You end up with Crohn's.

MCWHINNEY: And that's the end of it.

DEMERS: Was it common to be moved involuntarily, as you were?

MCWHINNEY: That was very common. They used to do that quite regularly. In fact, that was one of the platforms that Prison Justice Day was founded upon: involuntary transfers.

DEMERS: Of course, it's a huge deal to be moved against your consent. You were moved away from your family.

MCWHINNEY: Yeah, everything.

DEMERS: I think that when people think about prisoners being housed in prison—a prison is a prison. Some might have more or less, they've got to manage the population, shuffle people around a bit, but—you're in particular prisons because you're supposed to be kept closer to your home, closer to your family, and closer to your support system.

MCWHINNEY: Your support group, yeah.

DEMERS: You're still a part of your family. Your family wants to see you—you're support for them too, despite the fact that you're confined.

MCWHINNEY: Yeah, and they totally cut that off, you see. You may be serving a sentence in a penitentiary in British Columbia, and the next morning wake up in the Maritimes, in a penitentiary in New Brunswick, five thousand miles away from your family, your support group and everything.

DEMERS: You have similar issues to anybody who moves: all of a sudden you're starting from ground zero, you have to develop new relationships—except there's the added aspect that you're confined, and what's happened to you is entirely involuntarily.

MCWHINNEY: It's no wonder that prisoners become very embittered and resentful and recalcitrant toward the system. How do they expect to rehabilitate somebody under those conditions? It's impossible.

I was thinking earlier about the Harper government and the life-thirty-five sentence.[7] That's just a fast track to capital punishment in my mind. When someone enters a federal system, they assign certain programs for him and things like that. A guy doing life-thirty-five—what's the incentive for him to do programs, you know? I just fail to see that. What's the point?

He's never getting out, and so it'd be interesting to see how the correctional system approaches that in terms of programming for these sentences. I'd suspect that we're going to see more death through violence in the future. With these new, harsher sentences coming down, what's a guy care? He'll just kill you. I already witnessed that in the SHU, you know?

DEMERS: Prisons aren't geriatric centres either. With long sentences, you end up with a lot of elderly people in prison who need particular types of attention.

MCWHINNEY: The prison population is getting older and it's becoming more of an expense. As people get older, they get more vulnerable to sickness and disease.

DEMERS: And prisons aren't generally built with rails to hold yourself up in the shower, or—

MCWHINNEY: Oh no, none of that.

DEMERS: Or ramps to go up and down.

MCWHINNEY: Nope.

DEMERS: Or if you have to go outdoors for a particular amount of time—you're generally locked out, you can't come back in to go to the bathroom because of incontinence issues or anything.

MCWHINNEY: And prisons aren't wheelchair accessible, for the most part. When I was in Bowden I saw a lot of guys die in there, not just from illness, but by neglect. It was quite shocking. I was shocked by the number of men who were dying in there without treatment. There's no such thing as being proactive, or of employing preventative measures. There was a lot of cancer in Bowden. I saw a lot of guys dying from cancer. They just withered away. What's the point of keeping them in prison, you know? They're not a threat to society anymore. They're wheelchair bound for the most part, or bedridden, and they're just withering away. They're dying. Why keep them in prison? It didn't make a lot of sense to me. I think I touched upon that in that poem on Bowden that I wrote. "Where are you burying all the bodies" or something like that. I can't remember, but yeah, there were a lot of deaths there.

Letter to the Warden:
Extended Family Visit Program

AUGUST 31, 1984

Dear Sir:

Further to the documentation in your possession regarding the matter at hand, I am writing this letter to offer a personal perspective and to appeal to your sense of humanitarianism. There are only a few points that I wish to bring to your attention.

It has been suggested that I may be ineligible for the Extended Family Visit Program because there is some question regarding whether or not I have met the "six month living relationship prior to incarceration" clause. My relationship with Ms. Laura M. and her son David (age 12) dates back to November 1971. Between November 1971 and August 1973, I served two periods of incarceration at the Lower Mainland Regional Corrective Centre totalling 15 months. During the remaining 6 months, we did live together. My problem arises from the fact that between my release date in August 1973 and my arrest on the charge for which I am currently under sentence, there transpired only a period of two weeks. I would point out that, legally, mere cohabitation for any length of time does not in itself constitute a common law relationship. Conversely, however, total financial support over a 6-month period does constitute a legal and binding common law relationship. Since I maintained financial support during the entire 21-month period between November 1971 and August 1972, I would argue that we have, in fact, adequately met all relevant criteria. This would appear to be analogous to a man working on a remote oil rig, and while seeing his family only periodically, still maintaining his position by discharging his familial responsibilities.

I think that the program under discussion was designed, among other things, to serve at least partially as a rehabilitative vehicle. That is, families who were previously closely knit but whose cohesiveness has suffered due to current circumstances, are afforded an opportunity through this program to re-establish all of the positive aspects associated with the primary nuclear unit. In my case, due to the length of my current incarceration, the cumulative factors involved in producing an ideal family unit have not had opportunity for maturation. Thus, rather than this being a case of rehabilitation, I would argue that the program is ideally suited as a vehicle for habilitation or development, which is directly in line with the goals and ambitions espoused by the Correctional Service of Canada. This point is supported by the guidelines established during the symposium on the introduction of the Extended Family Visit Program to maximum-security institutions held here in August 1980, in which I was proud to participate.

Additionally, I wish to bring to your attention the fact that, since my return to this institution from the SHU a year ago, I have been a well-disciplined and productive member of the prison population. I attribute this stability to the strong relationship that Laura, David, and I have developed in spite of adverse conditions. I think that the natural progression from this point is obvious and hope that it will be included in your deliberations concerning the matter at hand.

I urge you to extend your support and am hopeful of a favourable reply.

Sincerely,
R. McWhinney, #7956.

Letter to Mom (Unsent)

JANUARY 14, 1985

Hello mom,

Just a short missive to say I have arrived safely, although somewhat exhausted. I am presently in the hospital here & I must admit the atmosphere is much less hostile. So far, I have only been here 10 hours, but the change in terms of the staff attitude is much easier. It appears that their concern is genuine, in terms of helping me toward recovery. I only wish I could accommodate them. Of course, I am speaking primarily in respect to eating. Although I have abandoned my fast & am fully prepared to start eating, I find it impossible to do so. The very thought of food is nauseating to my system. I have no immediate explanation for this, other than the fact that I am overcome by a profound state of depression, a state of despair that is virtually indescribable. Never in my life have I experienced such anguish. A state of total despair over the separation of Laura, David, Marie, & yourself. For the first time in my life I have met the reality of being in love. Although I am cognizant that this emotion is natural to most everyone, it has never been what one could consider an inherent part of my nature. This may be attributed to my institutional upbringing, which was devoid of all aspects of emotion—save anger. Since meeting Laura, I am so deeply & completely in love that I value our relationship above all else. Although I am not a religious person, I cannot help but speculate that my love for her is not unlike someone who comes to accept the existence of Christ in his life for the first time. The truth is that I miss you all to such a degree. I am moribund. The fact that you have accepted me into your life as well only serves to intensify my love & devotion. Your willingness to accept me for & as I am, unconditionally, touches my heart deeply. Well mom, I guess I will have the opportunity to prove these sentiments to you in the future. But, at the present time, the possibility seems so remote I feel so totally helpless. Please excuse the writing paper. But I have not had sufficient time to become established & this is all I have. Please ask Laura to send the 2 photos I provided S.B. as soon as possible. Or better yet ask S.B. to return them at once by registered mail. It is of extreme importance for which I will explain later. Also, I am enclosing a copy of a letter I received from S.B. with this letter to you. Please advise Laura it is the Warden's response to the submission I wrote to him on the 13th of January. I'm sorry to end this letter now, but I must lay down for a while as I am not feeling well. Please pass on my love to Laura ("my tender experience"), as well as David. I will begin a letter to her in a few hours.

Love,
Rik xxx

P.S. I've also enclosed 5 visiting forms

Involuntary Transfer:
False File Information

FOR INTER-REGIONAL INVOLUNTARY TRANS-
fers, the decision maker has 60 days in which to approve or deny the transfer. It has now been 6 months
and I have not received a decision in accordance with
Commissioner's Directive 540 Annex "A" page 6 of
7 paragraph 17 under the heading "Time Frame for
Transfer Decisions."

In addition, they cite a disciplinary charge #12302 as
support for transfer in spite of the fact that I have written & signed documentation that the above charge is an
error & is to be stricken from all records. Mr. Ingstrup,[8]
I anticipate you will respond by informing me to pursue
this through the appropriate channels (i.e., grievance
procedure), which I have already done. However, I have
absolutely no faith in regional headquarters reviewing
the grievance in an objective manner, particularly when
it is regional who makes the decision on the transfer
recommendations. Any system that falsifies files with

bogus information & violates the letter of the directives in order to effect a transfer cannot be expected to play fair. The fact that I have all of this documented is proof of their blatant disregard for abiding by the spirit of a duty to act fairly, or by a sense of decency, which you so ardently espouse in your "Mission Statement."

Are we, as prisoners, expected to be led by your office's example of duplicity & contempt? I am appealing to you to intervene on my behalf with respect to my transfer, a transfer based upon deliberate lies & failure of due process.

Rik McWhinney

List of Directives Violated
540 Annex "A" page 3 of 7 paragraph 7
540 Annex "A" page 4 of 7 paragraph 10
540 Annex "A" page 6 of 7 paragraph 17

Involuntary Transfer:
Duplication of Process

OCTOBER 20, 1991

Mr. Ingstrup,

In November 1989 I was recommended for involuntary transfer to Sask Pen for reasons of negative behaviour. I appealed this decision through the grievance procedure directly to your office. However, my appeal was not successful & I was subsequently transferred to Sask Pen in June 1990.

On May 17, 1991, I was segregated along with approximately 20 other prisoners for what the administration perceived as tension among the general population.

On June 10, 1991, I was informed by deputy Warden R.Z. to apply for a transfer to an institution of my choice & he would support it. On June 12, 1991, I applied for a transfer to Stony Mountain, which was supported by a positive Progress Summary Report from my Case Management Officer, S.G.

On August 27, 1991, I received notice from Regional Headquarters that my application had been denied due to the length of my sentence & the seriousness of my offence—despite the fact I have served more than the minimum of my sentence. I filed a grievance regarding this decision to your office on Sept. 12, 1991. I have yet to receive any comment on this matter from you as of this date.

On Oct. 8, 1991, I received notice of recommendation for involuntary transfer to Atlantic Penitentiary based upon my behaviour while at Edmonton Institution in 1985.

This amounts to a duplication of the process & reasons that were used to transfer me from Edmonton to support a further transfer to Renous.*

The fact is that I have been here in Sask Pen for 16 months & have only incurred one minor charge. I was elected by popular vote as President of the Lifers' Group here in August 1990 & maintained this position up until the date of my segregation. This fact in itself is evidence that my presence in general population does not cause any significant tension.

To cite my negative behaviour while at Edmonton Institution in 1985 as reason to support an involuntary transfer from Sask Pen to Atlantic Region is further

---

* Atlantic Institution is a penitentiary located in the rural community of Renous, New Brunswick.

proof that I have committed no offence in this institution to warrant such a transfer.

Mr. Ingstrup, I needn't remind you that it is your directives that state the administration has a duty to act fairly in this respect. To use & reuse the same information over & over again to bounce me from one prison to another across the length of this country is anything but fair. Therefore, I appeal to you to live by the letter & spirit of your Directives & Mission Statement.

Rik McWhinney

Submission of Facts
Surrounding Crohn's Flare-Up

ON 97-03-17, AT APPROXIMATELY 3:45 P.M.,
I asked my work supervisor B.G. to phone the hospital
to tell Health Care that I was feeling sick. B.G. phoned
and was informed that the nurse was on medi rounds.

At approximately 4:00 P.M., when R.D. the Health
Care nurse arrived at my cell to deliver my medication,
I informed him that I was feeling extremely uncomfortable (cramps, diarrhea & vomiting). He informed
me that he would call me up to Health Care at approximately 6:30 P.M.

At approximately 6:15 P.M. the pain and discomfort were becoming worse, so I proceeded to the unit
office and informed CX-2 S.R. to phone Health Care
and inform them of the situation. Mr. R. phoned Health
Care in my presence and was informed that I would be
called up to health Care as soon as the officer at Health
Care returned from the kitchen.

At approximately 6:30 P.M. I returned to the unit office and asked Mr. R. to phone Health Care to ascertain as to whether the staff member had returned from the kitchen and that I wanted to see the nurse. Mr. R. phoned Health Care in my presence once again and was told to inform me that Health Care was shut down and that I could see the doctor in the morning as well as something to the effect that the nurse was busy eating supper. Given my situation at that time, this flippant answer was totally unacceptable to me, so I went to my cell and slashed my lower right abdomen with a razor blade and then forced a Bic ballpoint pen through the incision to a depth of approximately 2 inches.

It was through this action that Mr. R. informed Health Care of my situation and then escorted me to Health Care. The nurse treated me for my discomfort from the Crohn's flare-up and dressed my self-inflicted wound.

I wish to state that Health Care officer R. over the past 3 years has always been very caring and understanding of my illness and its inherent deficits. My concern in this matter is that this problem never happens to a prisoner who requires medical attention in the future.

#274991A
R. McWhinney

Requests for Medical Transfer

COMPLAINT:
On 97-06-22, at approximately 10:15 P.M., I was experiencing a Crohn's flare-up. I proceeded to the duty desk and informed the officer of my condition, requesting to see a nurse.

The officer phoned the nurse at Stony Mountain, who informed me that nothing could be done that evening, but I could see the doctor in the morning. After threatening to inflict bodily harm upon myself if I could not see the nurse, I was taken to Health Care at Stony Mountain.

Upon seeing the nurse, who I assumed phoned a doctor, I was offered a Tylenol and Gravol, which I refused as inadequate.

I was then placed in a cell to spend the night in extreme discomfort and intense pain. The next morning, I saw a doctor who gave me six (6) steroid pills (Prednisone) to swallow, along with the advice that the pills should provide relief within 4 to 5 hours. However,

I did not experience the desired relief within the pre-scribed time frame. In fact, it took approximately three and a half days to recover from the flare-up.

After this experience, it is apparent to me that adequate treatment for this disease and its attending deficits are not being met in appropriate fashion at this institution. When I complain to the doctors here of my condition, I am met with suspicion, callous indifference, or benign neglect.

CORRECTIVE ACTION:

• I am requesting an emergency medical transfer to Millhaven Institution in the Ontario Region, where I believe I will receive appropriate treatment in addition to family support that resides in that region.

#274991A
R. McWhinney*

....

* Rik is asking for transfer from the Stony Mountain Institution in the rural municipality of Rockwood in Manitoba (a maximum/medium/minimum security pris-on, where he then had either a medium or minimum se-curity designation) to the maximum security Millhaven Institution in Millhaven, Ontario. Not only did Rik have family near Millhaven to advocate for him and provide support while he was ill and learning about what it was to live with Crohn's while incarcerated, but Rik also under-stood which prisons—and associated doctors—provided better care, as he was often in need of medical attention throughout his incarceration.

COMPLAINT:

On 97-08-07 I received a response to my complaint, which I submitted on 97-07-21. J.R., who responded to my complaint, deliberately lied or misrepresented the facts in her written response. She stated that my file indicates I have a substance abuse problem, and this factor cannot be ignored when considering appropriate medical treatment. I submit that there exists no active or passive evidence, on file or otherwise, to support this allegation. This can be supported by my behaviour over the past 8 years, as I have not been caught or suspected of drug involvement.

Furthermore, in March '97, I applied to participate in a voluntary drug urinalysis program. I may point out that this is not the behaviour or motivation of a substance abuser. In addition, I have never been selected for urinalysis testing on reasonable and probable grounds that would support suspicion of drug involvement. All of my tests have been conducted as a result of random selection or voluntary participation.

Most importantly, it is not possible, given my past prison record, that I would have been accepted for transfer on 97-04-16 to a minimum-security institution (Rockwood) from a maximum-security setting (Edmonton) if my file indicated a current problem with substance abuse.

J.R.'s spurious allegation is a calculated and deliberate attempt to shift responsibility away from her department for the inaction toward my medical problem on the night of 97-06-22. It is unethical for her to engage in such behaviour and a clear indication that she suffers from a major character flaw on a moral level, which is consistent with her job description.

CORRECTIVE ACTION:

- I am requesting that all reference to substance abuse, as described by J.R., be stricken and expunged from all relevant complaint and grievance documents.
- That J.R. be terminated from her place of employment within CSC so that her duplicitous talents can be better utilized (such as altering the Somalia documents in a manner she is accustomed to).

#274991A
R. McWhinney

COMPLAINT:

This grievance is in response to my [previous] complaint. J.R. made a deliberate attempt to obstruct the issue of my complaint of Crohn's flare-up by referencing her remarks to the treatment of the disease in and of itself. She then goes further by making false allegations of substance abuse in an attempt to absolve her department of responsibility for its lack of proper medical attention or treatment on the night of 97-06-22.

The regulations clearly state that all federal prisoners have a right to equitable medical treatment as enjoyed by civilians in free society—even if a substance abuse problem does exist, that should not preclude or exclude a person from appropriate medical treatment.

Apart from her disingenuous response to my complaint, it is abundantly clear that she is not only unfamiliar with Crohn's disease and its attending deficits, but is grossly incompetent as well, as evident by the fact she spells the name of the disease improperly (CHRON'S).

Her response to my complaint is replete with contradictions. A case in point where in summation she wrote "I believe the medical treatment received and proposed is appropriate." I have been assured by several staff that the nurse on duty the night of 97-06-22 has been reprimanded for this callous and flippant attitude toward my condition. If J.R. believes I received appropriate treatment, then why was the reprimand necessary?

Contrary to J.R., I do not consider it appropriate medical treatment, when complaining of flare-up symptoms, to be told to go back up and see the doctor in the morning. Crohn's disease sometimes requires the administration of narcotic analgesics to manage pain. Crohn's flare-up is another matter entirely, and more often than not is treated aggressively with narcotics. Incidentally, it is Crohn's flare-up that is the subject of my complaint. I believe it highly improper for J.R. to respond to a complaint against her department.

CORRECTIVE ACTION:

- I am requesting a medical emergency transfer to Millhaven Institution, where I believe I will receive appropriate medical attention as well as family support, as my family resides near there.

#274991A
R. McWhinney

COMPLAINT:

On 98-10-16 at approximately 9:00 A.M. I reported to Health Care complaining of a Crohn's flare-up. Dr. B. was completely indifferent to my suffering & appeared to be more interested in what I was in prison for & for how long. His advice was that I go back to my cell & take a pill. At approximately 11:00 A.M. I was given a shot of pain medication that was totally inadequate. As a result, it took me 7 days to recover.

Have You Tried to Solve Your Problem Before Filing This Complaint? No

I expressed my disappointment with the nurse, as well as several staff including the warden but all to no avail.

ACTION REQUESTED:

I am requesting an emergency medical transfer out of this region where I believe I will receive appropriate care & treatment.

#274991A
R. McWhinney*

. . . .

*   Rik is advised that he can request transfers at any time, but cannot request to transfer from a minimum- to a maximum-security institution, as he has. Rik was attempting

Regina General Hospital
(Fragment)

ON 2013-06-08 I WAS ADMITTED TO THE REGINA
General Hospital upon recovering from a seizure. Several hours later I attempted to leave the hospital, and
I was prevented from doing so by several members of
the nursing staff & hospital security who forcibly escorted me to another room & tied my hands & feet to
a bed in addition to placing a restraining strap across
my chest. I was then forced to take various medications that I later learned are contraindicated for a kid-
ney disease for which I was diagnosed 2 years previously [. . .]

....

to transfer to an institution where he had experienced a
positive relationship with a doctor. Rik is also advised that
"emergency medical transfers" are non-existent, except to
a Regional Psychiatric Centre. He is assured that his concerns about improper pain management will be relayed by
the chief of health services to the contractor to review the
subcontractor's decision and inmate medical file to determine appropriate management of "Chron's attacks."

VII) Posttraumatic
Stress Disorder

Introduction

ALTHOUGH RIK ONLY WROTE A SINGLE POEM about his experiences with posttraumatic stress disorder, PTSD structured his post-incarceration life, and it was something that he lived with while he was incarcerated. Rik's post-incarceration experiences stand as a powerful and important indictment of prison conditions, and they prompt us to consider through the lens of PTSD behaviours that are otherwise deemed destructive and anti-social. As we learn and think about trauma, what may become increasingly clear is that incarceration—a practice once thought to treat and correct—is in actuality a trauma-compounding response to trauma-induced behaviours.

While a growing body of research demonstrates that PTSD is prevalent among correctional officers,[1] there is a comparative dearth of research on PTSD among incarcerated and formerly incarcerated people. A recent French study found a high prevalence of PTSD among prisoners; this was especially the case if the prisoner's crime had been violent. The study also attributed the prevalence of PTSD to exposure to frequent trauma, especially during childhood.[2] As Rik makes clear in our conversation here, prison has the capacity to make monsters of men, and the trauma induced by living in such a violent and dysfunctional setting means that one is never free from its clutches.

Provided by Human Insecurities, Ltd.

The self-esteem composite index is down 14.21 points or 0.91%.

While posttraumatic stress disorder remains unchanged at 99.9 %.

Depression rose over 1,000 basis points after a strong rally
        on the emotions market.

Suicide ideation rose as well.

However, it may only be a short-term gain—

given the steep decline in rising expectations.

In Conversation V

MCWHINNEY: I didn't know it at the time, but I know now that solitary confinement was a huge contributing factor to my development of PTSD. I have a lot of dreams about it.

DEMERS: You tend to avoid sleep because of your dreams. What are your dreams like?

MCWHINNEY: Often I'm in solitary and some guys are getting beaten up by the guards. We're all up there banging our doors and it's just crazy. There's a lot of dreams where I'm in general population. The common thread in the dreams is violence and confrontation.

I remember I had this one dream where—I don't know where this came from—I'm in a barber's chair getting a haircut and seven guys are filling me full of holes. That never happened to me in prison—never—but that's a dream I had.

Why am I having dreams like that? Why am I having a dream where I'm in prison and seven guys are stabbing me?

I've had some dreams about violent situations that I was involved in with men that I know—so, actual events coming back to me in my dreams—but dreams like that are very rare. The majority of my dreams involve things that never actually happened.

Recollections that focus on experiences or things that actually happened generally come in flashbacks. I'll be doing something totally innocuous, like washing my dishes in the kitchen, and all of a sudden, I'll remember this case about a kid who burned himself to death—a kid who just set himself on fire, burned himself to death. And the screams, man. I have never, *ever* in my life—and hope to never again, ever—hear screaming like that again. I'll never forget that screaming. It has such an impact on you.

One day when I was living down in Winthorpe, close to my mom and sister, I'm in the kitchen washing dishes and it's a beautiful day—the sunlight's coming through the window. It's a beautiful day out. Then all of a sudden, these thoughts start to cross my mind—the screaming, and what that kid did to himself.

He didn't even belong in prison. He'd only been in prison a couple of hours. They'd sent him to the BC Pen from the Regional Psychiatric Centre in Abbotsford that afternoon. That evening I went out for exercise in a place we called the pool hall—it was just a big room, and there were a couple of pool tables and about five TVs, because you had no TVs in the cells at that time, so there were five TVs all hooked up to these earphones in the pool hall. There were also some card tables, and guys would be sitting playing bridge, or poker, or chess, or whatever.

And that kid came into that room that night. He had come from RPC that afternoon, and that evening, he came into the pool hall. Of course, I noticed him right away because I noticed everybody. And I'm studying him and saying to myself, "What's he doing here?" He's hanging out with the French guys, and he's speaking French with them, so I know he's French—and that's about all I know about him. I'm looking at him and I'm sizing him up—he's smaller than I am, he may be an inch shorter than me, maybe a hundred thirty pounds.

He lived in another range—on another wing. I lived in the east wing, and he lived in the north wing. But I heard these screams that evening. That's how far it travelled—from one wing to another, another part of the prison. Everybody heard him. So the next morning at breakfast time, word about what happened is all over the joint. This kid had taken some leather glue and smeared it all over himself—in his hair, on his face, his arms, his hands, his whole body. He had smothered himself with this leather glue, and he'd smeared it on his mattress and on his blankets—on everything—and he had lit himself on fire.

The guards couldn't get the cell door open. Those bars were so hot that the steel became malformed. The cell door was jammed shut because the bars were twisted in from the heat. That whole cell went up in thick, black, acrid smoke, because of the foam mattress—you know that pink Styrofoam.

After about an hour or so they got the fire out, and they had to cut him out of his cell. They had to cut the bars and get him out of there—remove what was left of him from his cell.

You couldn't go near the cell for the next two or three days. They had it all taped off and they moved everybody off that range to another range. They had the whole range taped off to clean up the area. Within a couple of days, I went up there and looked at that cell—I couldn't believe the damage that was done.

He was a young kid, and he was very, very mentally challenged. I don't know what he was in for. All I know is that he was a young kid, French, very mentally challenged, and very harmless. You could tell by looking at him that he wasn't a threat to anybody. And here's the ironic thing about it—his last name was LaFlamme. So, I don't know, maybe he saw something poetic in that. Who knows what was going on in his mind? So, you know, that comes back in flashbacks—that's a flashback.

Other flashbacks are somewhat similar, but it's different scenarios, different individuals. I don't want to get into all of those, but I could sum it up in those terms.

DEMERS: So these flashbacks are a product of these horribly violent incidents that emerge out of this environment. It's a place that drives people to do desperate things—things that they wouldn't normally do because they're going mad in solitary confinement, or because they have mental health issues in an institution that isn't equipped to understand or cater to special psychological needs. These are then violent things that have happened, that you've witnessed that come back unexpectedly—they invade new contexts. They pop up in places where they don't belong—not that they belong in prison in the first place.

MCWHINNEY: Yes. You could write a whole book about these incidents that I've witnessed, but I'm not sure that that would be all that interesting.

DEMERS: When people talk about conditions of confinement, about conditions that need to be improved—bad diet, lack of access to health care—the focus is often on present conditions. One of the reasons why it's so important to talk about PTSD is because people need to consider the long-term effects of incarceration. Rather than focus on these violent incidents,

I'm wondering if you've been able to pin down some of your triggers. For example, I don't know that you watch many television programs about prison anymore.

MCWHINNEY: That is interesting—and it's something I haven't really yet resolved in my mind. I know if a program's coming on and it's about prison, of course I'm attracted to it, especially if it's an investigative program, or something like that. If it's an American-produced prison drama, I won't watch it—not because it triggers flashbacks or nightmares, but because it doesn't hold any interest for me. For the most part, it's just garbage. I like shows that are based in reality and fact.

To answer your question, I haven't given a great deal of thought to it—I haven't really resolved it in my mind. I know there are some things that I watch on TV that have a triggering effect, but I can't really help myself, so I still watch them. Like those news briefs on Ashley Smith—when she's in her cell getting tear gassed and that, and pepper sprayed—that strikes a chord with me because I've lived that. That's happened to me, so that triggers me some, and I've had a few nasty nights because of this. But I watch these segments whenever they come on. I think somehow, morbidly, we're drawn to these things. I don't know if it's like people that go to car races just to watch the accidents or something like that.

DEMERS: It's something you relate to—something you've lived.

MCWHINNEY: Yeah, very much so.

DEMERS: You spent thirty-five years in prison, and you spent so much of it—

MCWHINNEY: Thirty-four.

DEMERS: —thirty-four years, and sixteen in solitary. So, to be invested in what somebody's just gone through in solitary at a moment when people are interrogating that practice—I don't think it's morbid to want to know how people are talking about something that you've had such an intimate experience of.

MCWHINNEY: That doesn't detract from the fact that these are morbid subjects, you know. When I watched that poor girl, Ashley, crouched on the floor with guards hovering over her, screaming at her and pepper spraying her . . . You know, that's not so much morbid as, for me anyway, as it is enraging. The morbidity factors in in terms of the unfairness and the inhumanity—the way that injustice manifests itself can be very morbid. That's the tragedy of it. And I suspect that will continue—it'll refine itself in many, many ways over time. They're always dreaming up new forms of torture.

DEMERS: So the effect of PTSD, there's flashbacks, and then there's dreams that lead to insomnia because you don't want to sleep. What else do you experience?

MCWHINNEY: There's the social factor too. When I'm in a populated area, like a restaurant or a store, people invade my space, and I get really uptight. You've seen it. We try to have a FOTO* meeting at Western Pizza and I have to get up and leave. I've got to go. The server hovers over me—Sister RéAnne spotted it right away. She went over and told her not to hang around me, and she was very good about it. She even came up to me and apologized, and now she doesn't do that any longer—she goes to the other side.

DEMERS: And those are the—

MCWHINNEY: Those are big triggers.

DEMERS: And this is because your experience is that it's dangerous for somebody to be close behind you—you always have to be completely aware of what's in your space?

MCWHINNEY: Yes. Especially if you don't know someone, or if you've got issues with him—maybe he's

---

* Friends on the Outside, a Regina-based group that meets for coffee and conversation on a weekly basis.

making a move on you. So you want him to keep his distance.

Out here in society, of course these are people I don't know. These are complete strangers. Totally harmless. I remember one case, in particular—I think I phoned my parole officer about this. I was down at the Cornwall Centre, at the Dollar Store, and I'm looking at some item on a shelf, but somebody was crowding me from behind. It turns out it was a twelve-year-old girl—twelve, thirteen, somewhere around there—but totally harmless, you know? She posed no threat to me, but I just freaked.

So I got out of there right away, I came so close to losing it. I was right on the verge of turning on her and saying, "What's your fucking problem?!" you know. "You got issues with me?" I've done this in the past with people, other people, generally men in Tim Hortons or whatever—men who are crowding me. I just snap. I try not to do that. Now, as a coping mechanism, I just leave. I go outside and I have a cigarette. That calms me down.

DEMERS: And this is in part because, if this would be happening inside a prison, where you spent most of your adult life, that's what you needed to do if somebody invaded your personal space—

MCWHINNEY: Oh yeah.

DEMERS: —you have to confront that person—

MCWHINNEY: Oh, right away.

DEMERS: —because that's a danger, and you need to be able to stand your ground and stop that situation from escalating, stop a confrontation from happening.

MCWHINNEY: Yes, exactly.

DEMERS: So that's a normal reaction. But once you're outside and in a normal social situation, where somebody might be close to you, you perceive this as threatening in spite of the fact that it's not meant to be a threat.

MCWHINNEY: Yes.

DEMERS: So this is why you don't like to go into crowded places, why you feel threatened by your server. This is also why you need to be close to an exit, right?

MCWHINNEY: Yes—I have to have an escape route. In prison you can only back up so far; after that you have to move forward. But discretion being the better part of valour, I choose to leave rather than confront. It serves another purpose too: I'm relieved once I'm out of that situation. I'm relieved of that tension, and that angst.

DEMERS: So you've learned to cope—but if somebody hasn't learned how to cope, how to remove
themselves from a situation, things can become
very volatile.

MCWHINNEY: Yes. A lot of people can't cope, so they
confront, and it can all end very tragically, especially if somebody dies as a result of a situation
like this.

DEMERS: So, one could viably see a situation where
some would argue that a person who is released
from prison and commits a violent act is inher-
ently violent or criminal, whereas a more nuanced
view might recognize that the institution has
played a part in conditioning a person to react
in a particular way.

MCWHINNEY: They've created a monster, you see.
PTSD and the reactions that stem from it are a
result of incarceration. A guy may have entered
the system somewhat damaged, but upon leaving, he's two or three times as damaged. And
that's what society is left to deal with, you know?
Especially if he can't cope or find coping skills
or mechanisms necessary to relieve himself of a
situation, or to escape a situation—because certainly there's no help for us out here. I'm required
to see a psychologist at least once a month. Those
are the terms of my parole. But there's nothing
she can do for me. For PTSD. They're just starting

now, in the wake of all these veteran suicides, to get some programs up and running for treating veterans who have PTSD, and that may include police officers, and—

DEMERS: —first responders.

MCWHINNEY: —yes, and firemen, because they all go through this too.

DEMERS: Because they witness violent situations as part of their profession.

MCWHINNEY: Yes—because they've been involved in, or witnessed, violence. But there's no help forthcoming for prisoners. You're left to your own upon release. I'm fortunate in the sense that I've got a great team behind me. That helps me a great deal. If it wasn't for this support, I don't know how I'd be coping.

DEMERS: Other coping mechanisms include addictions, right? Alcohol and drugs provide escape from dealing with dreams and flashbacks.

MCWHINNEY: Yes. And people get really depressed, you know? There's suicidal ideation. You struggle with that a lot—that's a hard one.

DEMERS: So you don't leave prison upon release. It continues to haunt you.

MCWHINNEY: I suspect I'll be in prison for the rest of my life—internally. I don't see any of this ever going away; perhaps it will diminish a bit in some respects, I don't know. But I'll carry all of this through to the grave. I suspect this has been the case for a lot of people. World War I victims, World War II victims. The horrors they've witnessed. Holocaust survivors—the nightmares they must have, you know? Wow.

DEMERS: I know one of the forms of treatment that excited you in particular was the possibility of having a service dog. What prevented that from happening?

MCWHINNEY: Money. That's all it is—it's just money. There may be some opposition toward it from management—pets aren't allowed here, that's their policy. But there's no way that the Salvation Army would want to become involved in a human rights issue in the court with their name splashed all over the newspapers. This has already happened a few times with respect to taxis and people who are blind, where a cab driver doesn't want a service dog in their car. This is a service animal—it's required, and it needs to be recognized as such.

I know that they wouldn't want to allow it, but they'd have no choice. So the only thing that prevents it for me really is the money, because these animals have to be certified, so they cost $10,000 to $15,000. I don't have that kind of money.

DEMERS: And because this is a relatively new form of therapy, there's no public insurance coverage.

MCWHINNEY: Veterans in Canada do have service dogs—I've got all kinds of articles on that. So it is recognized, you know, but it's financially prohibitive for me. Where am I going to get $10,000 for a service dog? I don't know how ex-servicemen acquire theirs, whether it's by using their own money or if they've got family. I have some limited means of support, but I'm on social assistance, I'm on SAID,* and they don't shell out $10,000 for service animals. In the end, I cope with it. That's all I can do. But there's experiences that I've lived that I'll carry with me right to the grave, because I'm still living them through the PTSD.

....

* Saskatchewan Assured Income for Disability, an income support program for people with disabilities.

VIII) Opportunities and Restorations

Introduction

IN THIS FINAL SECTION, WE SEE RIK ENGAGING in "pro-social" behaviours while benefiting from some of the programming that was made available to him. Rik's preference for the "opportunities" model of incarceration is something of a hornet's nest, nestled as that model is in the late-seventies turn away from the social safety net, and toward individual responsibility—a philosophy and social context responsible for a dramatic increase in the incarceration rate. While prisons are indeed ill-equipped to "correct," the shift in penal philosophy from rehabilitation to "personal reformation"[1] simply relieves the prison of its responsibilities and excuses its missteps and shortcomings by anchoring the successes and failures of corrections to the incarcerated individual. Rik did many good things during the last fifteen years of his incarceration. But as he points out in conversation, he achieved what he did *in spite of* his incarceration, not because of it. The grievances included here, alongside his letter to prisoner rights advocate Senator Earl Hastings, see Rik resisting coercive programming to the point that he was simply living out his sentence on cell lock-up.

It was only when Rik was given the opportunity to design and implement programs—peer counselling, HIV/AIDS prevention, and a Cat Club—that he really thrived. As we read his letters appealing to a Montana prison to keep their boxing club open due to the opportunities it provides at-risk youth, follow his search for an imprimatur to bolster the status of an inmate-directed program, and read about the extraordinary amount of communal thought and compassion that went into caring for the feral cat population at a prison farm annex, we can fully understand Rik's belief that programming needs to be initiated and run by prisoners. The Rockwood Cat Club was a particular source of pride for Rik, whose intense bond with the cats saw him dubbed "the Catman of Rockwood" (a reference to the infamous Birdman of Alcatraz, Robert F. Stroud). This particular program, which Rik describes in detail below, led to calls from the Headingley and Regina Correctional Centres asking how to start their own programs. It should be noted that although the Cat Club instilled accountability and responsibility, the program was born of compassionate rebellion, as it started with prisoners hiding cats destined to be euthanized in their cells. From protecting cats from a death penalty to berating a zoo manager for the conditions of scarlet macaw confinement, Rik's intense compassion for animals is an inversion of lessons learned while incarcerated, not the culmination of a successful correctional program. Rik kept the certificates he earned from organizations external to the prison, and the letters and articles that documented his various interventions and achievements, in a portfolio that he used to narrate who he was. As Rik says in conversation about the work he was able to achieve during the later years of his incarceration, "I finally felt I was somebody."

In Conversation VI

DEMERS: One of the themes that comes up through your history of incarceration is anger management. Can you tell me a little bit about your anger?

MCWHINNEY: I was very angry from a very early age, you know? I grew up in a broken home, and went to reform school at the age of nine. Once I got into reform school at that age, nine years of age—of course I was very rebellious and angry. And I just graduated up through the system, you know, from reform school to provincial jails, from provincial jails to penitentiaries—it was my whole life. It's all I knew. And I became very adept at surviving it, at navigating the treacherous waters.

But I was fortunate to survive it. I can recall quite a few times where I was just left for dead, laying on the floor. But I'm still here. It's a rough experience though—a very rough experience. And it's what you make of it too. I didn't help

myself any by living the way I did, with my attitude. I was probably my own worst enemy, with
all my anger and bitterness, which came out in
the form of violence. I reasoned emotionally. I
wore my heart on my sleeve. I had no ability or
even inclination, in terms of critical thinking, or
conversing, of attacking a problem in a mature
manner. I would just lash out and, as a result,
get myself buried deeper, into more trouble.
I just wasted my life, hey? A terribly wasted life. I
think I've summed it all up in the FOTO [Friends
on the Outside] brochure: "A whole lifetime of
highs, lows, antipathies, and despairs. 34 years
of animal screams, murders, and suicides." That
pretty much sums it up. It's a shame because I could
have accomplished so much had I gone in
another direction. It's too late now, but I'm better
off now than I ever was—I've got a good support
team behind me, some good friends, for which
I'm thankful, and which is very helpful.

I cut myself from all that prior lifestyle, the
criminal life, and now I'm much more at ease,
much more peaceful, and much happier, even
though I have collateral issues in terms of health
and things like that. I'm not getting any younger,
but I'm more at peace with myself now than I ever
was at any point in my life. I have a lot of regrets,
but I deal with them as best I can, and I can't
undo something that's already been done. If I
had the opportunity to do a lot of things over
again, I would do them a lot differently, but I

think everybody, given that choice, would say the same thing.

DEMERS: I think you also began a transformation before you left prison—

MCWHINNEY: Yeah.

DEMERS: —and went along a positive path and did many positive things that affected people's lives inside and out. You've done a lot for animals. And when you think about the impact that people have, and the decisions that people make, you certainly made bad decisions, and served a lot of very hard time. As a result of those decisions, you got pulled into a system that took your life away for more than three decades. But that turn that you took, and what you've accomplished since, I think is so much more than many people who don't experience incarceration, who don't go through that turmoil that you did—I don't think that many people actually accomplish a lot of the things that you did, once you turned things around, in their entire lifetime.

MCWHINNEY: And I ran into a lot of opposition too. Many of those things that I did while in prison were—for lack of a better term—more pro-social, but they were very difficult to do in terms of the rules and regulations governing prisoners within the system. I had to navigate, or negotiate, ways around it in order to get something done. And it usually took the form of a political, or semi-political, approach. I was always active—very active in prison politics, where I would have some standing or recognition in terms of not only representing myself, but other prisoners. I'd serve on inmate committees, lifers' groups, and things like that, and I'd use those positions as a form of negotiation to achieve what I wanted, or what other people wanted. That was very reward-ing, but at the same time it was very frustrating, because it went unrecognized, particularly by the National Parole Board.

DEMERS: And on a larger scale, it's rare to see news about the achievements of people who are incarcerated.

MCWHINNEY: You know, it's interesting that the vast majority of these programs with respect to service dogs originated in prisons. A civilian, a person from the outside, would come in and teach these programs to inmates. They'd give them dogs that they would live with in prison, and they would train these animals, and then they'd sell them off, or donate them or whatever to an organization—CNIB, you know, the Canadian National Institute for the Blind, and then they'd get another dog and train it. The prisoners themselves were the main facilitators, or co-facilitators.

That's a valuable, valuable program—prisoners training dogs to help the blind. And it helps not only the dog and the person who ultimately receives that dog, but it also helps the prisoner.

In many respects, through that program, they become more empathetic, they become more responsible, more pragmatic. These programs have a way of bringing about change in a person. It's a humanistic approach that's very rewarding for everybody. It's a valuable program that should be enhanced and fully supported.

DEMERS: If I remember correctly, one of the justifications for shutting down the prison farms was that the benefits were too abstract—they weren't directly training people for specific jobs upon release. When they tracked people post-release, the people who spent time in a farm annex weren't getting jobs in the agricultural sector. In other words, the farm annexes weren't offering vocational training, so they offered no tangible benefits—you don't get a job in empathy.

MCWHINNEY: Yeah, that's the way they view that. But these programs are essential. How the government misses that—that's just mean-spirited. It's a shame, because when you see the system move away from the punitive aspect toward a more rewarding set of programs, it changes a person's whole perspective—it moves them from a life they once lived toward a better way of living.

Aside from empathy, your self-esteem and self-confidence are developed and reinforced. These are important things. I hate to use the term "rehabilitate," you know, but these are ways of changing a person to be a better person, and to become a fuller person.

I've seen guys come into the joint who are totally—you know, aside from being illiterate or semi-literate—lacking in basic life skills. Programs only came in 1989. Before that they resisted them. Once programs became implemented, they instilled those traits—like your self-esteem, your self-worth. And I think, for the most part, they largely ignored that. You had to go out on your own and fight, or be at odds with the system, to implement change. Change was highly resisted.

I remember when they introduced the peer counselling program in prison. We wanted that for twenty-five years before they first introduced it. I think I shared a tape with you one time on capital punishment—the question the host asked me, "Well, what brings about change?" And I said, "Well, what's required here? What's needed?" I said, "Programs." Programs, because at that time when that tape was made—that was around 1986, I believe, or '85, there were no programs.[2] None whatsoever. They weren't introduced until 1989. But then I'm not sure that most have had any effect on actually bringing about changes in prisoners.

DEMERS: And why is that?

MCWHINNEY: For multiple reasons. But I think it was just a case of, well, this is policy that's been handed down by our superiors, and we've just got to do it.

First of all, the program facilitator is a guard. So there's that rift there to begin with. As a peer counsellor, I had many guys come in to see me, and they just said, "I've had it, McWhinney. I can't handle this anymore. This program is driving me nuts. What the hell does she know about drugs? Why is she telling me about drugs? I don't want to be in that program. She's never done drugs in her life, you know? What does she know about drugs?" To which I would respond—well, look at it from this point of view. A person doesn't necessarily have to have brain damage in order to become a brain surgeon. One doesn't have to have lived that experience, per se, to speak on it. Also, they may be coming at it from a different angle. I mean, they're just primarily focused on prevention, and "just say no," without delving into the causes, the underlying causes of it, and things like that. What contributes to addictions? Now, they contribute to it. Prison is a breeding ground for drug addiction. Boy, I've seen guys that never had a thing to do with drugs their entire life come to prison, and man, they're right into it just to escape the horrors of their situation, to escape the reality of it, you know, as often and as frequently as they can. And some guys go right off the deep end. They end up dying from it. I've known guys dying from drugs in prison, whereas before that they never had anything whatsoever to do with drugs.

I felt very good about programming, just not the manner in which they delivered programs, because they're forced upon people. We were screaming for programs back in the early seventies—we wanted programs, but we wanted to deliver them. We wanted to be trained—educated and trained—so we could deliver them and facilitate them, which I eventually ended up doing myself, you know. AIDS education, peer counselling—whatever I could do, but I had to initiate that on my own. They didn't offer it to me.

We wanted to deliver programs ourselves because then they had authenticity. I had more credibility speaking to my peers in a program setting than a prison guard did. It's an adversarial system to begin with. It's us versus them. So who's going to listen to somebody that you resent, you know? And that you may even harbour a great deal of hatred toward. You're going to take advice from them? No. You're going to resist it with every fibre of your being. So that person has no credibility, whereas a person speaking to his own peers has more credibility, and that's why I ended up being so successful in the programs that I delivered, and that others did with the programs that they delivered.

It's very rewarding—not just for the client, but for the facilitators themselves. It helped me in terms of my own self-confidence, self-esteem, assuredness. It helped me build myself up. I finally felt I was somebody. You're a piece of meat—a nothing, a nobody, you know, not even recognized as a human being. But if you become a somebody, somebody that's respected, and maybe looked up to, and sought out for advice, for counselling and things like that—that goes toward reinforcing your own sense of self-worth, you know? That helped me tremendously, and it helped others who embarked upon that road. It does a tremendous service. Beyond the facilitator and the client, it's a great advantage for the institution as well, because I'm a tool. Why not use me instead of treating me as an object to be punished and degraded? Why not build me up, so I become a team member—you know what I mean? You're able to work with me, and I'm able to work with you, rather than having two opposing sides at each other's throats constantly, you know?

DEMERS: Where was it that you started doing the programming? Was it in Edmonton Max?

MCWHINNEY: Yeah—in the early nineties.

DEMERS: Was it a case of a good warden, as well that—

MCWHINNEY: A very good warden who I just despised. I hated him, but once I got to know him and understand what he was dealing with—and once I saw that he was not only able but willing to encourage me and help facilitate my own self-growth and development—I said, "Hey, this guy's an asset," you know? "In fact, he's not only an asset to me, but I've become an asset to him as well." Even though we were on opposing sides, we could work together.

DEMERS: So, what was it that he was dealing with? How and why did you despise him, and what did you come to understand?

MCWHINNEY: Well, the gangs were just starting to enter the prison system at that time and there was a lot of violence going on. It was just gratuitous, you know? Senseless, stupid violence. And of course, as a warden, he had to deal with it, but his way of dealing with it was to get tougher: lock the system down, tighten it up. It became very, very difficult to even function in that place, you know? To move from point A to point B without being searched and questioned and watched. Before, you had some limited freedoms—you could move from point A to point B with no interference, but now, everything's tightened right up, and guys would complain, saying, "What's the joint become so tight for?"

Guys would say, "Well, ask the warden, it's his decision."

So everything fell back on him. The screws were being tightened on us and we had no one else to blame but the warden, because the last thing we're going to do is blame ourselves. But then he asked me if I could get a restorative justice program started.

I agreed to participate, provided he would do something in return for our group. I was president of a lifers' group, and I had never had the warmth of an animal's touch for twenty-five years—and neither had many of my contemporaries. Some hadn't seen a cat or a dog, other than in a newspaper or magazine or on T V.

So I said, "Well, there's a staff member who works in the gym. He's got a nice dog. A purebred boxer. Will you consider letting him bring him in one night for a lifers' meeting so the lifers could interact with this dog, and I'll see what I can do about getting the lifers to participate in this restorative justice thing?" He said, "You've got a deal." That's when I realized, hey, we can work together here, you see? So that's what opened the door. And then later he approached me and he said, "What do you think about a peer counselling program?" I said, "I don't know. I don't know anything about it," and I said, "I have to look at it. Give me a couple of weeks."

So I did some research, and I said, "Hey, this has some benefits to it. This could work." So I went back to him and I said, "I'll do it, but I'm not going to approach it on the level that it's handed down from Ottawa or from higher-ups, you know? A program that's designed and implemented the way you want it. I want to have some input into it as well, because I've got my own set way of doing things."

He said, "Sure. You've got carte blanche." That was an eye-opener—a warden saying, "Hey, yeah, feel free. You've got freedom—within certain limits. I mean, I'm not going to hand you the keys to the front door." So that worked out very nicely. I designed a peer counselling program, got it going. And you know what happened? CSC, the Correctional Service of Canada, came to me and offered to buy it off me. I said, "No, it's not for sale." They ended up co-opting it anyway and taking it over as their own. I knew that was going to happen—I didn't care as long as I got some benefit and some of my peers got benefit from it, you know?

DEMERS: So how did you run it? How did it work?

MCWHINNEY: I've got it written up here somewhere. I'd have to dig it up, but basically what it was is conflict resolution. A lot of that, you know? And critical thinking and counselling. A lot of counselling. I dealt with a lot of suicide ideation. Guys that were just feeling rough and couldn't get any help. But the majority of it, because it's a prison setting—an adversarial system, naturally—the majority of it was conflict resolution. Some beef between some guy and some guard, you know? Get them together, get them to sit down and iron out their differences.

And it worked out fine. It got to a point—I'll give you an example. Two guys doubled up, double bunked. Two guys in a cell, refusing to come out of their cell. They're screaming threats and that through their door. "No, we ain't coming out. You come in and get us." So the keeper who's running the institution after hours, the head guy in charge of the institution for the night, he comes and pulls me out of my cell and says, "We got a problem upstairs, Rik." I say, "Yeah, what's that?"

He says, "You know, two guys are double bunked upstairs on the range above you refusing to come out of their cells, and because of the situation—it's a double bunk situation—it can be very dangerous, not only for them, but for my staff, as well. I've got staff suiting up outside right now—suiting up, ready to go in like gang busters and drag these guys out of there. Now, somebody's going to get hurt. We want to try and prevent that. You, as a peer counsellor, can you resolve this so I don't have to send my staff in there?"

"Yeah. I don't know if I can resolve it, but I can try." So I went up and talked to the guys through the door, came back, talked to the keeper, went back to the guy, talked to him some more, came back, talked to the keeper, went back to talk to the guys some more, came back, talked to the keeper, made arrangements, headed up—bang, they come out of their cell. Nobody was hurt. Nobody assaulted. Nobody hit, nobody hurt, nothing. Not a punch thrown, you know? Very passively resolved. That guy came up to me after, about a month later, after he did about thirty days in the hole, he came up to me and thanked me. He knew he would have gotten a beating, you know? Instead, all he did was thirty days in the hole.

DEMERS: I imagine you have to be pretty respected on both sides to be able to do that type of negotiation.

MCWHINNEY: Yeah. Very much so.

DEMERS: Because if not, then you become the adversary for either side—it would be a difficult position to maintain.

MCWHINNEY: Was it ever. You have to have a certain amount of cred, so to speak. But, you see, I had over twenty years then. So I was well respected. And I had experience. I mean—there was a time when I was locked up in a cell refusing to come out, you know, and threatening the guards. I'd been there, done that, bought the shirt, wore the shirt [*laughs*]. So it was nothing new to me. I knew what was going on in this poor guy's head, and I also knew what was going on in the staff's minds too.

Someone could—there's a few, very immature rookies, who are all gung-ho and can't wait to get in there and flex their muscles and beat some poor con half to death, you know? But at the same time, I know the majority of the staff that are suiting up, they would much rather just have a nice quiet evening, get through their shift with no altercations and go home, greet their wife and kids.

They're the majority, and they knew me well—I'd been in that joint for many, many years, and they all knew me very well and respected me. So they were very appreciative of my contribution, of my effort toward resolving that issue. And that's just one case. I did several like that—maybe about a half a dozen or so. So that's the peer counselling program—the conflict-resolution end of it.

DEMERS: It's probably a better job than most of the jobs that you've had inside prison.

MCWHINNEY: You know something—it was the best job I ever had, because it was so rewarding. That and when I was in Rockwood, when I looked after the cats. I'd say that job was the best. But I was my own boss, hey, and all I did was play with cats all day, which I just loved, you know?

In that, I wasn't really different from anyone else. We wanted programs, but we wanted them in a different format. We wanted to be able to deliver the programs, and we also wanted it to be on a voluntary basis. As it exists, they force you into programs, which doesn't work: the program in and of itself becomes ineffective. A guy is going to be there and he's just going to become a class clown—he's just going to be disruptive. He's not going to pay attention, he's not going to learn anything, because, first of all, he resents even being there. Why? Because he was forced to be there. I think I wrote a letter on that too—a complaint. I wrote a letter and I sent it out to Senator Earl Hastings.

DEMERS: September 27, 1993—it's regarding coercive programming at Edmonton Institution. You write that "change of behaviour cannot be coerced, but it can be facilitated."

MCWHINNEY: Precisely. This is the only way, in that setting, to improve—or even in the first place instill—your own sense of self-worth and self-esteem. But instead they go in the opposite direction. At the time I wrote that, they had me on cell lock-up—they wouldn't let me work, I got zero pay. I wasn't getting any pay, so I couldn't buy the necessities that I needed to survive, like shampoo or toothpaste or any of that. How can I? I can't go to the canteen and buy it, because I've got no money and they're not paying me. Why? Because they won't let me work. Why won't they let me work? Because I refuse to participate in programs. And you know the program they wanted me to participate in? Orientation. And you know what their orientation program was? How the institution operates. I'd already spent thirteen years in that institution. I know how it operates; I don't need no orientation program.

DEMERS: And it doesn't matter in the end, how many contradictions or how many ironies exist within the system, because you just live it. I mean you're forced to live it. It sounds very Kafkaesque.

MCWHINNEY: It's very Kafkaesque, yeah—the psychological and administrative mind games that they put you through, with transfers and segregation. There's no way of communicating and educating people on the outside by any means other than through our own visitors, who have limited resources themselves—contacts and things like that. With the exception of the few grassroots movements, like prisoners' rights groups—like Claire Culhane. She was a big advocate for prisoners in Canadian federal prisons who spoke out against the inhumane conditions that we were forced to live in, and which the public was by and large mostly ignorant of—either by design or by choice, through apathy, or a general lack of communication.

DEMERS: It's not a cause that most are particularly sympathetic toward. There's no real soapbox—I mean, if someone stands up on one, the city square generally empties out, because there's very little sympathy.

MCWHINNEY: Yeah. By and large.

DEMERS: It's got to be so frustrating to be living in those conditions and to know that there isn't much hope of finding an ear.

MCWHINNEY: That's what leads to a lot of the discontent, and the refusal to follow the straight and narrow. It turns you the opposite way—and it's a pity that people can't see that. I think many people who work within the system recognize it within a short time. They say, "Hey, this is counterproductive here, what we're doing."

DEMERS: You've talked about the line between inmates and guards, with their respective codes, but the antagonism extends with all of this discourse in society—people draw a line, and put you on one side of it, and talk about you as though you're worthless.

MCWHINNEY: Yeah. And so, in turn, as a way of rebelling, we would *embrace* that. We'd say, "You say I'm bad? Okay, I'm bad. I'll show you what bad is then," and become even worse. It's self-perpetuating.

Like I've said before, true change can only come from within. The desire and the will to change oneself—that's not because of the system, it's in spite of the system that change comes about. I certainly never had—I had very, very little help in accomplishing the things I did in prison to better myself, to better conditions for myself and for others. In fact, there was a lot of opposition, and sort of roadblocking.

But with sheer determination and will, you steer around it, or you just keep pounding at it until you reach your goal.

DEMERS: So it's like the steel door.

MCWHINNEY: Yeah, metaphorically—sure.

DEMERS: But you're an advocate for restorative justice—which is part of the reason why you talk about how real change comes from within, and in spite of the system. In restorative justice, it's dialogue that's productive, that's educative, that helps one to understand the effects they have on other people—you believe that opening up these channels for dialogue would be much more productive than caging.

MCWHINNEY: Exactly. Dialogue—and that's where the empathy enters into it, you know? You're hit with a realization of the enormity of your offence and the effect that it had on the victim, and they in turn come to understand the situation that led up to that offence, you know, or what led you to that offence. And these are myriad because there's so many different reasons why a person would go down a particular road. I mean, social, economic—and most importantly, mental health.

There are many, many—too many people who are in prison because they're basically *non compos mentis*, you know? They don't have the mental ability to effect change in their lives, and they fell through the cracks somewhere along the line. A lot of people would be surprised by the wide range of mental health problems that exist in prison today.

FASD—fetal alcohol spectrum disorder—is a big contributor. When a person who suffers from that malady falls through the cracks, what do they do in order to survive—without a job, without social supports or coping mechanisms? They run afoul of the law, end up in prison, which just exacerbates the situation—makes it even worse. If they survive that, they don't come out any better. In fact, in most cases, they come out worse, because prisons aren't designed or equipped to deal with these issues regarding mental health. Ashley Smith is a good case in point, you know. Boy, there are thousands, literally thousands of Ashley Smiths in Canadian prisons today as we speak.

The prison system has made some headway in terms of at least recognizing it as a problem, and making some lame attempt to address it, but by and large it remains the same—or worse. Nothing good comes of these thousands of interactions. People either end up dying in prison, or if they happen to survive the experience, they're released back out into an unsuspecting community and society, much worse for wear.

Once people enter the system, the penitentiary system, or the correctional system, as it is—and it's sort of a misnomer, but—they become locked into it, you know? They basically don't see any escape for themselves. Some of them accept it for what it is, and some lash out at it and become a problem not only for themselves, but for other people around them, and for the system in and of itself. They become what they like to term a "disciplinary problem." They don't care for the rules or regulations, or anything like that.

It's a very sad situation. A lot of it is based on class: you see very, very, very few millionaires in prison. People always talk about the deterrent factor—that's a misnomer in and of itself. I mean, what does it mean to weigh one's need to escape their past or present circumstances against any deterrent value whatsoever?

Some guys are quite comfortable in prison because they feel secure, and they establish their own relationships to a point that they never achieved outside, living on the streets.

You take a look outside here, you see these guys outside here [the Salvation Army], and they're basically homeless, you know? For them, prison may be a relief—it might give them some sense of security, you know? They've got shelter, a roof over their head, and three meals a day, if you choose to call them that. I ran into a lot of people that were in prison who lacked the social skills to deal effectively with the problems that they encountered. They'd have a number of issues—like with anger, you know, anger management issues, which are compounded by substance abuse issues, and an anti-social sort of attitude—and that all feeds into it. For the most part, they can't help themselves.

Prison, yeah—I mean, you just have to take a walk through a prison and you'll see the overrepresentation of the Native population versus the white population, the poor versus the rich, people with mental health issues—you can't escape the fact that these guys for the most part were just cast aside at some point in their lives, at an early age, you know? And they said, "Well, I'll just live this way, you know, and I'll choose to live this way, and to hell with everybody else," you know? "I'll do what I want." I mean, you just have to take a look around in prison, and you can see that it's very—crime is very class-driven, you know? Like I said before, there's very, very few millionaires in prison. So few, in fact, that you could probably discount them altogether.

Induction/Orientation Programming: Grievance No. 1

COMPLAINT:

I recently received a letter from AID,* as per attached, encouraging me to apply for a social security number & birth certificate at a cost of $15.00.

However, a recent decision by the Unit Program Board to deny me employment because of my refusal to participate in an orientation/induction program prohibits me from earning the money for application fees. My reason for refusing to participate in induction programming is based upon many reasons. The primary issue is that it is a flawed plan gone awry: induction programming is a liberal bourgeois concept conceived by nascent social engineers who resort to coercive practices, denying employment to prisoners who refuse to lend themselves to manipulation.

....

* The full name of this organization—assuming this is an acronym—isn't included anywhere in Rik's papers.

CORRECTIVE ACTION REQUESTED:

- That mandatory attendance in induction be discontinued as it contravenes the Charter of Rights as well as the mission statement of Corrections Canada.

#274991A
R. McWhinney

Induction/Orientation Programming: Grievance No. 2

COMPLAINT:

On 92-10-18 I submitted my name to do some volunteer work for the Lifers' Group. On 92-10-22 my name was stricken from the list of volunteers. The reason given for this rejection was that I could not volunteer because I was not actively seeking employment. On 92-10-24 I applied for employment in the laundry. On 92-10-25 my application was rejected because I have not participated in orientation. I object to this practice of treating me like a circus animal where I am required to jump through hoops only to be met with obstacles that are Catch-22 in their nature. I refuse to participate in any program that, by its title, "Orientation," suggests that those who participate are disoriented. I have presently served 19 years of a life sentence & strongly feel any information forthcoming from such a program is irrelevant to my present situation.

CORRECTIVE ACTION:

- I be given a formal apology for subjecting me to this runaround.
- That I be given suitable employment in an area of my choice in accordance with the Commissioner's Directive.
- That authorities in Edmonton Inst. desist in attempting to coerce me into orientation.

#274991A
R. McWhinney

Induction/Orientation Programming: Grievance No. 3

COMPLAINT:

For the past year I have been receiving from the Program Board written notice that my status remains unemployed, non-pay, & cell lock-up. They also state this is due to my refusal to submit to coercive attempts by the board to force me into an induction/orientation program.

Apart from all the faults & deficits associated with the orientation program, my refusal to participate remains based upon principle. I have resided in various maximum-security institutions for the past 20 years & have always opposed muscling & strong-arm methods, often on a violent & physical level. My resolve on the matter is strengthened by the Canadian Charter of Rights.

I refuse to be muscled by nascent social engineers who display the ambivalent smugness of unavowed totalitarianism.

CORRECTIVE ACTION:

• That <u>mandatory</u> orientation be discontinued as it contravenes the Charter of Rights as well as the mission statement.

• That the orientation program be revised to address its failures.

• That I be paid retroactively to Dec. 1992 at level 2-k pay for lost employment opportunities & economic hardship imposed upon me.

• That I be given the immediate opportunity to seek employment of my choice in accordance with Commissioner's Directives.

#274991A

R. McWhinney[3]

Letter to Senator Earl Hastings

SEPTEMBER 27, 1993

Dear Senator Earl Hastings,

There exists a disturbing and potentially dangerous policy being practised at Edmonton Penitentiary for the past year. Prisoners, many of them lifers, are finding their jobs or work placement eliminated and are being told to participate in programs or to remain on cell lock-up, unemployed, and with zero pay.

This coercive policy is based upon the Rousseauist argument that man must be forced to be free. Over the past 20 years I have experienced numerous models of prison practice. I have seen medical models, process models, punitive models, opportunities models, and the living unit model. These models are operational ideals: they shape social policy and the management of prisons. Their perfection lies in the total subordination of design to function; that is, to make it work, not to question its very existence. However, ideals are not reality, nor can the concept dog bark. Everyday life in prison is experienced as arbitrary and irrational—in spite of the appearance of order and endless routine.

The so-called medical model is passé. This model implies that the criminal is sick and can be cured, usually by experts. Its most valuable legacy is the word "correctional" itself. The major corollary of this is the realization that a cure cannot be coerced. The medical model is in decline insofar as it is merely a model and rationale for corrections. However, its continued decline does not imply its disappearance any more than the medieval preference for punishing the body has disappeared. The real impact of this decline can be measured in the related decline of the rehabilitative ideal.

Surveying the state of rehabilitation in 1973, Robert Martinson concluded that all such programs had been comprised by linking them to punitive measures; for example, linking parole to participation in such programs. In 1974, an important book was published, Norval Morris's *The Future of Imprisonment*, which took up the challenge of separating the rehabilitative ideal from the medical model. If I recall correctly, his essential point was that change in behaviour cannot be coerced, but it can be facilitated. Under the medical model, the incentive to reform becomes a barrier to the treatment prescribed. One is forced to participate, and therefore reform is rejected.

My own experience illustrates this point quite clearly. For the past year I have been rejecting management's coercive efforts to force me into programming. Of course I realize that I will never be released and will die in prison. This raises the question: What possible purpose will be served by forcing me to comply with an induction program? Those that force prisoners to participate will only serve to polarize and alienate the very people they propose to help. While incarcerated in a medical model prison in the early seventies, I was asked somewhat naively by a so-called professional if my bitterness and hostility toward authority figures was based upon revenge. I fixed upon her my best cynical eye and replied, "Au contraire . . . if anything, it is based upon contempt!"

I remain resolute and determined not to succumb to management's bullying and strong-arm methods. Yet, I am available and willing to work with alternatives. The opportunities model is a case in point. Many prisoners will avail themselves of programs provided they are voluntary.

Rik McWhinney

Letter to HIV/AIDS Organizations

THURSDAY, OCTOBER 21, 2004

To Whom It May Concern:

I am a serving prisoner in a federal institution. I am also a trained educator/facilitator for HIV/AIDS harm reduction and prevention. Recently, prisoners were assigned a mandate by the Regional Infectious Disease Coordinator and National Infectious Disease Program Coordinator to create projects/activities designed to educate federal prisoners in prevention/harm reduction in relation to HIV/AIDS. As you are no doubt aware, the incidence of this disease in prison is on a steady rise. In our attempt to address this problem, we prisoners are extremely motivated to educate our peers in the safe practise of harm reduction and prevention through a unique and intensive education program.

In our efforts to accomplish this, it is important that we stress to our clients that this initiative is for the most part prisoner-driven and separate from Correctional Service Canada core programming, thus lending a greater degree of credibility or authenticity to the project. To further our aims and objectives with respect to this initiative, it is vital that upon completion of the course, our clients receive recognition or accreditation from an established HIV/AIDS society or foundation for their effort in this discipline. It is our plan to award certificates of competency upon completion. In an effort to further enhance this recognition, it is our sincere hope that your organization would lend its name to sponsoring us. Please understand that in requesting this we are not asking for funding or any work-related input from your organization, but solely the lending of your organization's name as an imprimatur of sponsorship toward our effort. We strongly feel that by doing so we can further our achievements in creating a strong and supportive partnership in battling this pernicious and deadly disease. In addition, we cannot let it go unsaid that the loan of your name as a sponsoring agency to our effort would serve as a positive incentive for many prisoners who are ignorant or complacent toward the dangers of this disease.

Sincerely,
Rik McWhinney
Inmate Peer Counsellor
Inmate Committee Chairman

Letter to Montana State Prison

MARCH 26, 2004

Dear Sir:

On behalf of the Cougar Boxing Club, it is with great regret that I write this letter. While words alone are difficult to find in expressing our disappointment with the recent decision to cancel your boxing program, we nevertheless feel compelled to ask you to please reconsider the matter.

Your program, as it existed, served a multi-purpose objective for all participants involved and was of great benefit to the young men of our club. No doubt you are aware that many adolescent boys and girls are drawn to our club as it provides a diversion from straying beyond the boundaries of society. Once they become involved and learn they are accepted—their self-esteem, with egos strengthened and intact—they discover the error of their past ways.

It was participation in your boxing program that enhanced their commitment to a new or rediscovered lifestyle. As a result, they are much happier and responsible citizens, who are willing and able to contribute to the community in which they feel a part of.

Although the evidence of this is for the most part anecdotal, it is of no less significance. I have been approached many times in private by young men who expressed their gratitude for the opportunity to participate in your boxing program with the chance to discover where his errant ways may have led him. Not a "Scared Straight" venue by design or purpose, but having the same effect. A sort of "There, but for the grace of God go I."

I do not hesitate to share that your boxing program is a very respected and valued tradition, which is looked upon favourably and not without some envy and nostalgia within the correctional system here in Canada. I have had many opportunities to discuss your program with people employed by Corrections Canada, and they have confirmed that a boxing program such as yours is only capable of emanating from a progressive and enlightened prison administration. It is on this note that we urge you to please rescind your decision and keep the tradition intact.

Sincerely,
Rik McWhinney
Coach and Motivational Co-coordinator,
Cougar Boxing Club

Letter to WWF

MARCH 3, 2003

Dear Silia,

I just received your promotional material in the mail twenty minutes ago. I am currently a supporting member of WWF. I am very impressed with your mission statement and am eager to join your organization in its efforts. Please understand that I am a serving federal prisoner and have been for close to three decades. It is for this reason that I am unable to enroll in your monthly program. However, this does not preclude me from encouraging others to join your fine program. Please accept my hard-earned prison wages in the amount of $100.00 so that I may become a supportive member. Could you please send me several more of your fantastic window decals? I am enclosing a self-addressed, stamped envelope to accommodate this. Thank you for seeking my support to help the animals.

Sincerely,
Rik McWhinney

Letter to Valley Zoo

JUNE 18, 2003

Dear S.V.,

During the month of October 2002, I enrolled in the adopt an animal program at the Valley Zoo.

I sent you sixty dollars ($60.00) to adopt a scarlet macaw. On June 1, 2003, I visited the zoo to see this bird. Locating the scarlet macaw presented great difficulty as the exhibit was unmarked. After seeking directions from one of the zoo guides, I stood in front of glassed-in aviary which contained two exotic looking parrots. There was no way to determine if one of these birds was the scarlet macaw that I had adopted, for unlike the other exhibits there was no sign or legend attached. The two birds in question were so despondent and inactive that I seriously wondered if they were in fact alive, or donated to the zoo by some local taxidermist! I do not hesitate to inform you that macaws in general are curious, intelligent, and social birds that require a great deal of stimulation and social interaction. Upon close examination of this aviary, it became apparent by the conspicuous absence of toys or other diversions, that these parrots were suffering the effects of severe sensory deprivation! This raises the question as to whether or not you actually care for these poor unfortunate creatures, or rather view them as a means or a tool for ripping off the public for their money under the guise of some bogus adoption program. I am now convinced that you people suffer a moral turpitude consistent with your propensity to inflict damage upon these defenceless birds. In fact, you are of such amoral character as to engender in the mind a pernicious casuistry which leads one to weigh your faults with your wrongs, and to excuse the former because the latter exceed all measure! In light of this situation, I wish to inform you that I am withdrawing my support of your facility and will actively encourage others to do likewise.

Sincerely,
Rik McWhinney

COPIES TO:
Feathered Friends of Edmonton
World Wildlife Fund of Canada (WWF)
World Society for the Protection of Animals (WSPA)
Society for the Protection of Animals Abroad (SPANA)
People for the Ethical Treatment of Animals (PETA)

Rik enclosed the following printed document:

ACTIVITIES: Macaws are curious and intelligent. They love puzzles, and will often unpuzzle themselves right out of a locked cage. Give them interlocking toys, "parrot puzzle" toys—toys with a nut or something that has to be extracted, anything which may confound them for at least an hour or two. Give them lots of chew toys. UNTREATED lumber cut into chunks are great, and you can "dye" the pieces by soaking them in Kool-Aid (sans sugar). Macaws love acrobatics and appreciate a swing or a rope to twirl on. Things to climb on are dandy too. It seems that most macaws like the TV as well. Many enjoy a bath. If you have the time and ambition, you can teach a macaw to eat with a spoon, and do other various tricks.

Letter to Veterinarian

JANUARY 10, 2004

Dear Doctor,

Rusty is a 14-year-old male cat with a history of feline urologic syndrome. Recently he has been exhibiting signs of discomfort. He will wake suddenly from a deep sleep & begin turning in circles, then sit on his rump with hind legs splayed & extended forward parallel to his head, while aggressively pawing or kneading the floor in front of him. This is followed by much licking & nipping at his genital area, but not in a general grooming context. He seems quite agitated, almost as a female preparing for labour, while trying to find a comfortable position in which to deliver her litter. It is quite obvious that he is experiencing pain or extreme discomfort while this is occurring.

Upon palpation through the abdominal wall there does not appear to be evidence of uroliths. However, the bladder wall feels somewhat thick & fibrous & there is possibly some distension of the bladder itself. But, then, I am not experienced at this & may be reacting based solely on Rusty's urological history & strong suspicion that he has been receiving a steady diet of fish products. I am certain that he is in extreme discomfort during the above-described behaviour. Because he is an outside cat & I reside in an institution, it is almost impossible to detect the presence of dysuria.

A Resident Pet Program in a Canadian Federal Prison

APRIL 2004

Rockwood Institution Cat Population Maintenance Project

HISTORY

Rockwood Institution is a minimum-security facility which houses up to 167 federally sentenced men. The units consist of 25 separate houses which accommodate between 6 and 8 inmates and provide an independent living environment. The institution is also a fully equipped farm operation which produces pork, beef, dairy products such as cheese and milk, corn, potatoes, and grain.

The farm has a number of buildings such as barns and sheds which are highly appealing to stray cats, especially in the winter. As a consequence, Rockwood becomes home to numerous strays who consistently, and naturally, reproduce. Although offenders and staff generally learned to accept these cats as partners on the farm grounds and in its buildings, some problems did occur. In the first place, some inmates became so attached to specific cats which they had successfully tamed that they then introduced these cats to the housing units, where there were no rules or standards to monitor cleanliness or proper care. The second problem resulted simply from the natural reproductive processes of fertile wild cats.

As a result of the lack of proper cat care products, and in the absence of an effective population control program, the cats became a health concern to staff and for some inmates. Traditionally, the solution was to call the Humane Society once the number of cats was felt to be out of control, to have the animals trapped and, in most cases, euthanized. In 1996, when the Health and Safety Committee indicated that it was time to once again reduce our cat population, some of the staff decided that they did not support the previous method of cat population control and chose to look at other options.

One possibility which came to mind was the "catch, neuter and release" program, which has been documented in other areas and which could possibly be considered as a viable option in this case. It was decided that a "Cat Club" consisting of interested staff would be established to explore available options and prepare a proposal for the Health and Safety Committee.

IN THE BEGINNING

Support was gained from the Deputy Warden and the Warden of the institution for the cat project. The objective was to propose a humane program which would eliminate the unhealthy presence of cats in the inmate houses, and to reduce our overall cat population to what would be considered an acceptable number.

As a first step, the Humane Society was approached to see what support or suggestions they could provide, as most of the people involved in the Cat Club did not really know where to start. The Humane Society recommended a local vet who apparently was interested in exploring and maintaining feral cat colonies. This generous doctor and his staff were intrigued by the prospect of establishing a feral cat colony at a federal penitentiary, and they immediately agreed to assist. The animal clinic provided abundant information regarding the establishment and maintenance of feral cat colonies, they provided free medical services, including spaying and neutering of all the cats on the property. They recommended an approach to capturing the cats and provided the humane traps to accomplish the task.

Once the project was proposed and supported by the Health and Safety Committee on a 3-month trial basis, the Cat Club invited inmates to assist with the project. Information sessions were held with the inmates and staff to advise everyone of the proposal and the objectives of the project. Inmates were advised that the intent was to have all the animals spayed or neutered and to have them tested for potential disease. They were advised that hiding cats in the residences would not be a kindness to the cats as it could result in the complete annihilation of the cat population if our project did not succeed in reducing health concerns.

In the beginning, two inmates cooperated with the Cat Club and agreed to trap all the cats on the grounds. They also convinced other inmates at the institution to stop hiding cats in the houses, and to cooperate in ensuring that all the cats were spayed and neutered. Full cooperation was obtained and over the winter months, every cat at Rockwood was caught, neutered, and released.

An interesting by-product of the initiative was the need for an adoption program. As the cats were taken to the vet, it became apparent that a number of the females were already pregnant. The first few pregnancies were terminated as part of the principle of population control, but it became apparent that the inmate population was opposed to this strategy. Inmates again began to hide pregnant cats to ensure that the kittens would not be aborted. In order to maintain their cooperation, it became necessary to assure them that the females would be permitted to carry their kittens to term if we could provide a controlled environment where we could ensure that the kittens would not be added to our feral population. It is noted that the staff at the animal clinic were also relieved that terminations would no longer be performed.

Another consequence of mixing people who care with the cats is the initiative and emotional reasoning which can evolve when it is apparent that euthanasia may prove to be necessary. Some of the cats which were tested were identified as positive for a contagious disease called feline immunodeficiency virus (FIV). Two cats with this disease were euthanized in order to eliminate the risk of infecting the rest of the colony. However, when it was discovered that one of the most beloved cats at the farm was also infected, it became evident that euthanasia in this case simply was not a solution. Once again, the clinic, the Cat Club, and the inmates got together to come up with a more appropriate solution.

The solution: to set up some of the inmate houses as approved residences for sick cats. From this idea evolved the cat health-care program and there are now approximately 4 to 5 houses which are approved to have cats. This aspect of the project is dependent on the number of inmates willing to volunteer to look after a sick cat, either on a long-term basis, as is the case with FIV, or on a short-term basis, if a cat requires special medical attention. There are always a number of inmates willing to volunteer when necessary; staff have also agreed to take a sick cat home for a short time. In the case of approved house cats, the Cat Club provided all the necessary equipment to ensure that the cat was well cared for and that its presence in the house did not present a health concern.

In order to maintain some house cats and a feral cat colony, the Cat Club did some fundraising through the sale of baked goods, raffles, and collection of donations. The funds raised were used to purchase food, litter and boxes, leashes, brushes, and anything else needed to ensure that the cats are all properly cared for.

Current Status

THE CAT POPULATION

The cats at Rockwood Institution are now welcomed by both staff and inmates. There are approximately 20 to 30 cats who remain on the property at any one time. The population fluctuates at times due to deaths and new arrivals. These are reported by the inmates to a staff member of the Cat Club and close monitoring is maintained to ensure that deaths are natural and that new arrivals are taken to the vet clinic as soon as possible.

Shelters have been built to protect the cats from the elements and one or two inmate volunteers have been tasked with feeding all the feral cats at specific feeding stations throughout the institution. These inmates are also usually the ones who identify health concerns and trap the sick cats for the members of the Cat Club, who then make arrangements with the vet.

All the cats who have been to the vet for spaying and neutering are named and photographed and a record is maintained of their health status. The photo album assists the staff and inmates in identifying cats who belong to the colony versus new cats who have not been neutered or medically cleared. A tattoo imprinted in their ear by the vet also assists in identifying the cats when they are tame enough for people to get close enough to see them.

THE CAT CLUB

The Cat Club consists of concerned staff who are willing to volunteer their time and energy to ensure that the cats at Rockwood maintain a healthy life. Member-ship is completely voluntary and status in the club is not reflective of title at work. As a consequence of the club's contribution to the care of the cats, any health and safety concerns which may have existed in the past have been eliminated.

Club members take part in fundraising, transport the cats to and from the vet's office, and oversee the overall administration of the project. They also distrib-ute information regarding health, disease, and care of cats. They respond to questions and concerns expressed by staff and inmates. They also administer the funds raised for the project.

Club meetings occur as needed. Proposals and prob-lems are discussed at the meetings and members vol-unteer to take on specific projects which may come up.

THE INMATES

Like the Cat Club, the inmates at Rockwood Institution have volunteered their time and energy to assist in the care and control of the cat population at the institution. They have expended countless hours of their leisure time in trapping the cats, caring for them during illness, and delivering food to various feeding stations.

THE CAT HEALTH PROGRAM

As previously mentioned, there are a number of cats who have been identified as having some long-term health concerns. These animals will live a relatively happy life, without excessive health-care cost, if they are properly cared for by designated inmates. To destroy these animals is an option, but not one which is favoured by the vet and his staff, the staff involved at Rockwood, or the inmates. Consequently, it was agreed that in some cases, it would be appropriate to accommodate these cats in the inmate residences.

Members of the Cat Club staff approached interested inmates who had demonstrated or expressed their willingness to care for cats. The inmates were advised that the cats would be sick and may be subject to a short life relative to a healthy cat. They were given instructions regarding the level of care required and the need for high standards of cleanliness as related to food and water dishes, and especially regarding the litter box.

Other inmates were approached to provide short-term health care for cats who required the administration of medicine for a specific period of time, or for cats who required post-op care. In this case, it was made very clear to these inmates that the cat would have to be released to the farm grounds once the special care was no longer required. Although it became difficult at times to release the cats due to the emotional attachments which formed very quickly between caregiver and cat, the emphasis expressed on the welfare of the cat and the project always resulted in the appropriate decision being made.

General standards have been established in order to ensure that the cats who reside in the houses do not present any health hazard. To start with, all the inmates in the house are approached by staff to ascertain that there are no health concerns or personal dislike of cats. If all the inmates in the house are in agreement with having a cat reside with them, one inmate is designated as caregiver. It then becomes his responsibility to care for the cat with the support and assistance of a staff member from the Cat Club. Food and litter supplies are provided. The cats are not allowed outside unless accompanied by an inmate and the cat must remain on a leash until it returns indoors.

THE FELINE FUND

On an informal basis, some inmates had taken the initiative to submit a fundraising proposal. The idea was to refurbish an old shack near the ball diamond in which they would sell hot dogs and pop to the visiting teams and their guests during league games. The proposal was approved, and the initiative was successful. Funds raised were all donated to the care of the cats. A Feline Fund was established through the finance department at the institution where the offenders can deposit money from their fundraising efforts and a designated member of the staff Cat Club can withdraw money to purchase supplies and emergency medical attention.

The Feline Fund represents the first time the care of the cats has crossed into the need for official administrative intervention. In other words, the account is an official account maintained by the finance clerk and subject to policies governing the establishment and maintenance of accounts at a federal penitentiary. Up until this time, the staff of the Cat Club had elected a treasurer and the money was simply maintained in a cash box in the safe. No official processes were invoked to access the money and the treasurer basically operated on trust.

The need to establish an official account suggests again that perhaps it is time to formalize this project.

THE VET

Dr. Peter Schwartz of the Assiniboia Animal Hospital represents the foundation of the project. Without his generous contribution and his dedication to the establishment of feral cat colonies, the project at Rockwood Institution would most likely have been doomed to financial ruin. In these days of fiscal restraint, it is unlikely that the members of the Cat Club could have presented a financially viable project compared to the relatively minor monetary cost of having all these poor animals destroyed. Dr. Schwartz and his staff have provided most of their services and medication at no cost to the institution, or to the Cat Club. Consequently, we have had the opportunity to demonstrate that it is possible to maintain a healthy cat population at the institution, and we have been able to involve the offenders in a constructive and thought-provoking program. It is evident from people's reactions and from the publicity provided to the project that this is a humanitarian approach.

Conclusion

RIK'S MOST PRIZED POSSESSIONS WERE THE books that had journeyed with him as he was involuntarily transferred across the country over the course of his long incarceration. Paroled and living in his Salvation Army bachelor pad, he kept these books on a small bookcase in view of his couch. Dog-eared anthologies that contained several centuries worth of canonized poets were shuffled in among books about prison. While American political prisoner George Jackson's books acted as a bridge between these poets and penologists, Claire Culhane's *Barred from Prison* trilogy and Rik's copy of the 1977 MacGuigan report told the story of his early adulthood.

"Rick McWhinney" is listed among the named contributors at the back of the MacGuigan report, but the fact that his name is listed doesn't mean that we can dive into its pages and find his speech. In some ways, Rik's existence in the MacGuigan report is a lot like his existence in the penitentiary system itself. In the report,

Rik is one of the "inmates," and we can only intuit his presence when that term is used. In the report, as in the penitentiary, "inmate" denotes a collective subject position, one dispassionately written into passages that brim with violence and despair. Like many of the other "inmates" in these reports, Rik was separated from his family at a very young age, and he went on to live in institutions that subjected him to horrific abuse. These are the practices we condone when we don't have the time to listen to other people's stories.

Rik read and spoke endlessly about prison not only because he never left, but because he struggled to understand what it meant, and he tried to understand who he was in relation to his experience. Inquiries and subcommittee reports were a source of fascination, but the string of expert studies that concluded time and again that prison was failing was also a source of frustration. For someone who had spent more than three decades inside, these findings were merely variations on a set of old and familiar themes. The most recent itemized list of problems in the penitentiary system can be found in the *Standing Senate Committee Report on the Human Rights of Federally-Sentenced Persons* (2021), chaired by Salma Ataullahjan. As it was for Rik, the penitentiary system today is plagued by conditions that are unconducive to rehabilitation; a broken internal grievance system; geographical dislocation from family (which affects women and Indigenous prisoners in particular); inadequate access to health care and mental health care; and, in spite of recent legislation revamping the practice of segregation, prolonged and indefinite solitary confinement.[1]

The history of the prison is a history of senseless repetition. Rik began his incarceration when the practice of solitary confinement was being challenged in BC Federal Court, and he passed away months before the BC Court of Appeal upheld a 2018 decision that the practice was unconstitutional. When the case pertaining to the 1970s practice of solitary confinement at BC Pen was making its way to the courts, then correctional investigator Inger Hansen recommended that a special study be conducted on the practice. The subsequent Study Group on Dissociation, chaired by James Vantour, released its report a week before Justice Heald handed down his 1975 decision. Though critical of the effects of solitary confinement, the Vantour report concluded that segregation was an administrative necessity, but that physical and human resources were required to ensure that adequate living, working, and exercise spaces were provided.[2] Justice Heald's decision was in line with the findings of the report. In 2019, in anticipation of the BC Court of Appeal upholding the 2018 decision regarding the unconstitutionality of administrative segregation practices, the Government of Canada drafted Bill C-83, which would eventually legislate Structured Intervention Units (SIUs) into being. Rik passed away months before the bill's passage. To be clear, the term "Structured Intervention Unit" designates new policies and procedures, and not the creation of new "units" within the system. On its webpage, Correctional Service Canada refers to SIUs as "part of a historic transformation of the federal correctional system that saw the abolition of administrative segregation."[3]

The unofficial story, uncovered by research into these units, is that oversight of the implementation process has instead been eliminated, and the units have yet to meet the standards established by the bill. Had Rik been alive, he would have ranted and railed about the sixteen years he spent in solitary confinement after the court decision in 1975, and he would have slipped in some lines from "Slash Solitary" for good measure:

The warden quickly did arrange
For that unit's notorious name
To be included in cosmetic change,
While the results remained the same.

To rename a practice of ill-gotten fame
Is but a pseudo transformation,
Yet cause and effect remain the same,
Denies not death nor mutilation.

Rik wouldn't have been smug in his delivery of this verse, nor would he have been flippant (*plus ça change!*). The ongoing battle over solitary confinement wasn't simply entangled with his own bitterness, traumas, and sleepless nights either. For Rik, solitary confinement was a practice that claimed lives, and it pained him to see it continue. Although Rik had more than earned the right to leave his horrific experiences of the penitentiary system behind him, he continued to speak about these experiences in churches and university classrooms because he hoped that he might change people's minds about an institution they took for granted.

After presenting his poetry and relaying some of his story to my class, a student asked Rik what should be done to fix prisons. How could we prevent the things that had happened to him from happening to other people? Rik's response was immediate and reasoned. "Well, they should be abolished," Rik said. "Prisons aren't suited for dealing with the people and the problems they inherit. In fact, they create problems. I mean, there are some people who likely need to be kept away from society, to keep society safe—the Clifford Olsons and Robert Picktons—but these people are very, very few. And while they should be kept away for society's sake, I don't know what that would look like. It probably wouldn't look like prison as we know it; anyone kept in an institution that's run by the state should be treated humanely. No measure of vengeance or violence can ever repair the harm that someone may have done, but we can keep society safe. Aside from containing a dangerous few, there should be no such thing as prison."

Although it might currently be difficult to imagine, it's likely that the very existence of an institution called "prison" will someday be a matter of historical record, part of a bygone era wherein the symptoms of social inequities were disappeared rather than examined for their underlying causes. The work of scholar-activists like Angela Davis and Ruth Wilson Gilmore has given the movement for penal abolition a high-profile voice south of the border, but its Canadian counterpart took off at around the same time as Rik entered prison. Rik was especially touched by the work of Claire Culhane, who became a vocal abolitionist after speaking with the men incarcerated in BC Pen in the mid-seventies, and Ruth Morris and the Quaker Committee on Jails and Justice began their advocacy work in Toronto in the late 1970s, culminating in their founding of the International Conference on Penal Abolition in 1983, a biannual conference that Rik attended on a day pass when it was held in Toronto in 2000.

We live in a society that's almost entirely unsympathetic toward incarcerated people, and it's that culture of indifference that allows the practice of incarceration to continue even as we read testimony and reports about its routinized violence or watch leaked CCTV footage documenting injury and death. Though legitimized by positive polling numbers, a consistently high recidivism rate—as well as chronic unemployment, broken families, psychological damage, and various physical health problems acquired or neglected within the prison environment—speaks incessantly of the institution's failure. We perpetually turn to reform in an attempt to solve the problems of the penitentiary system, but as Senator Kim Pate points out "prison reform is tantamount to rearranging the deck chairs on the Titanic."[4]

Abolition might seem like a radical, even nonsensical idea if conceived in terms of subtraction—the closing of prisons—but abolition is ultimately about adding and supporting. With redistributed funds, institutions and community support programs that address the root causes and inequities that lead people into confrontations with the law in the first place will be better able to thrive. To phase out prisons, the first step is to fund the communities that people leave behind when they enter the prison system, ensuring that people have food and housing security, access to health care, and access to an education system that provides a diverse array of supports for different learning needs. Empathy and mutual service will do more to restore our communities than punishing those who face constant barriers and who are already, every day, being punished by their circumstances.

Notes

INTRODUCTION

1   After touring the country's penitentiaries with a parlia-
    mentary committee in 1976–77—during the early years of
    Rik's federal incarceration—Gérard McNeil and Sharon
    Vance wrote that "the huddled, caged figures we saw in
    those cells came back to haunt us at night." "Brooding
    silences during the day [and] nightmares later" was the
    standard experience of politicians and staffers who were
    merely afforded a passing glance at prison conditions as
    part of the same parliamentary inquiry. Gérard McNeil
    and Sharon Vance, *Cruel and Unusual* (Ottawa: Deneau
    and Greenberg, 1978), 2, 5.

2   I use the word "incorrigible" here in both its colloquial and
    technical sense. Rik used the word to describe himself as a
    child. Until 1960, children could be sent to training school
    if they "proved unmanagable or incorrigible." *Kirk Keeping
    v. Her Majesty the Queen in Right of the Province of Ontario*,
    CV-17-0578-00 (2018), 9–10. Rik entered the training
    school system in 1960 or 1961. Regardless of the official
    reason given for his admission, "incorrigible" is what Rik
    understood himself to be.

3   "Locked Up," *W5*, CTV News, March 8, 2019, web, 11:57,
    https://www.ctvnews.ca/w5/it-felt-like-a-prison-for-kids-
    w5-investigates-allegations-of-abuse-at-ontario-training-
    schools-1.4327718.

4   Colin Perkel, "Police Looking Into Case of Student at
     Notorious Ontario 'Training School,' " Global News,
     November 15, 2018, https://globalnews.ca/news/4665954/
     ontario-training-school-police/.
5   Colin Perkel, " 'Yeah, I'm Alive:' Boy Survived Training
     School Beating 55 Years Ago," National Post, December 6,
     2018, https://nationalpost.com/pmn/news-pmn/canada-
     news-pmn/yeah-im-alive-boy-survived-training-school-
     beating-55-years-ago.
6   Kirk Keeping v. Her Majesty the Queen in Right of the Province
     of Ontario, 11.
7   Ibid., 12.
8   Ibid., 12–13.
9   Canadian Press, "Survivors of Ontario 'Training Schools'
     Say Their Suffering Is Being Erased by Redevelopment
     Project," National Post, September 6, 2016, https://
     nationalpost.com/news/canada/survivors-of-ontario-
     training-schools-say-their-suffering-is-being-erased-by-
     redevelopment-project.
10   Ibid.
11   Mark MacGuigan (Chair), Report to Parliament by the
     Subcommittee on the Penitentiary System in Canada
     (Ottawa: Supply Services of Canada, 1977), 2.
12   Claire Culhane, Barred from Prison: A Personal Account
     (Vancouver: Pulp Press, 1979), 115.
13   Joseph Archambault (Chair), Report of the Royal Commission
     to Investigate the Penal System of Canada (Ottawa: King's
     Printer, 1938), 109.
14   Ibid., 213–15.
15   Ibid., 60–1.
16   Ibid., 114–20, 126–44.
17   Ibid., 109–19.
18   Chris Clarkson and Melissa Munn, Disruptive Prisoners:
     Resistance, Reform, and the New Deal (Toronto: University
     of Toronto Press, 2021), 22.
19   Ibid., 34–55.
20   MacGuigan, Report to Parliament by the Subcommittee on
     the Penitentiary System in Canada, 5.
21   Ibid., 15.
22   McNeil and Vance, Cruel and Unusual, 14.

23 Ibid., 24. Steinhauser was sympathetic to prisoners. Prisoners argued that "the guards were as angry with her as they were with the hostage-takers and the shot that killed her had been fired deliberately," a claim that "seemed extreme until a public inquiry learned that the guns had been handled carelessly after the shooting, making it impossible to determine which guard had fired the fatal shot." Ibid., 45.

24 Culhane, *Barred from Prison*, 14.

25 MacGuigan, *Report to Parliament by the Subcommittee on the Penitentiary System in Canada*, 15.

26 McNeil and Vance, *Cruel and Unusual*, 1.

27 Ibid., 47.

28 Ibid., 48–9.

29 Ibid., 46–9.

30 Culhane, *Barred from Prison*, 13.

31 McNeil and Vance, *Cruel and Unusual*, 38.

32 J.W. Swackhamer (Chair), *Report of the Commission of Inquiry into Certain Disturbances at the Kingston Penitentiary during April, 1971* (Ottawa: Information Canada, 1973), 56.

33 Ibid., 57–8.

34 Culhane, *Barred from Prison*, 13.

35 MacGuigan, *Report to Parliament by the Subcommittee on the Penitentiary System in Canada*, 26.

36 Culhane, *Barred from Prison*, 14.

37 McNeil and Vance, *Cruel and Unusual*, 51–2.

38 Ibid., 52.

39 Swackhamer *Report of the Commission of Inquiry*, 33–4.

40 MacGuigan, *Report to Parliament by the Subcommittee on the Penitentiary System in Canada*, 32.

41 Ibid., 21–2.

42 McNeil and Vance, *Cruel and Unusual*, 53–4. While large sections of the prison had been damaged during the uprising, prisoners weren't being transferred out in greater numbers because transfer was looked upon as a reward. In the meantime, at least one prisoner was serially gang raped while the guards turned a blind eye. MacGuigan, *Report to Parliament by the Subcommittee on the Penitentiary System in Canada*, 27–8.

43 Culhane, *Barred from Prison*, 120–2.

44   Ibid., 122.
45   McNeil and Vance, *Cruel and Unusual*, 18–19.
46   Michael Jackson, *Prisoners of Isolation: Solitary Confinement in Canada* (Toronto: University of Toronto Press, 1983), 54.
47   Ibid., 78.
48   Ibid., 58.
49   Immediately after it was opened, Kent was the site of disturbances as prisoners and guards clashed over programming. Each group reacted to the other's violence in turn. See Claire Culhane, *Still Barred from Prison: Social Injustice in Canada* (Montreal: Black Rose Books, 1985), 62–9. Culhane details the continued unrest within the prison system through the remainder of the seventies and well into the eighties in *Still Barred from Prison* and *No Longer Barred from Prison: Social Injustice in Canada* (Montreal: Black Rose Books, 1992), an updated and renamed reprinting of *Still Barred*.
50   Jackson, *Prisoners of Isolation*, 186.
51   *Kirk Keeping v. Her Majesty the Queen in Right of the Province of Ontario*, 26
52   Gerald Fauteux (Chair), *Report of a Committee Appointed to Inquire into the Principles and Procedures Followed in the Remission Service of the Department of Justice of Canada* (Ottawa: Queen's Printer, 1956), 47–9. During this time, a number of prisoners were subject to medical experiments conducted by drug companies, university researchers, and federal government agencies as a matter of normal operating procedure. See Geraint B. Osborne, "Scientific Experimentation on Canadian Inmates, 1955 to 1975," *Howard Journal of Criminal Justice* 45, no. 3 (2006): 284–306, and Margaret A. Somerville and Norbert Gilmore, *A Report on Research on Inmates in Federal Penitentiaries* (Montreal: McGill Centre for Medicine, Ethics, and Law, 2000). Somerville and Gilmore wrote their report for the Correctional Service of Canada after Dorothy Proctor revealed that she was subject to LSD experimentation while incarcerated at the Kingston Prison for Women in the 1960s, leading to the publication of a series of exposés in the *Ottawa Citizen*. The report was among the papers that Rik left behind. On the final page of the report, Rik taped a

note containing the following: "Ricky C. given L S D in solitary in exchange for cigarettes. Started seeing polar bears coming out the walls. George W. given aversion therapy ECT in solitary. Rik McWhinney given aversion therapy ie Haloperidol administered with no antagonist while in solitary."

53 McNeil and Vance, *Cruel and Unusual*, 134–45.

54 Henry A. Nasrallah, "Haloperidol Clearly Is Neurotoxic. Should It Be Banned?," *Current Psychiatry* 12 (2013): 7.

55 See "Regina General Hospital (Fragment)" in section 6 of this volume.

56 Rik was making a coded reference here to a prisoner quoted in the 1977 MacGuigan report: "How do you expect me to be rehabilitated when I never was habilitated." MacGuigan, *Report to Parliament by the Subcommittee on the Penitentiary System in Canada*, 10.

57 Bob Gaucher, "*The Journal of Prisoners on Prisons*: An Ethnography of the Prison-Industrial Complex in the 1990s," in *Writing as Resistance: The Journal of Prisoners on Prisons Anthology (1988–2002)*, ed. Bob Gaucher (Toronto: Canadian Scholar's Press, 2002), 5–6.

58 Claire Culhane's books, cited above, which include grievances and unpublished, prisoner-produced letters, press releases, and log book entries, are also, in some respects, compendiums of historically and regionally situated Canadian prison writing, as is Michael Jackson's *Prisoners of Isolation*, which collects the testimony of the lead plaintiffs in *McCann v. The Queen*.

59 Ioan Davies, *Writers in Prison* (Oxford: Basil Blackwell, 1990), 7.

60 Ibid., 4.

II) SOLITARY CONFINEMENT AND
SPECIAL HANDLING UNITS

1 Michael Jackson, *Prisoners of Isolation: Solitary Confinement in Canada* (Toronto: University of Toronto Press, 1983), 77.

2 Ibid., 68.

3 Ibid., 73.

4   Gérard McNeil and Sharon Vance, *Cruel and Unusual* (Ottawa: Deneau and Greenberg, 1978), 32–3.

5   J.W. Swackhamer (Chair), *Report of the Commission of Inquiry into Certain Disturbances at the Kingston Penitentiary during April, 1971* (Ottawa: Information Canada, 1973), 4.

6   Ibid., 34.

7   McNeil and Vance, *Cruel and Unusual*, 30.

8   Jane B. Sprott and Anthony Doob, "Solitary Confinement, Torture, and Canada's Structured Intervention Units," February 23, 2021, https://s3.amazonaws.com/tld-documents. llnassets.com/0024000/24852/torture-solitary-sius-sprott-doob-23-feb-2021.pdf, 1.

9   Anthony Doob and Jane B. Sprott, "Understanding the Operation of Correctional Service Canada's Structured Intervention Units: Some Preliminary Findings," October 26, 2020, https://johnhoward.ca/wp-content/uploads/2020/10/UnderstandingCSC_SIUDoobSprott26-10-2020-1.pdf, 29.

10   Sprott and Doob, "Solitary Confinement, Torture, and Canada's Structured Intervention Units," 2.

11   Ibid., 1.

12   The document "In Remembrance" is collected in section 3 of this volume.

13   According to Michael Jackson, the cells were eleven by six and a half feet. Jackson, *Prisoners of Isolation*, 48.

14   Rik met American Beat poet Allen Ginsberg at a poetry reading before he started his first federal sentence, and he corresponded with him for a number of years while incarcerated. Two of Ginsberg's letters to Rik can be found in Rik McWhinney, "The McWhinney-Ginsberg Correspondence," in *Sentences and Paroles: A Prison Reader*, ed. P.J. Murphy and Jennifer Murphy (Vancouver: New Star Books, 1998), 121–2.

15   See Jackson, *Prisoners of Isolation*, 51–2, 66–7, 73–4.

16   Shortly after it opened, Michael Jackson visited and observed that "the Millhaven SHU 'library' was a cell furnished with an empty bookcase, the 'music room' was a cell with a shelf on which a single guitar rested, and the 'gym' was a double cell equipped with a punching bag

and exerciser." Michael Jackson, *Justice behind the Walls: Human Rights in Canadian Prisons* (Vancouver: Douglas and McIntyre, 2002), 8.

17 As Gérard McNeil and Sharon Vance note, "the twenty-five year minimum was the price demanded for abolition of the death sentence in 1976. But everyone in the prison, from administration to prisoners, feared the prospect of mingling with men who knew they must spend the rest of the century behind bars without hope of release." This led to the grudging adoption of Warren Allmand's "faint hope" provision that judicial review be granted after fifteen years of a sentence had been served. McNeil and Vance, *Cruel and Unusual*, 20–1.

18 In his personal account of his incarceration, Edward Hertrich discusses his entry into Millhaven, the sometimes violent entry of others, and the reputation that follows prisoners when they're transferred elsewhere. Edward Hertrich, *Wasted Time* (Toronto: Dundurn, 2019), 84–97, 124–34.

19 The US federal penitentiary in Marion, Illinois. The prison opened in 1963 to replace Alcatraz. Having attended a talk by Edgar Schein on brainwashing among American POWs returning from Korea in the 1960s, psychiatrist Dr. Martin Groder adapted brainwashing techniques in a "control unit" he opened at Marion in 1973. He used a combination of complete segregation with therapeutic programming as a behaviour-modification strategy, rendering prisoners docile, making them into blank slates that would be susceptible to rehabilitation. The prison was reclassified as the highest-security prison in the United States in 1978, and by 1983 the whole institution was on permanent lockdown. Administrators from across the country and abroad visited the prison. As rehabilitation was abandoned in favour of basic population management, Marion became a model prison for the spread, during the late twentieth century, of the supermax model. Sharon Shalev, *Supermax: Controlling Risk through Solitary Confinement* (Cullompton, UK: Willan Publishing, 2009), 18–22.

III) ADVOCACY AND (A) PRISON(ER'S) POLITICS

1   "CAC" refers to the Citizen's Advisory Committee. CACs be-
     gan to form in 1965 following a Commissioner's Directive
     by Commissioner Allan McLeod and became nationally
     organized after the McGuigan Report of 1977 suggested
     that they should be operational at all institutions. CACs
     are meant to stand in as impartial observers and advisors
     regarding penitentiary policies, programs, and services
     while also acting as a liaison between communities and
     prisons. (Correctional Service Canada, "Citizen Advisory
     Committees Resource Manual," Government of Canada, last
     modified March 5, 2015, https://www.csc-scc.gc.ca/cac/1-
     eng.shtml; Correctional Service Canada, "Citizen Advisory
     Committees," Government of Canada, last modified March
     10, 2022, https://www.csc-scc.gc.ca/cac/index-eng.shtml).
2   "CX-1" denotes a correctional officer, while the "CX-2" des-
     ignation, for example, signifies a "primary worker" who
     requires more training and is higher on the pay scale.
3   Broadcast on CBC Radio Edmonton, August 10, 1995.
4   List reprinted from *Cell Count* (no. 30: 6–7). *Cell Count* is
     a publication of the Prisoners' HIV/AIDS Support Action
     Network.
5   A debate on the reinstatement of the recently abolished
     death penalty in Canada, held at Edmonton Max Peni-
     tentiary in 1987. The debate is hosted by Ron Collister,
     and features Bill Domm (Conservative MP) and Warren
     Allmand (Liberal MP), who represent the death penalty
     reinstatement and death penalty abolition positions, re-
     spectively. In 1988, Domm—an ardent death penalty ad-
     vocate—initiated a "free vote" on the reinstatement of
     capital punishment in the House of Commons; the motion
     failed. The Edmonton Max panel also included George
     Oake, assistant managing editor of the *Edmonton Journal*,
     and Roy Farran, a *Calgary Herald* columnist and former
     solicitor general of Alberta. The audience is composed of
     inmates from Edmonton Max, who are invited to partic-
     ipate in a Q&A by the host as the debate draws to a close.
     Included here is the transcription of an exchange between
     McWhinney and the debate participants.

IV) PRISON CULTURE IN THE TIME OF THE CODE

1 Donald Clemmer, *The Prison Community* (Boston: Christopher Publishing House, 1940).

2 For classical deprivation arguments, see Gresham Sykes, *The Society of Captives: A Study of a Maximum Security Prison* (Princeton, NJ: Princeton University Press, 1958); Gresham M. Sykes and Sheldon L. Messinger, "The Inmate Social System," in *Theoretical Studies in Social Organization of the Prison*, ed. Richard A. Cloward et al. (New York: Social Science Research Council, 1960), 5–19; and Erving Goffman, *Asylums: Essays on the Social Situation of Mental Patients and Other Inmates* (New York: Anchor, 1961). On the importation model, see John Irwin and Donald R. Cressey, "Thieves, Convicts and the Inmate Culture," *Social Problems* 10, no. 2 (1962): 142–55; Timothy Hartnagel and Mary E. Gillan, "Female Prisoners and the Inmate Code," *Pacific Sociological Review* 23, no. 1 (1980): 85–104; and Geoff Asher, *Custody and Control: The Social Worlds of Imprisoned Youth* (Sydney: Allen and Unwin, 1986).

3 Joseph Archambault (Chair), *Report of the Royal Commission to Investigate the Penal System of Canada* (Ottawa: King's Printer, 1938), 54.

4 Roger Ouimet (Chair), *Report of the Canadian Committee on Corrections—Toward Unity: Criminal Justice and Corrections* Ottawa: Queen's Printer, 1969), 315.

5 Ibid., 315.

6 Rose Ricciardelli, *Surviving Incarceration: Inside Canadian Prisons* (Waterloo, ON: Wilfrid Laurier University Press, 2014), 120.

7 Ibid., 134.

8 See, for example, Elizabeth Comack et al., *Indians Wear Red: Colonialism, Resistance, and Aboriginal Street Gangs* (Halifax: Fernwood, 2013), and Joe Friesen, *The Ballad of Danny Wolfe: Life of a Modern Outlaw* (Toronto: McClelland and Stewart, 2016).

v) THE KEEPERS AND THE KEPT

1   Eddie Bunker was an infamous career criminal who be-
    came a writer of semi-autobiographical prison fiction and
    a Hollywood actor after he was released from prison for
    the final time in 1975.

2   See Robert M. Kaplan, "The Bizarre Career of Aubrey
    Levin: From Abuser of Homosexual Conscripts to Molester
    of Male Prisoners," *Forensic Research and Criminology
    International Journal* 2, no. 5 (2016): 182.

3   Richard Poplak, "Dr. Shock," *The Walrus*, April 8, 2020,
    https://thewalrus.ca/doctor-shock/.

4   As the recent report of the Standing Senate Committee on
    Human Rights makes clear, the grievance system remains
    fundamentally flawed to this day; it is severely backlogged,
    submissions are made in a context of intimidation and fear
    of reprisal, and grievances are subject only to internal re-
    view by the csc. Salma Ataullahjan (Chair), *The Standing
    Senate Committee Report on the Human Rights of Federally-
    Sentenced Persons* (Ottawa: Senate Printing Service, 2021),
    https://sencanada.ca/content/sen/committee/432/RIDR/
    reports/2021-06-16_FederallySentenced_e.pdf, 179–80.

5   Rik's grievance is upheld in part. While his assertion that
    noon-time meals were never delivered is acknowledged,
    the security concern that a glass shiv was found—leading
    to a thorough search of the unit for additional weapons—
    outweighed concerns about proper meal delivery.

6   A trail of signatures and delays, especially at Edmonton
    Institution, meant that Rik's grievance was upheld in part.
    He was right to point out that his application for trans-
    fer was not addressed in a timely fashion. The response
    also points out, however, that while his case-management
    team rates him as suitable for medium security, the poten-
    tial receiving institution, which is ultimately responsible
    for making the decision regarding transfer, did not. The
    letter outlining the denial of transfer was accordingly not
    removed from his record.

VI) THE BODIES OF THE CONDEMNED

1   There is slight variation between the graffiti on the wall
    in BC Pen and the note Rik left behind in Edmonton Max.
    The quote from the wall of BC Pen begins with "My eternal
    soul" and ends with "day on fire." Paul Grescoe, "A Jail Out
    in the Open," *Maclean's*, June 9, 1980, 13.

2   Mark MacGuigan (Chair), *Report to Parliament by the
    Subcommittee on the Penitentiary System in Canada* (Ottawa:
    Supply Services of Canada, 1977), 93.

3   Ibid., 94.

4   The obligation to provide essential health care to incar-
    cerated people is enshrined in section 86(1) of the
    Corrections and Conditional Release Act, while rule 24
    of the United Nations Standard Minimum Rules for the
    Treatment of Prisoners states that "prisoners should en-
    joy the same standards of health care that are available
    in the community, and should have access to necessary
    health-care services free of charge without discrimina-
    tion on the grounds of their legal status." UN General
    Assembly, Resolution 70/175 (December 17, 2015), https://
    undocs.org/A/RES/70/175. According to the Office of the
    Correctional Investigator, "On a consistent basis, delivery
    and access to health care services remains the number one
    area of offender complaint to the Office. . . . The feder-
    al correctional system faces serious capacity, accessibility,
    quality of care and health service delivery challenges and
    constraints." These include "bed space at the five regional
    treatment centres (psychiatric hospitals); aging and in-
    appropriate infrastructure; lack of 'intermediate' mental
    health care units; management of self-injurious offenders;
    recruitment and retention of mental health care profes-
    sionals; sharing of information between health care and
    front-line staff; meeting the needs of aging inmates; op-
    erational dilemmas—prison vs. hospital, inmate vs. pa-
    tient, security vs. treatment; infectious diseases, drugs in
    prison and harm reduction; informed consent and invol-
    untary treatment." Office of the Correctional Investigator,

"Access to Physical and Mental Health Care," Government of Canada, last modified March 14, 2016, https://www.oci-bec.gc.ca/cnt/priorities-priorites/health-sante-eng.aspx.

5   The 1971 prison uprising at Attica Correctional Facility in western New York.

6   Jeffrey St. Clair and Alexander Cockburn, "CIA Shrinks & LSD," *Counterpunch*, October 18, 1999, https://www.counterpunch.org/1999/10/18/cia-shrinks-lsd/. The LSD experiments were being run under the purview of Dr. George Scott, a staff psychiatrist for the CSC whose research was funded by the CIA and the Canadian Department of National Defence. Mike Blanchfield, "Canada: LSD Experiments 'Good Research Back Then,' " *Ottawa Citizen*, July 10, 1998, retrieved via the Media Awareness Project, http://www.mapinc.org/drugnews/v98/n548/a11.html?9595. Asked to reflect on the early '60s experiments shortly after Proctor had come forward, Scott pointed out that he did not personally conduct the experiments, and he questioned the veracity of Proctor's claims. Mike Blanchfield, "I Was Reduced to a Lab Rat," *Ottawa Citizen*, July 21, 1998, retrieved via Media Awareness Project, http://www.mapinc.org/drugnews/v98/n602/a02.html?7434. Although notes confirm that Scott held a series of intensive psychiatric sessions with Proctor, ultimately deeming her a sociopath—and qualifying her as a research subject in the process—Scott maintained that he had no recollection of Proctor, noting of his patients that "their names are as sticky as postage stamps, as far as I'm concerned. . . . That's probably 30,000 patients ago" (Blanchfield, "Canada: LSD Experiments"). In another interview, he dismissed the entire affair, ultimately concluding, "I'm happy with myself. I don't give a shit" (St. Clair and Cockburn, "CIA Shrinks & LSD"). When the Proctor suit was filed, Scott had just lost his licence to practise medicine due to an unrelated case in which he was found combining sodium pentothal, electroshock therapy, and Ritalin—as well as prescriptions for birth control—to seduce female patients using a method called narcoanalysis, knocking them out, implanting erotic suggestions,

and then waking them up with the Ritalin (St. Clair and Cockburn, "CIA Shrinks & LSD").

7   Rik is referring here to Bill C-53, the *Life Means Life Act*. The bill, sponsored by Peter MacKay, made it to a second reading in the House of Commons shortly before the end of the 41st Parliament in June 2015, but it never became law. The bill proposed life without parole for certain crimes, and it outlined some instances where the sentence of life without parole would be mandatory. To remain constitutional, the bill included a clause that someone serving such a sentence could appeal to the minister of public safety for exceptional release after thirty-five years.

8   Commissioner of the Correctional Service of Canada from 1988 to 1992, and again from 1996 to 2000.

VII) POSTTRAUMATIC STRESS DISORDER

1   See, for example, Cheryl Regehr et al., "Prevalence of PTSD, Depression and Anxiety Disorders in Correctional Officers: A Systematic Review," *Corrections* 6, no. 3 (2021): 229–41, and Nina Fusco et al., "When Our Work Hits Home: Trauma and Mental Disorders in Correctional Officers and Other Correctional Workers," *Frontiers in Psychiatry* 11, no. 493391 (February 2021), https://doi.org/10.3389/fpsyt.2020.493391.

2   B. Belet et al., "Trouble de stress post-traumatique en milieu pénitentiaire," *L'Encéphale* 46 (2020): 493.

VIII) OPPORTUNITIES AND RESTORATIONS

1   Mark MacGuigan (Chair), *Report to Parliament by the Subcommittee on the Penitentiary System in Canada* (Ottawa: Supply Services of Canada, 1977), 37–8.

2   The two-part *Crossfire* special on Capital Punishment aired on CBC Alberta on February 19 and 26, 1987.

3   On the basis of his grievance, it was decided that long-term prisoners should be approached in a manner that

seems less coercive (i.e., by memo), and that Rik was entitled to some back pay since he participated in orientation
in October 1993. Rik has added the following handwritten
note to the form: "I have never taken orientation as you
indicate above & never will. I am opposed to all forms of
coercive programming & refuse to be muscled into com-
plying with a flawed program gone awry."

CONCLUSION

1   Salma Ataullahjan (Chair), *The Standing Senate Committee
    Report on the Human Rights of Federally-Sentenced Persons*
    (Ottawa: Senate Printing Service, 2021), https://sencanada.
    ca/content/sen/committee/432/RIDR/reports/2021-06-16_
    FederallySentenced_e.pdf, 39–40.
2   James Vantour (Chair), *Report of the Study Group on
    Dissociation* (Ottawa: Solicitor General of Canada, 1975),
    24–7.
3   Correctional Service Canada, "Structured Intervention
    Units," last modified August 18, 2021, https://www.csc-scc.
    gc.ca/acts-and-regulations/005006-3000-en.shtml
4   Kim Pate, "A Canadian Journey into Abolition," in *Abolition
    Now! Ten Years of Strategy and Struggle against the Prison-
    Industrial Complex*, ed. The CR10 Publications Collective
    (Oakland, CA: AK Press, 2008), 77.

Bibliography

Archambault, Joseph (Chair). *Report of the Royal Commission to Investigate the Penal System of Canada*. Ottawa: King's Printer, 1938.

Asher, Geoff. *Custody and Control: The Social Worlds of Imprisoned Youth*. Sydney: Allen and Unwin, 1986.

Ataullahjan, Salma (Chair). *The Standing Senate Committee Report on the Human Rights of Federally-Sentenced Persons*. Ottawa: Senate Printing Service, 2021. https://sencanada.ca /content/sen/committee/432/RIDR/reports/ 2021-06-16_FederallySentenced_e.pdf.

Belet, B., F. D'Hondt, M. Horn, A. Amad, F. Carton, P. Thomas, G. Vaiva, and T. Fovet. "Trouble de stress post-traumatique en milieu pénitentiaire." *L'Encéphale* 46, no. 6 (2020): 493–99.

Blanchfield, Mike. "Canada: LSD Experiments 'Good Research Back Then.'" *Ottawa Citizen*, July 10, 1998. Media Awareness Project, http://www. mapinc.org/drugnews/v98/n548/a11.html?9595.

———. "I Was Reduced to a Lab Rat." *Ottawa Citizen*, July 21, 1998. Media Awareness Project, http://www.mapinc.org/drugnews/v98/n602/a02.html?7434.

Canadian Press. "Survivors of Ontario 'Training Schools' Say Their Suffering Is Being Erased by Redevelopment Project." *National Post*, September 6, 2016. https://nationalpost.com/news/canada/survivors-of-ontario-training-schools-say-their-suffering-is-being-erased-by-redevelopment-project.

Clarkson, Chris, and Melissa Munn. *Disruptive Prisoners: Resistance, Reform, and the New Deal*. Toronto: University of Toronto Press, 2021.

Clemmer, Donald. *The Prison Community*. Boston: Christopher Publishing House, 1940.

Comack, Elizabeth, Lawrence Deane, Larry Morrissette, and Jim Silver. *Indians Wear Red: Colonialism, Resistance, and Aboriginal Street Gangs*. Halifax: Fernwood, 2013.

Correctional Service Canada. "Citizen Advisory Committees." Government of Canada, last modified March 10, 2022. https://www.csc-scc.gc.ca/cac/index-eng.shtml.

———. "Citizen Advisory Committees Resource Manual." Government of Canada, last modified March 5, 2015. https://www.csc-scc.gc.ca/cac/1-eng.shtml.

———. "Structured Intervention Units." Government of Canada, last modified August 18, 2021. https://www.csc-scc.gc.ca/acts-and-regulations/005006-3000-en.shtml.

Culhane, Claire. *Barred from Prison: A Personal Account.* Vancouver: Pulp Press, 1979.

——. *No Longer Barred from Prison: Social Injustice in Canada.* Montreal: Black Rose Books, 1992.

——. *Still Barred from Prison: Social Injustice in Canada.* Montreal: Black Rose Books, 1985.

Davies, Ioan. *Writers in Prison.* Oxford: Basil Blackwell, 1990.

Doob, Anthony, and Jane B. Sprott. "Understanding the Operation of Correctional Service Canada's Structured Intervention Units: Some Preliminary Findings." October 26, 2020. https://johnhoward.ca/wp-content/uploads/2020/10/UnderstandingCSC_SIUDoobSprott26-10-2020-1.pdf.

Fauteux, Gerald (Chair). *Report of a Committee Appointed to Inquire into the Principles and Procedures Followed in the Remission Service of the Department of Justice of Canada.* Ottawa: Queen's Printer, 1956.

Friesen, Joe. *The Ballad of Danny Wolfe: Life of a Modern Outlaw.* Toronto: McClelland and Stewart, 2016.

Fusco, Nina, Rosemary Ricciardelli, Laleh Jamshidi, R. Nicholas Carleton, Nigel Barnim, Zoe Hilton, and Dianne Groll. "When Our Work Hits Home: Trauma and Mental Disorders in Correctional Officers and Other Correctional Workers." *Frontiers in Psychiatry* 11, no. 493391 (February 2021). https://doi.org/10.3389/fpsyt.2020.493391.

Gaucher, Bob. "*The Journal of Prisoners on Prisons*: An Ethnography of the Prison-Industrial Complex in the 1990s." In *Writing as Resistance: The Journal of Prisoners on Prisons Anthology (1988–2002)*, edited by Bob Gaucher, 5–30. Toronto: Canadian Scholar's Press, 2002.

Goffman, Erving. *Asylums: Essays on the Social Situation of Mental Patients and Other Inmates*. New York: Anchor, 1961.

Grescoe, Paul. "A Jail Out in the Open." *Maclean's*, 9 June 1980.

Hartnagel, Timothy, and Mary E. Gillan. "Female Prisoners and the Inmate Code." *Pacific Sociological Review* 23, no. 1 (1980): 85–104.

Hertrich, Edward. *Wasted Time*. Toronto: Dundurn, 2019.

Irwin, John, and Donald R. Cressey. "Thieves, Convicts and the Inmate Culture." *Social Problems* 10, no. 2 (1962): 142–55.

Jackson, Michael. *Justice behind the Walls: Human Rights in Canadian Prisons*. Vancouver: Douglas and McIntyre, 2002.

———. *Prisoners of Isolation: Solitary Confinement in Canada*. Toronto: University of Toronto Press, 1983.

Kaplan, Robert M. "The Bizarre Career of Aubrey Levin: From Abuser of Homosexual Conscripts to Molester of Male Prisoners." *Forensic Research & Criminology International Journal* 2, no. 5 (2016): 182–4.

Kirk Keeping v. Her Majesty the Queen in Right of the Province of Ontario, CV-17-0578-00 (2018).

"Locked Up." *W5*. CTV News, March 8, 2019. Web, 11:57. https://www.ctvnews.ca/w5/it-felt-like-a-prison-for-kids-w5-investigates-allegations-of-abuse-at-ontario-training-schools-1.4327718.

MacGuigan, Mark (Chair). *Report to Parliament by the Subcommittee on the Penitentiary System in Canada*. Ottawa: Supply Services of Canada, 1977.

McNeil, Gérard, and Sharon Vance. *Cruel and Unusual*. Ottawa: Deneau and Greenberg, 1978.

McWhinney, Rik. "The McWhinney-Ginsberg Correspondence." In *Sentences and Paroles: A Prison Reader*, edited by P.J. Murphy and Jennifer Murphy, 121–2. Vancouver: New Star Books, 1998.

Nasrallah, Henry A. "Haloperidol Clearly Is Neurotoxic. Should It Be Banned?" *Current Psychiatry* 12, no. 7 (2013): 7.

Office of the Correctional Investigator. "Access to Physical and Mental Health Care." Government of Canada, last modified March 14, 2016. https://www.oci-bec.gc.ca/cnt/priorities-priorites/health-sante-eng.aspx.

Osborne, Geraint B. "Scientific Experimentation on Canadian Inmates, 1955 to 1975." *Howard Journal of Criminal Justice* 45, no. 3 (2006): 284–306.

Ouimet, Roger (Chair). *Report of the Canadian Committee on Corrections—Toward Unity: Criminal Justice and Corrections*. Ottawa: Queen's Printer, 1969.

Pate, Kim. "A Canadian Journey into Abolition." In *Abolition Now! Ten Years of Strategy and Struggle against the Prison-Industrial Complex*, edited by The CR10 Publications Collective, 77–85. Oakland, CA: AK Press, 2008.

Perkel, Colin. "Police Looking Into Case of Student at Notorious Ontario 'Training School.' " Global News, November 15, 2018. https://globalnews.ca/news/4665954/ontario-training-school-police/.

———. " 'Yeah, I'm Alive:' Boy Survived Training School Beating 55 Years Ago." *National Post*, December 6, 2018. https://nationalpost.com/pmn/news-pmn/canada-news-pmn/yeah-im-alive-boy-survived-training-school-beating-55-years-ago.

Poplak, Richard. "Dr. Shock." *The Walrus*, April 8, 2020. https://thewalrus.ca/doctor-shock/.

Regehr, Cheryl, Mary Carey, Shannon Wagner, Lynn E. Alden, Nicholas Buys, Wayne Corneil, Trina Fyfe, Alex Fraess-Phillips, Elyssa Krutop, Lynda Matthews, Christine Randall, Marc White, and Nicole White. "Prevalence of PTSD, Depression and Anxiety Disorders in Correctional Officers: A Systematic Review." *Corrections* 6, no. 3 (2021): 229–41.

Ricciardelli, Rose. *Surviving Incarceration: Inside Canadian Prisons*. Waterloo, ON: Wilfrid Laurier University Press, 2014.

Shalev, Sharon. *Supermax: Controlling Risk through Solitary Confinement*. Cullompton, UK: Willan Publishing, 2009.

Somerville, Margaret A., and Norbert Gilmore. *A Report on Research on Inmates in Federal Penitentiaries*. Montreal: McGill Centre for Medicine, Ethics, and Law, 2000.

Sprott, Jane B., and Anthony Doob. "Solitary Confinement, Torture, and Canada's Structured

Intervention Units." February 23, 2021. https://s3.amazonaws.com/tld-documents.llnassets.com/0024000/24852/torture-solitary-sius-sprott-doob-23-feb-2021.pdf.

St. Clair, Jeffrey, and Alexander Cockburn. "CIA Shrinks & LSD." *Counterpunch*, October 18, 1999. https://www.counterpunch.org/1999/10/18/cia-shrinks-lsd/.

Swackhamer, J.W. (Chair). *Report of the Commission of Inquiry into Certain Disturbances at the Kingston Penitentiary during April, 1971.* Ottawa: Information Canada, 1973.

Sykes, Gresham. *The Society of Captives: A Study of a Maximum Security Prison.* Princeton, NJ: Princeton University Press, 1958.

Sykes, Gresham M., and Sheldon L. Messinger. "The Inmate Social System." In *Theoretical Studies in Social Organization of the Prison*, edited by Richard A. Cloward, Donald R. Cressey, George H. Grosser, Richard McCleery, Lloyd E. Ohlin, Gresham M. Sykes, and Sheldon L. Messinger, 5–19. New York: Social Science Research Council, 1960.

Vantour, James (Chair). *Report of the Study Group on Dissociation.* Ottawa: Solicitor General of Canada, 1975.

RICHARD "RIK" MCWHINNEY was born in Saint Boniface, Manitoba. He spent his early childhood between Winnipeg, Toronto, and Beamsville before beginning a life of incarceration at the provincially run Brookside School in Cobourg, Ontario at the age of nine. He was an avid reader and animal lover. He passed away peacefully in Regina, Saskatchewan on January 19, 2019 at the age of sixty-seven.

JASON DEMERS is an assistant professor in the Department of English at the University of Regina. He resides in Regina, Saskatchewan.

www.ingramcontent.com/pod-product-compliance
Lightning Source LLC
Chambersburg PA
CBHW022132020426
42334CB00015B/855